The daughters of the Marquis de Sade

BDSM Pictures from the early times of nude photography

Jürgen Prommersberger: The daughters oft he Marquis de Sade
Regenstauf , Januar 2016

First Edition by
CreateSpace Independent Publishing Platform

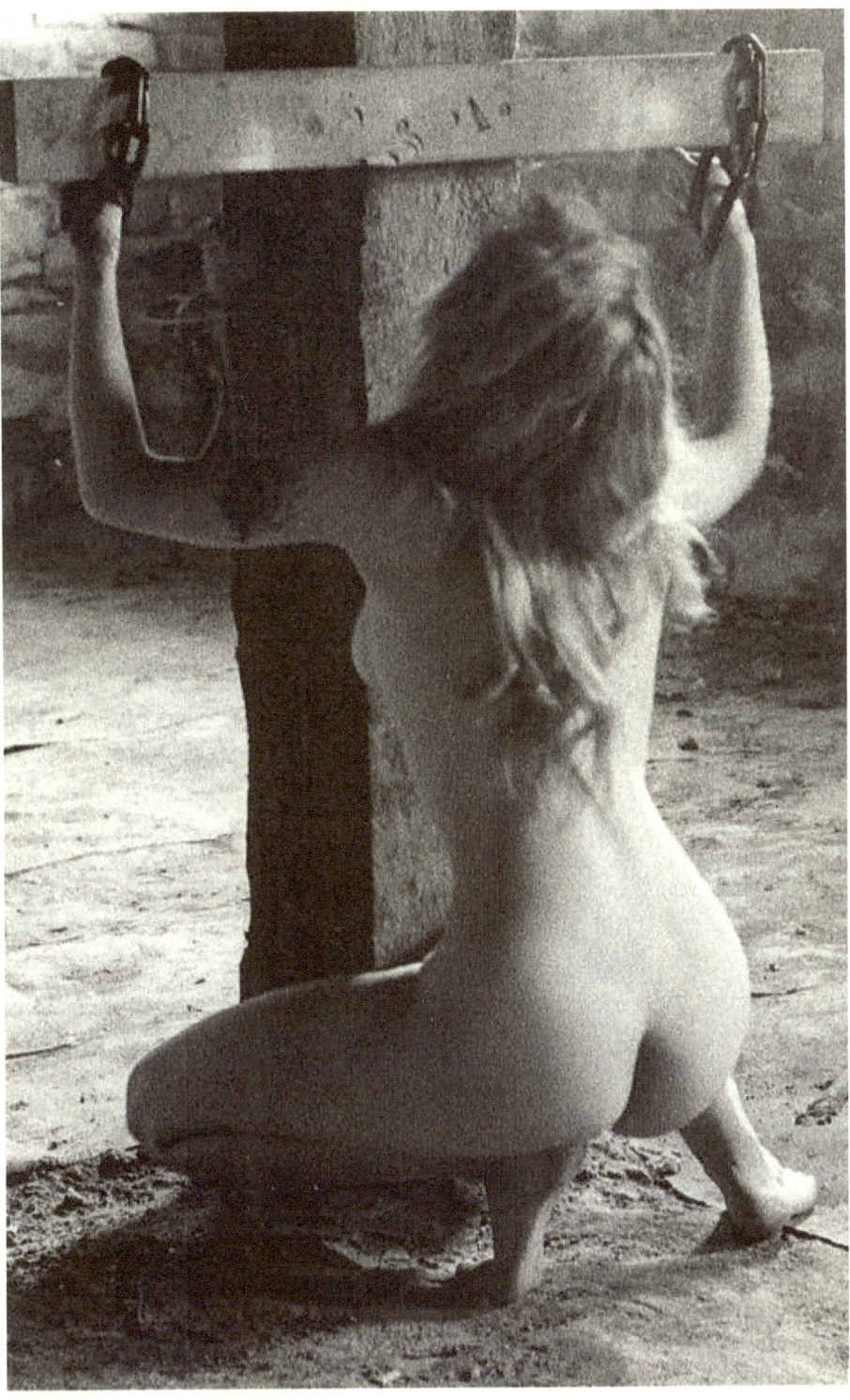

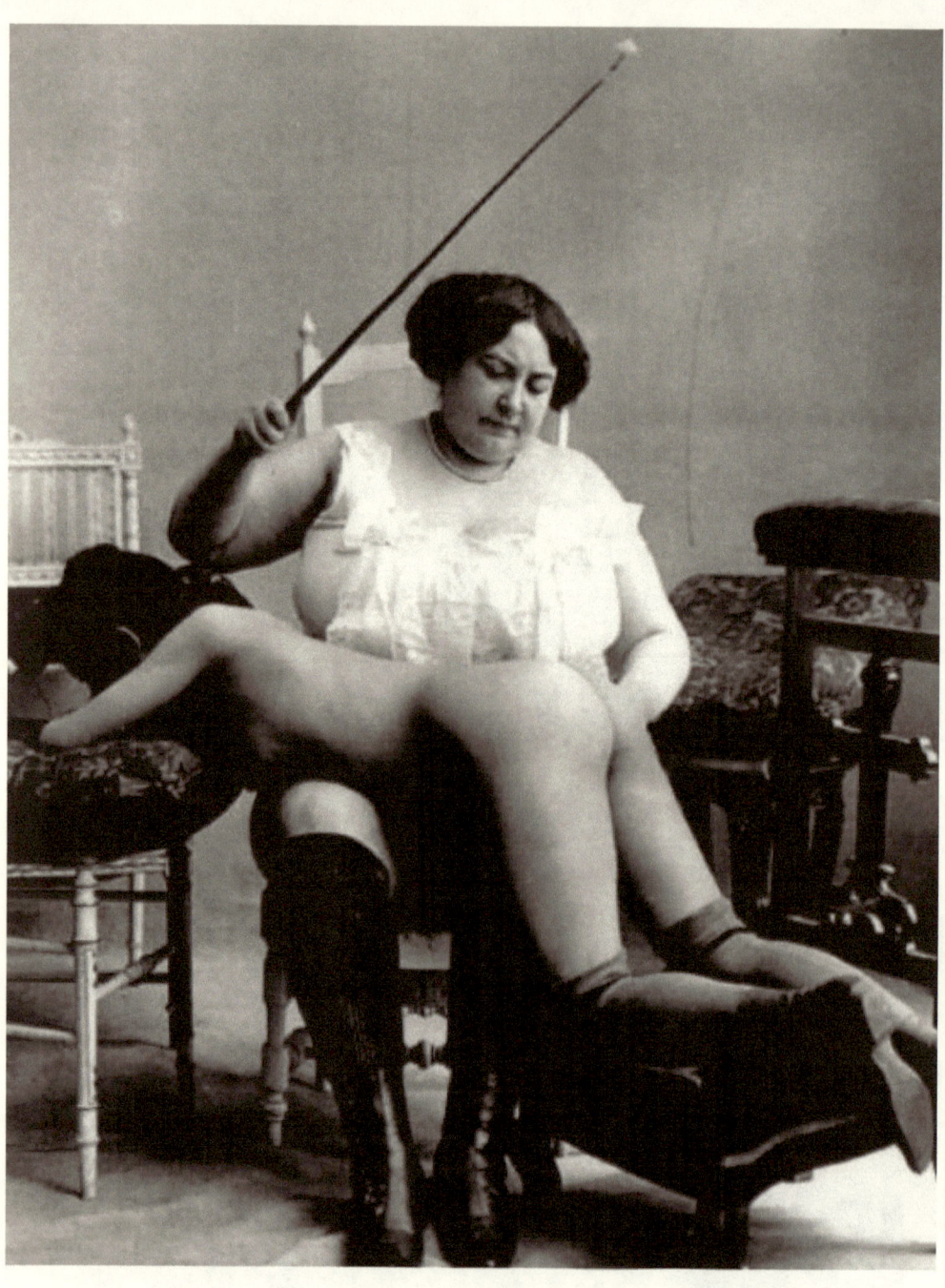

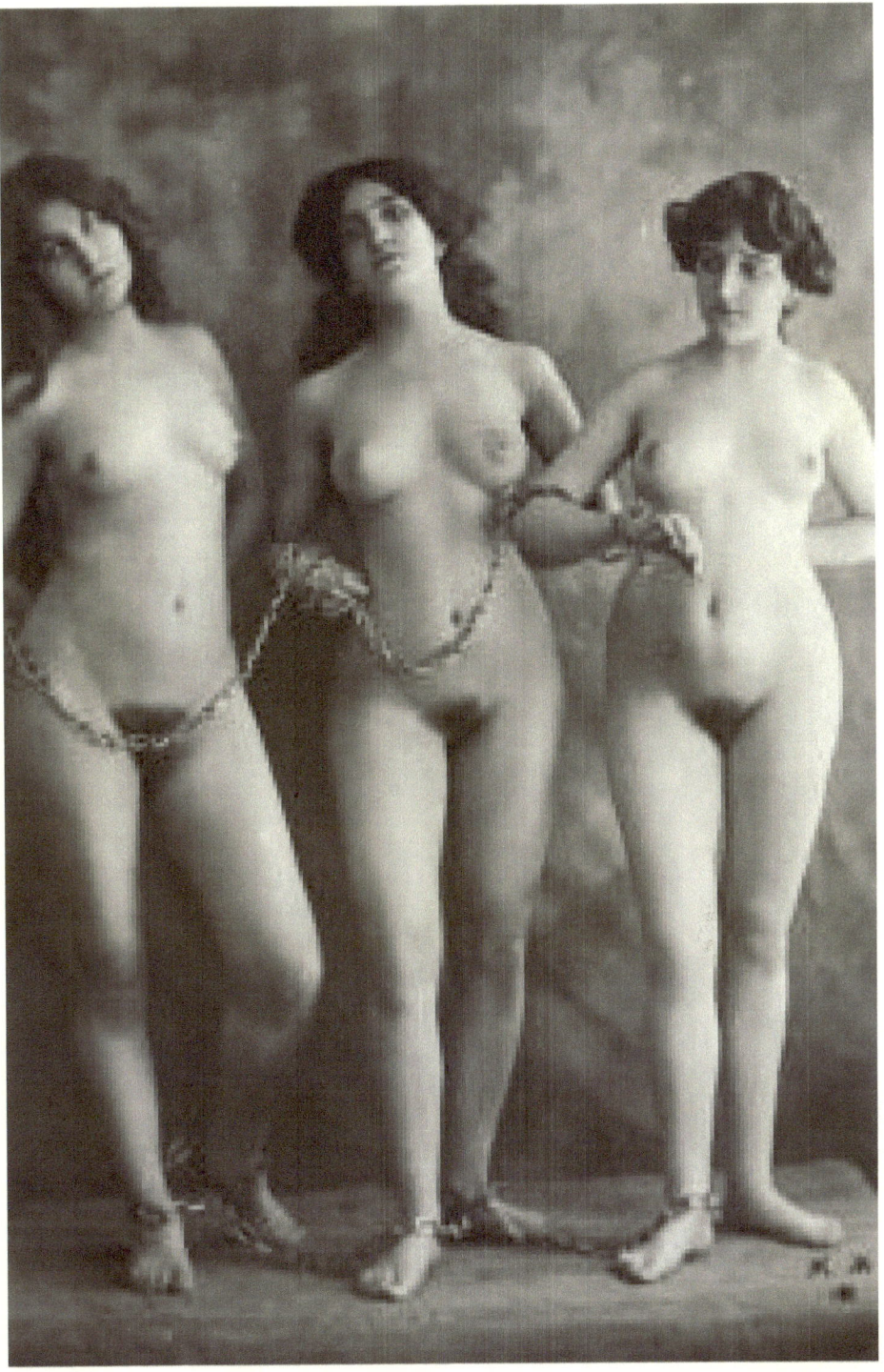

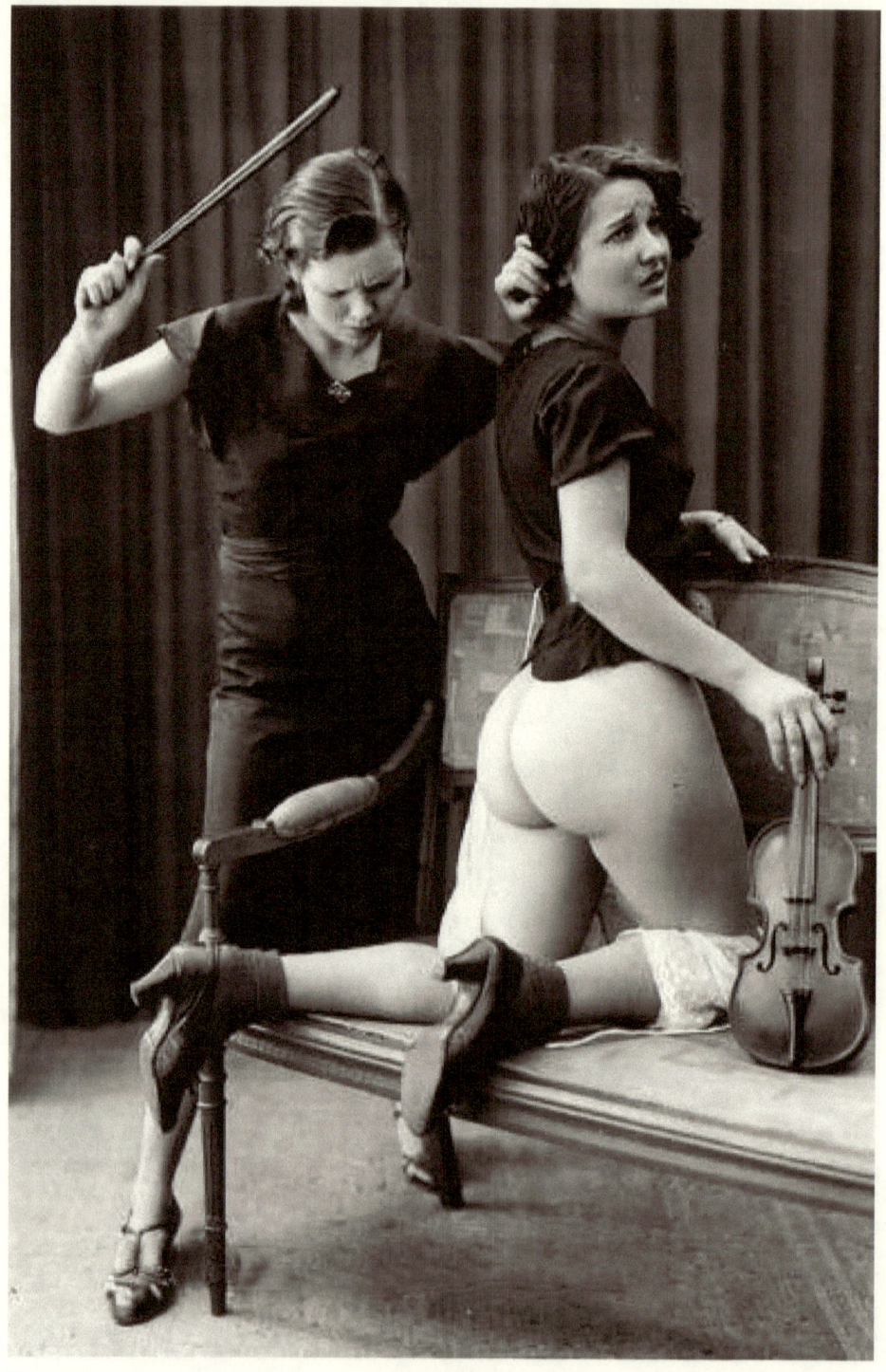

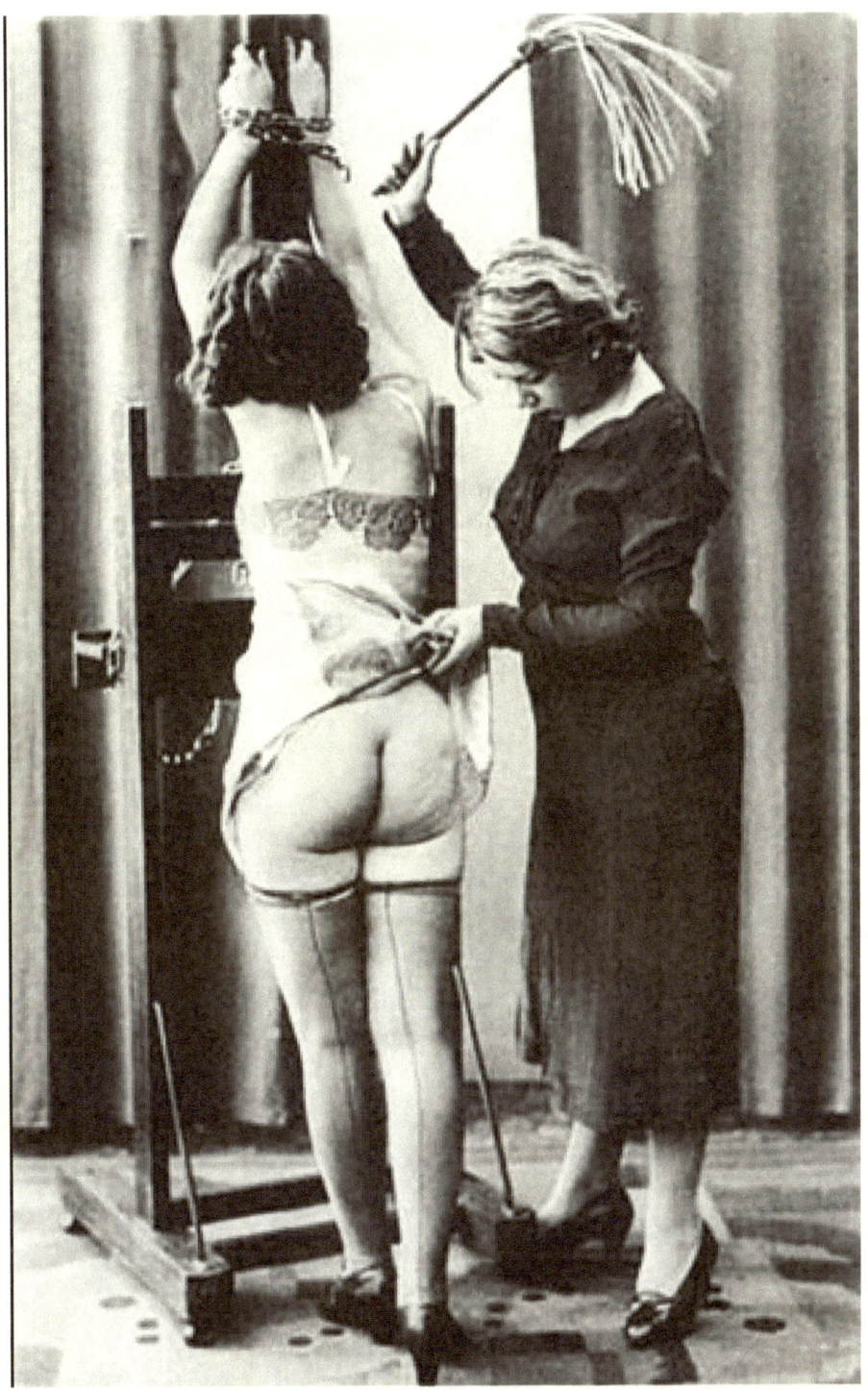

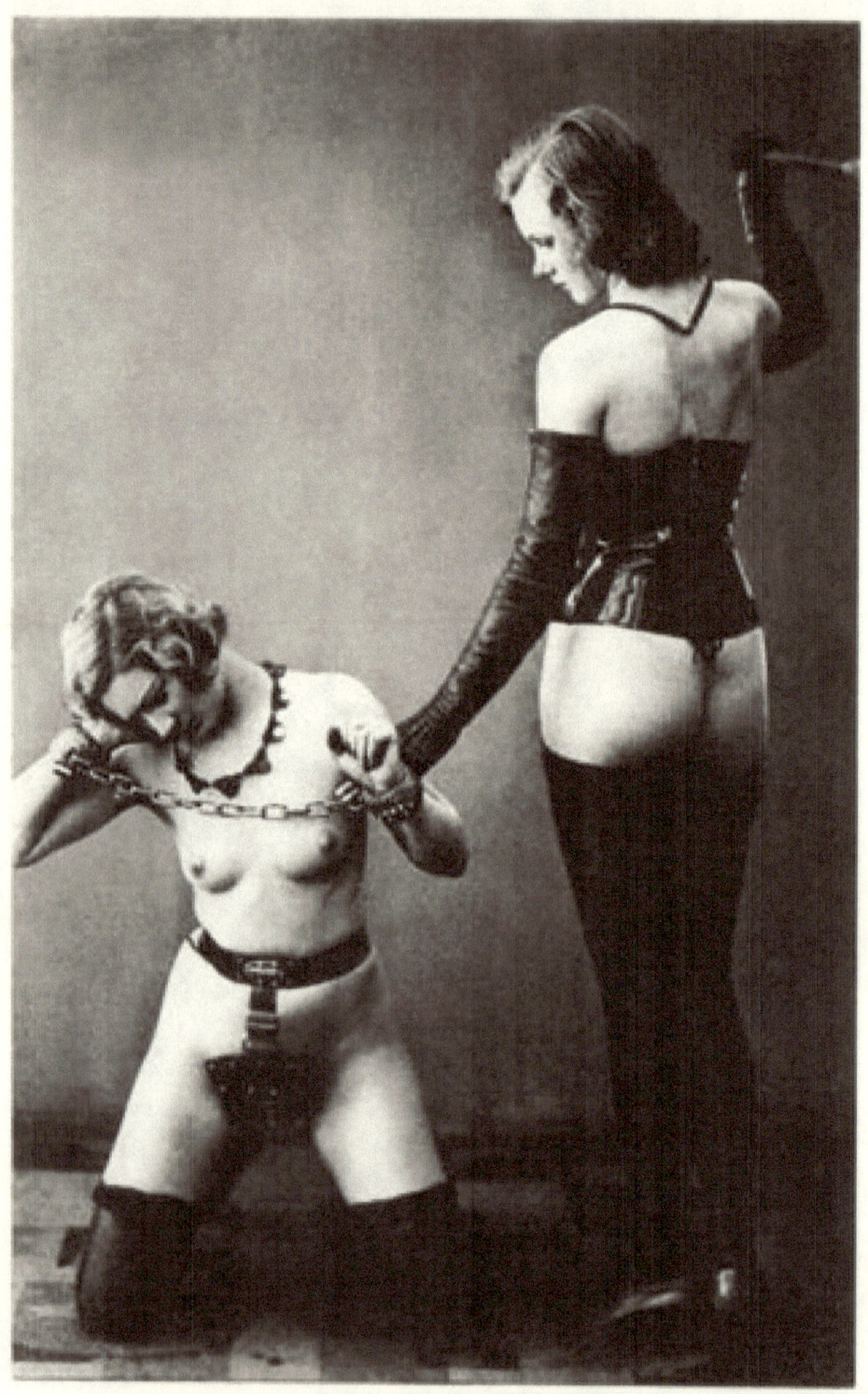

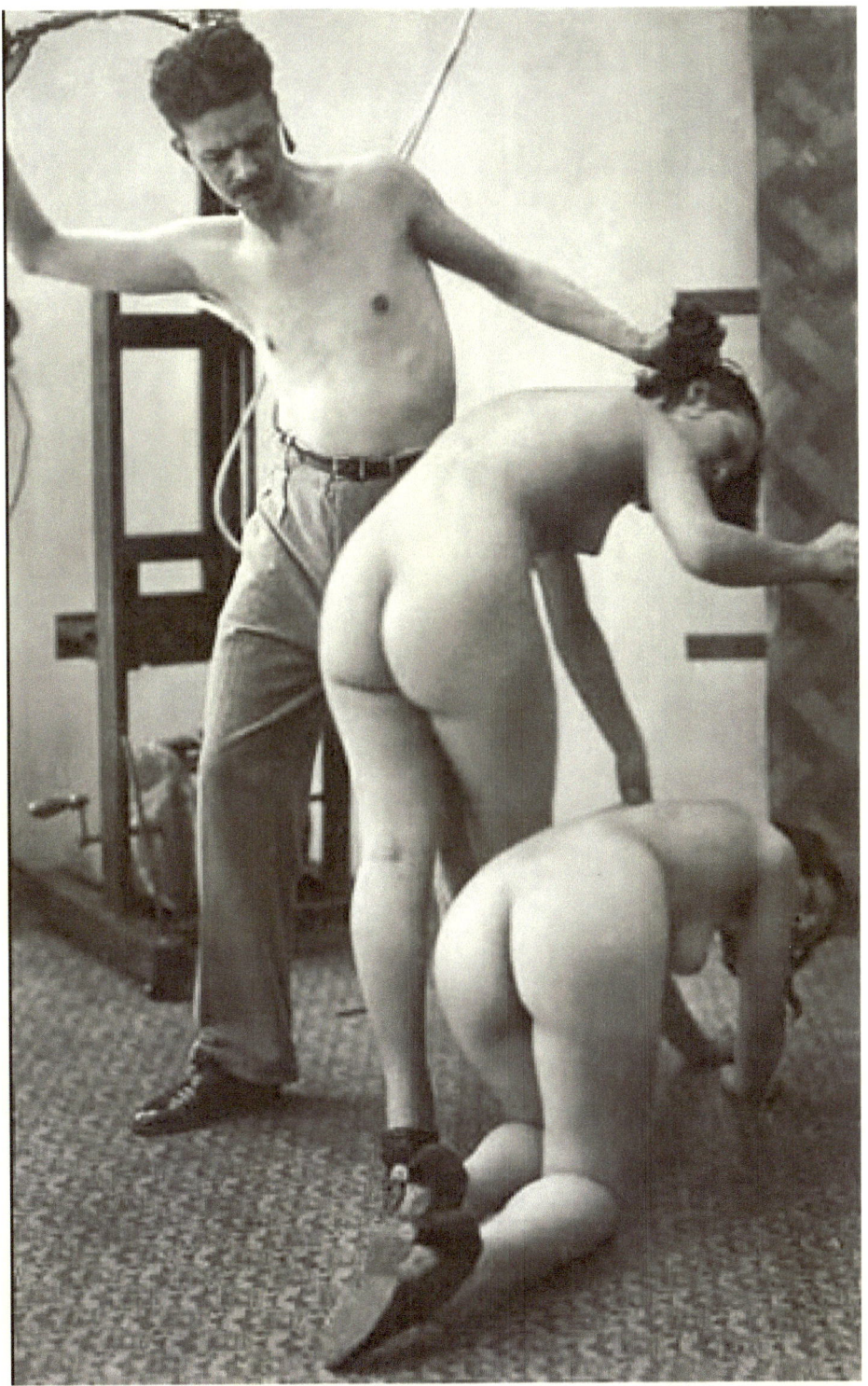

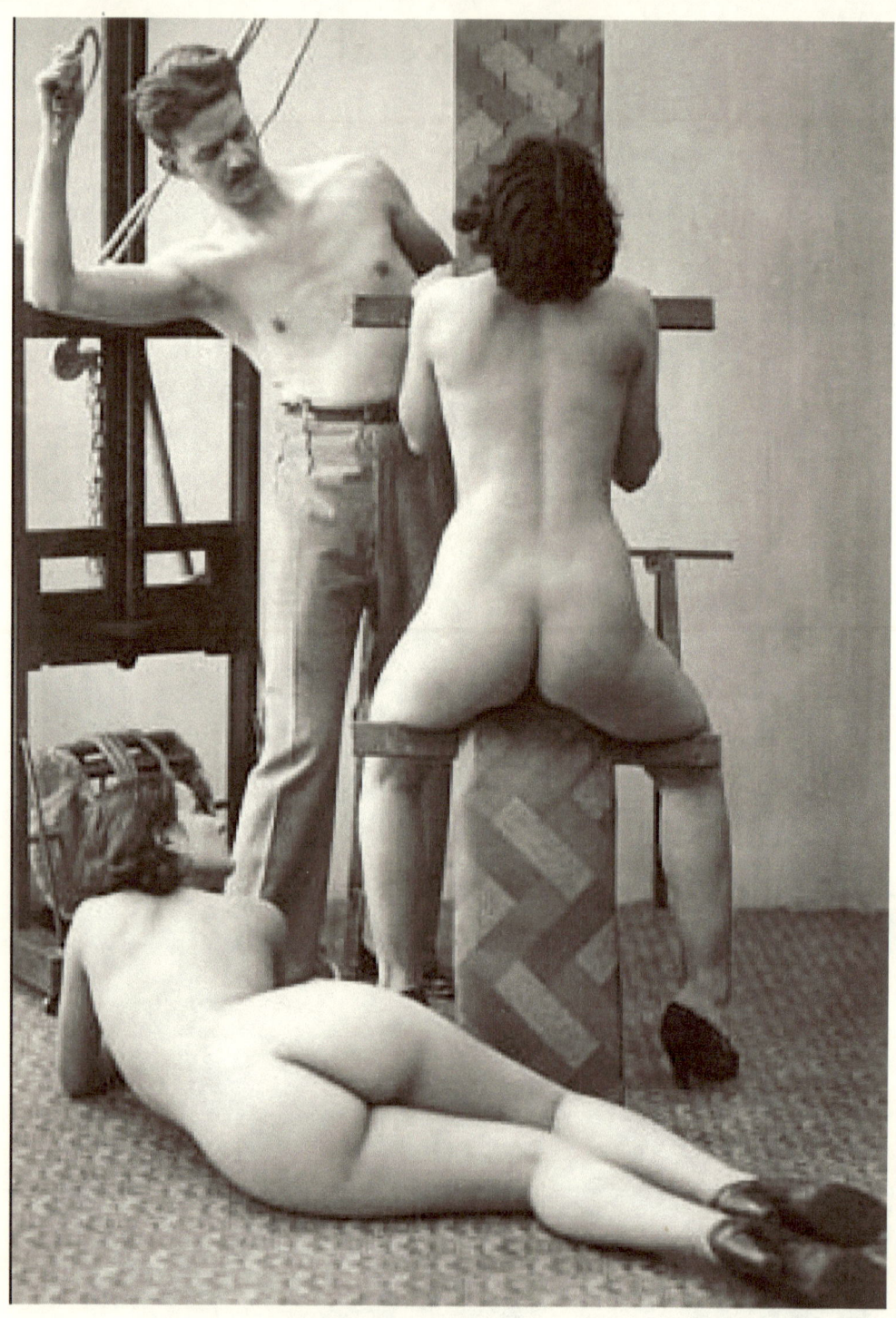

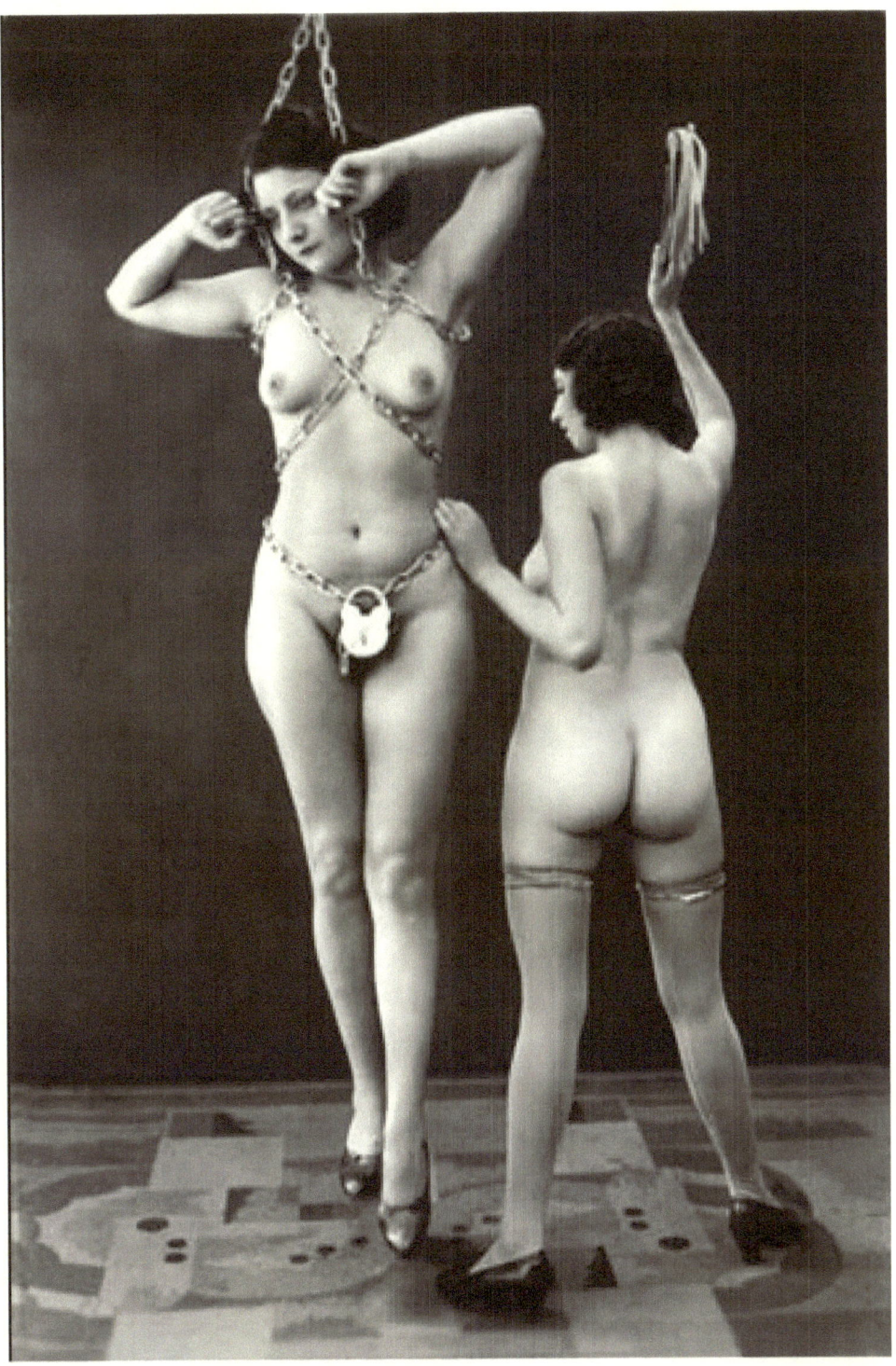

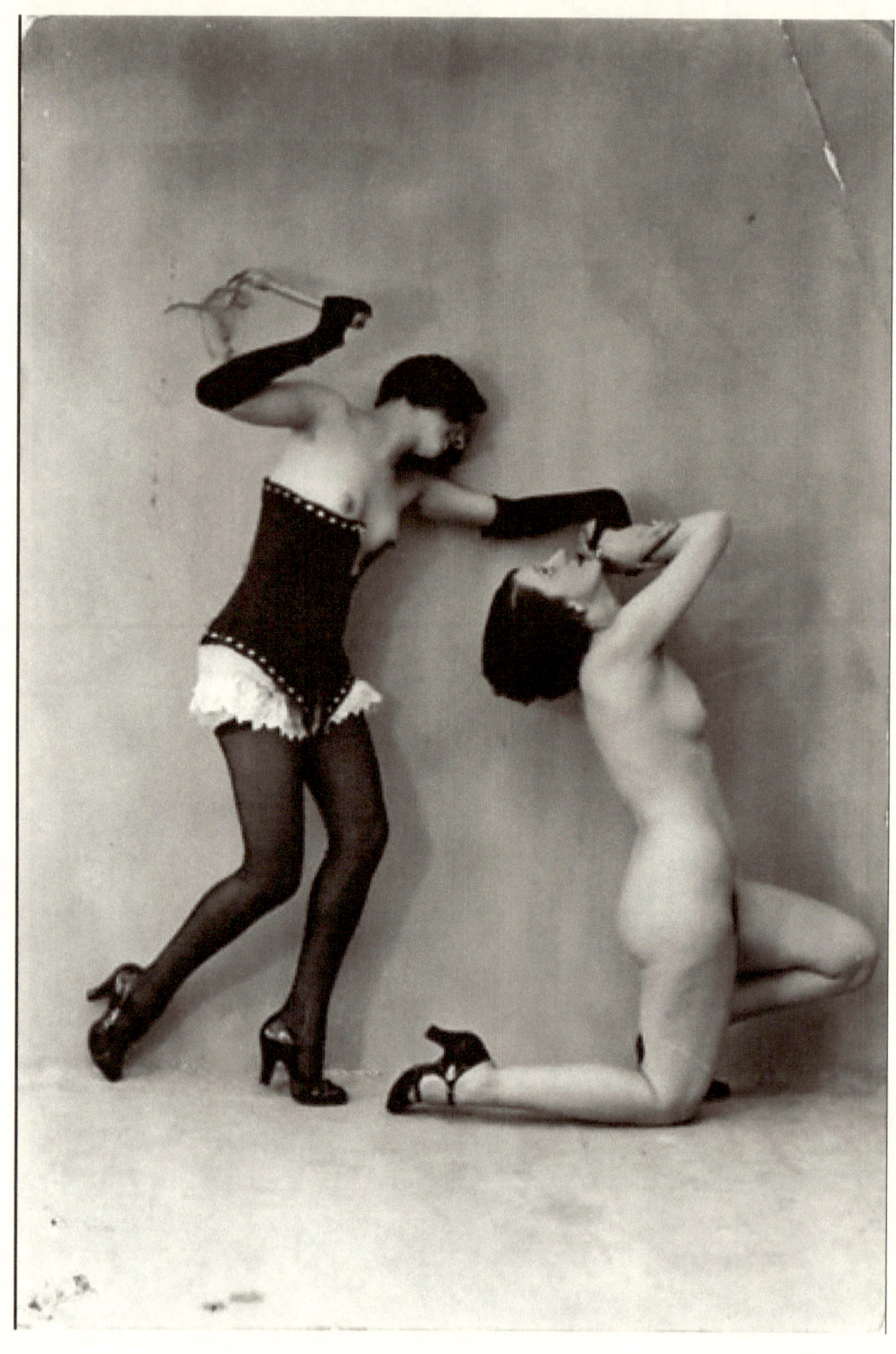

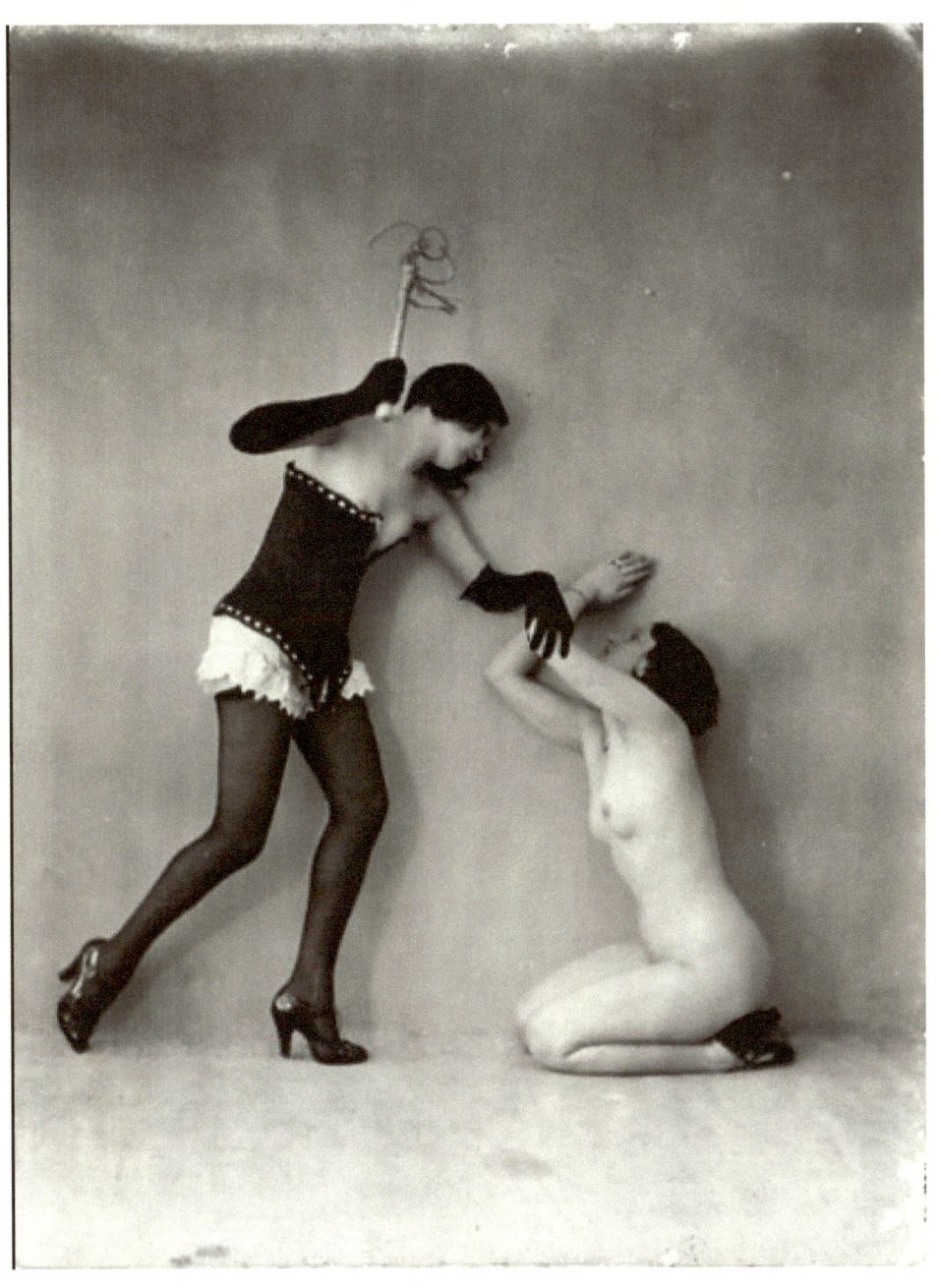

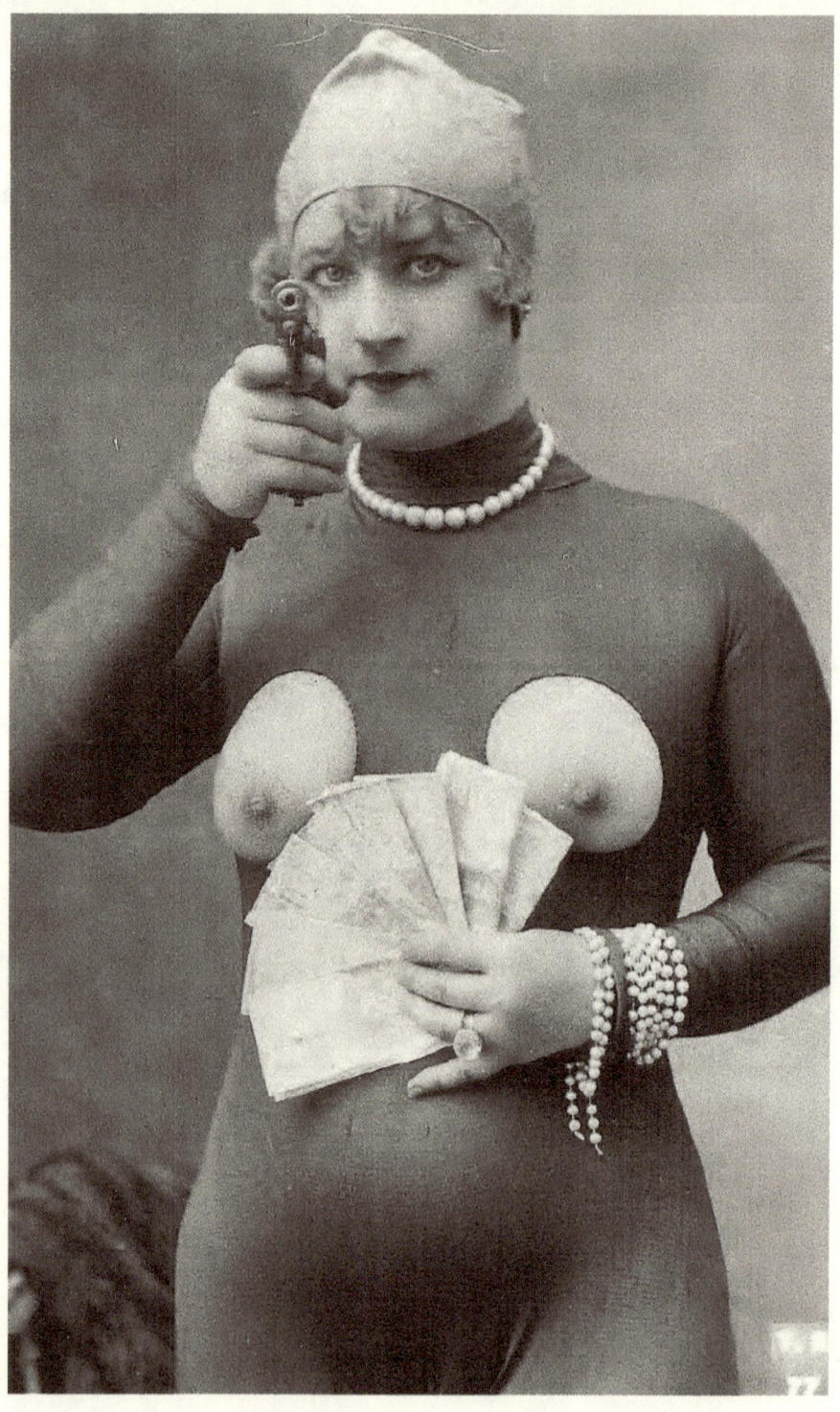

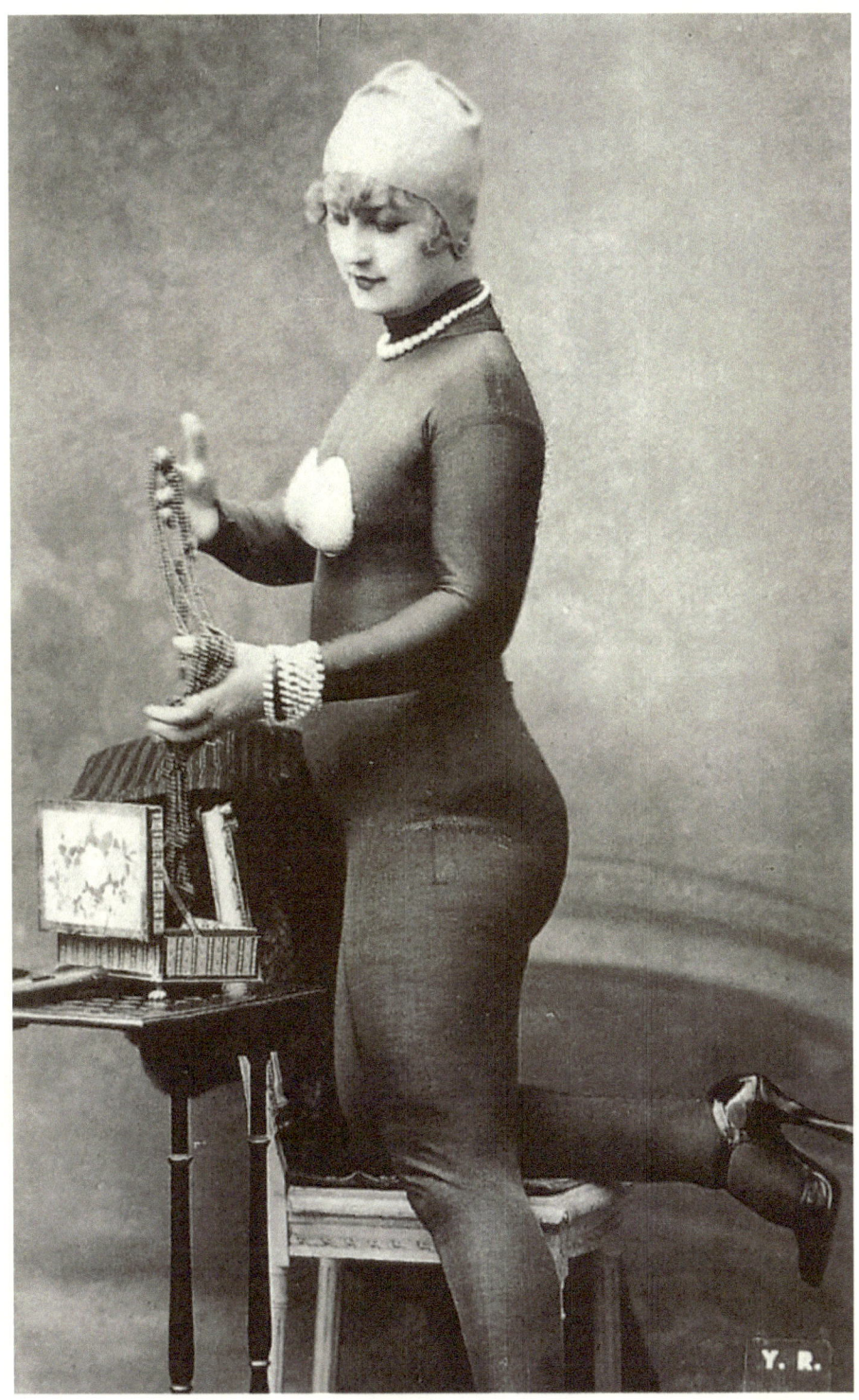

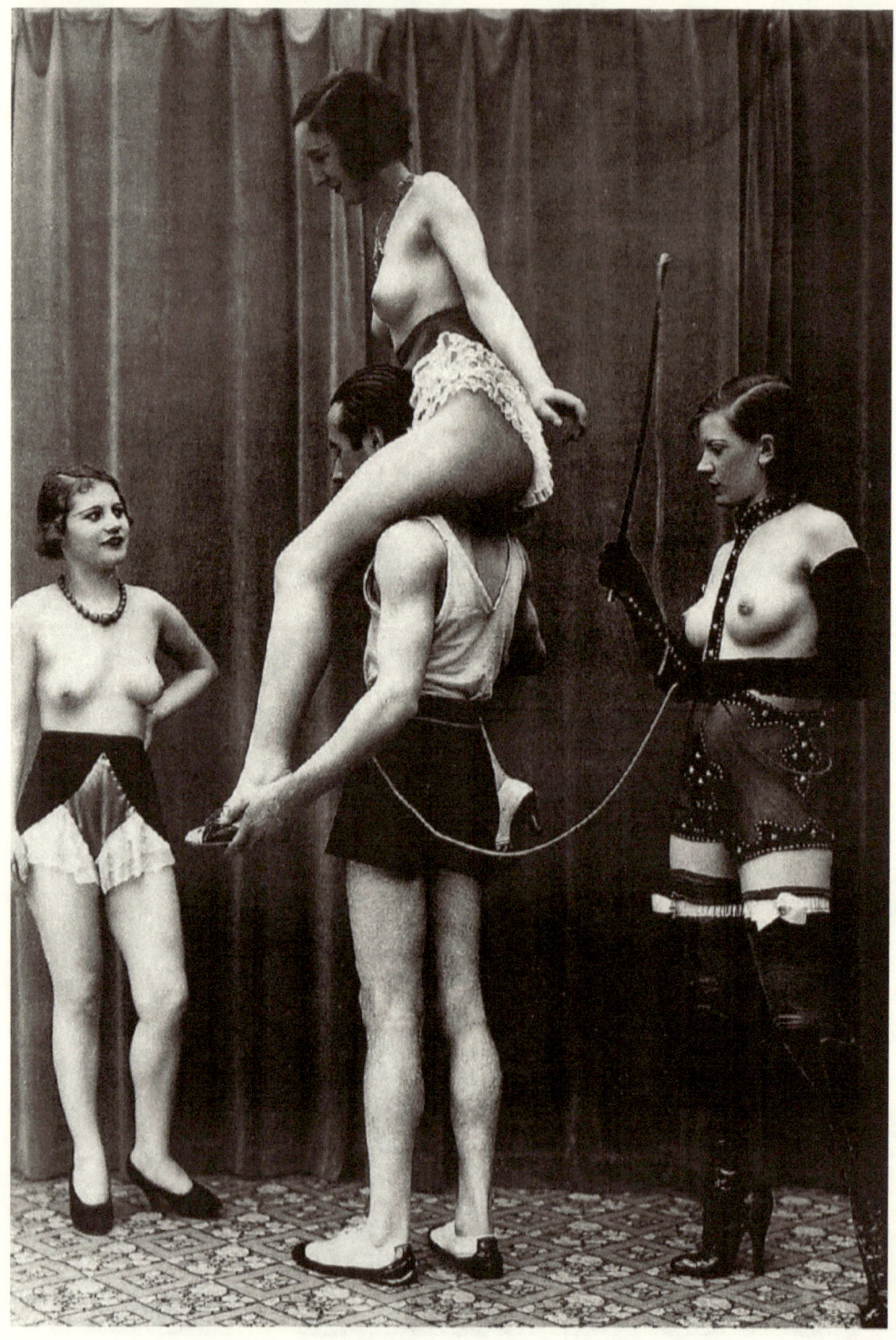

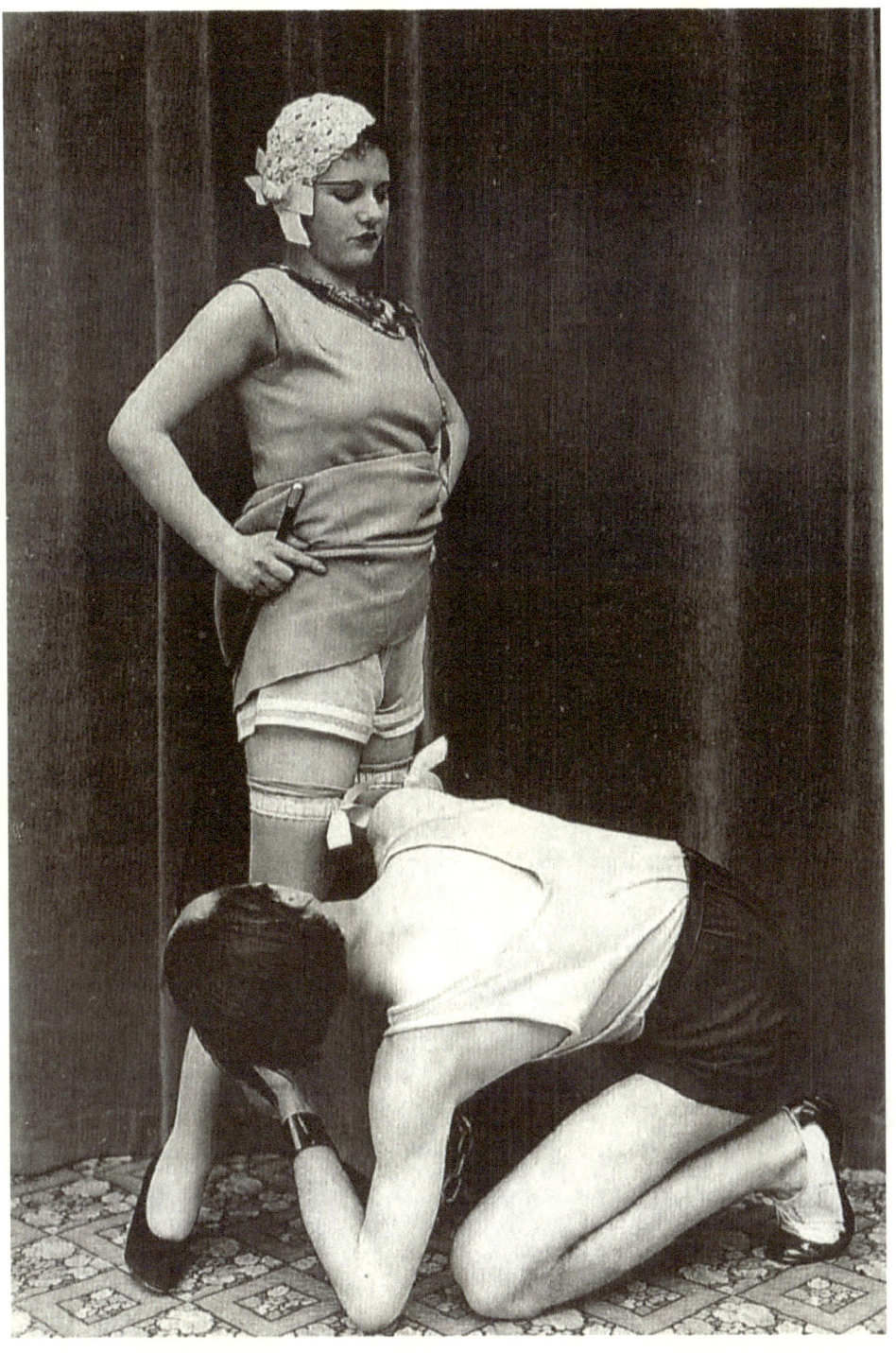

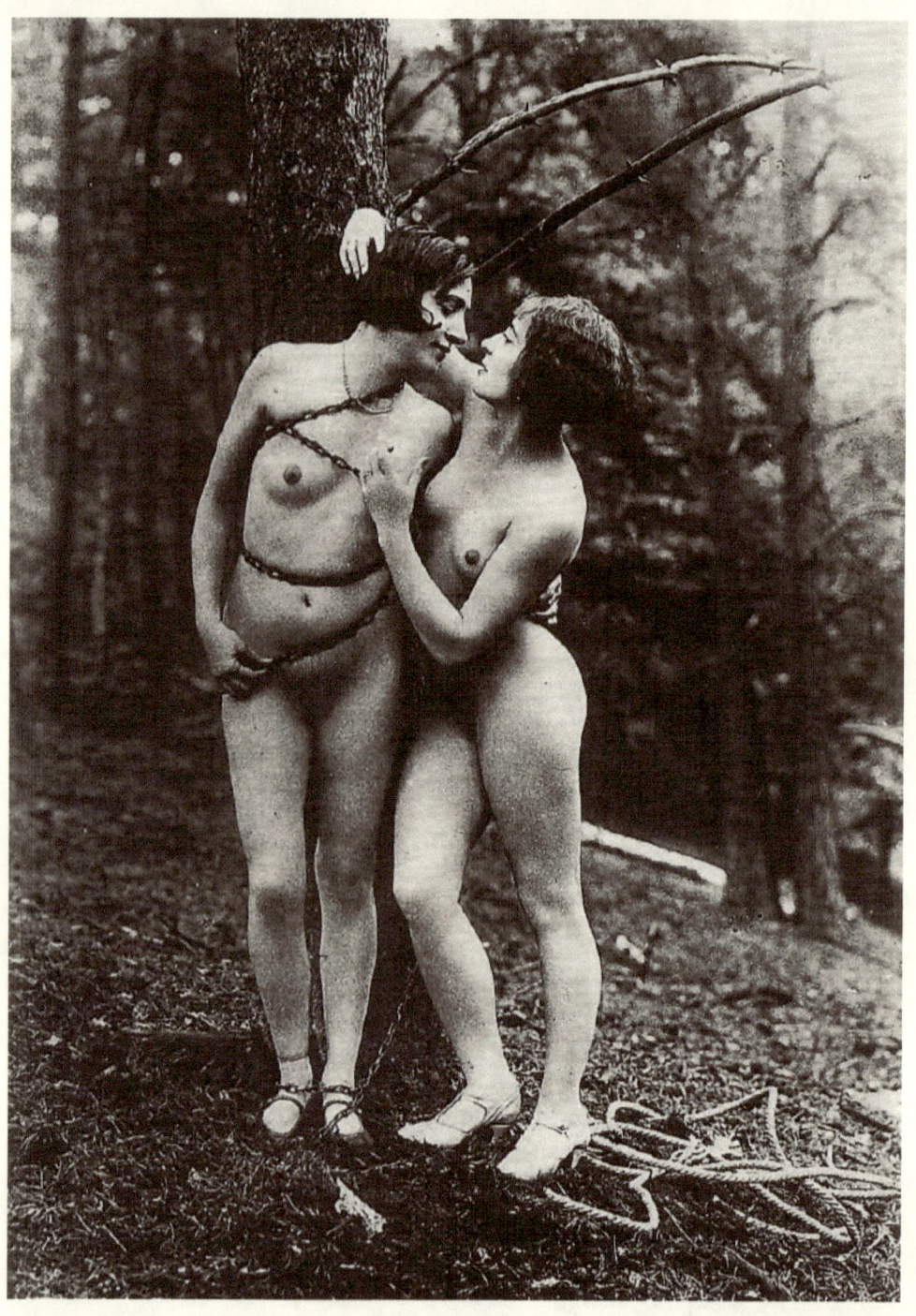

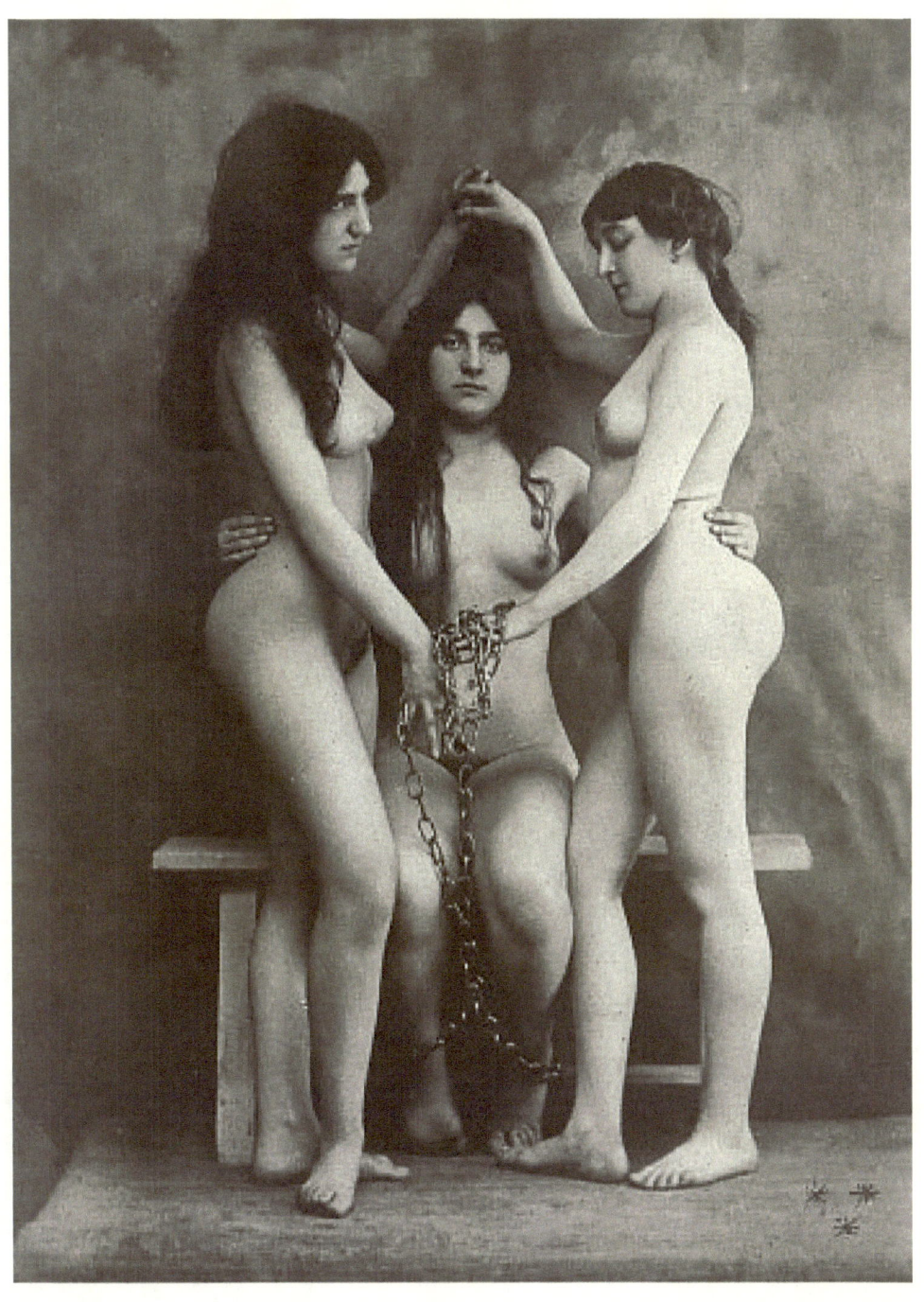

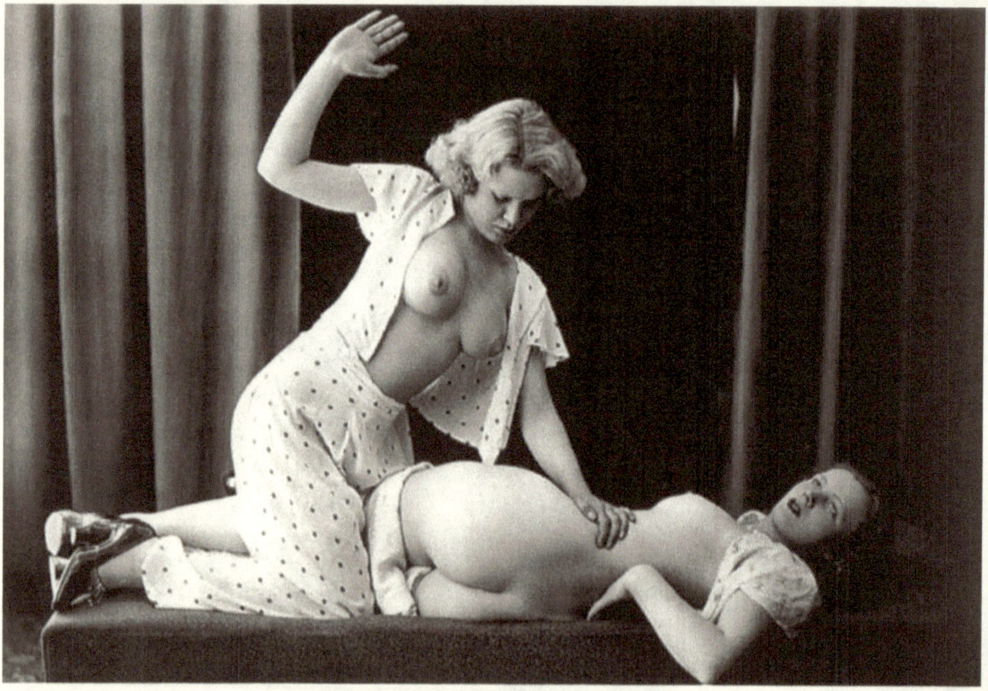

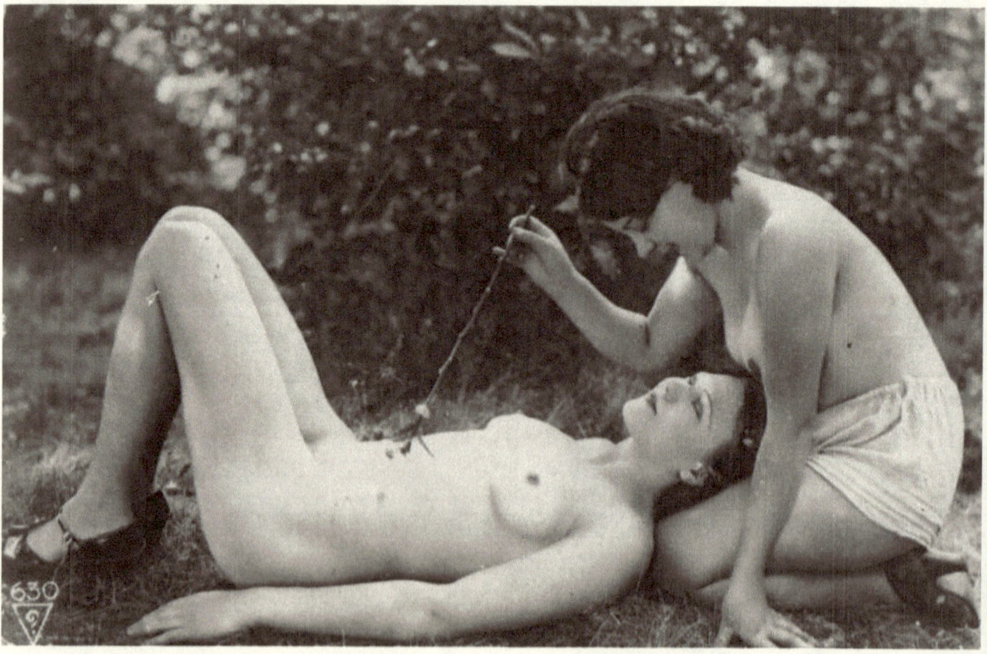
630

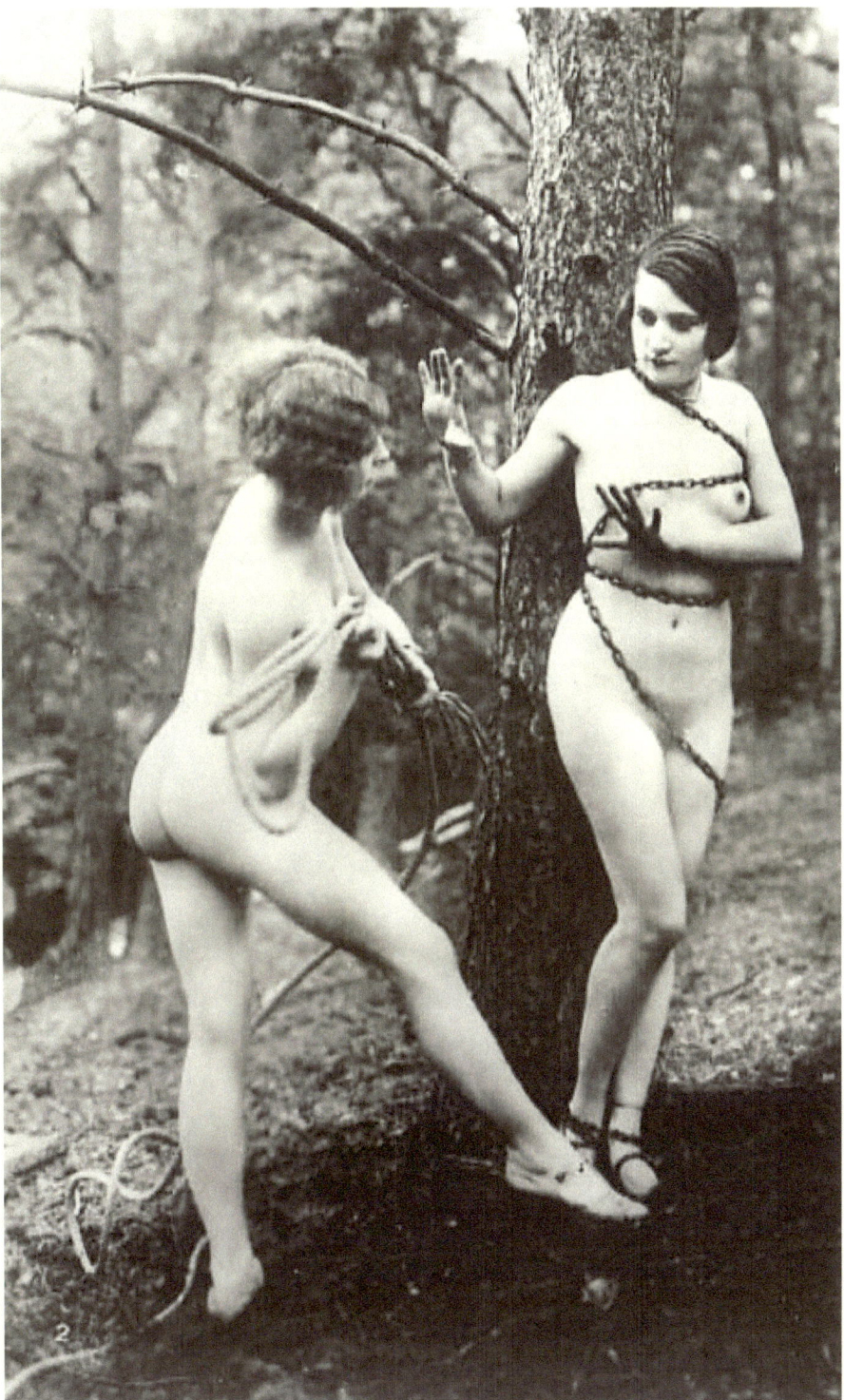

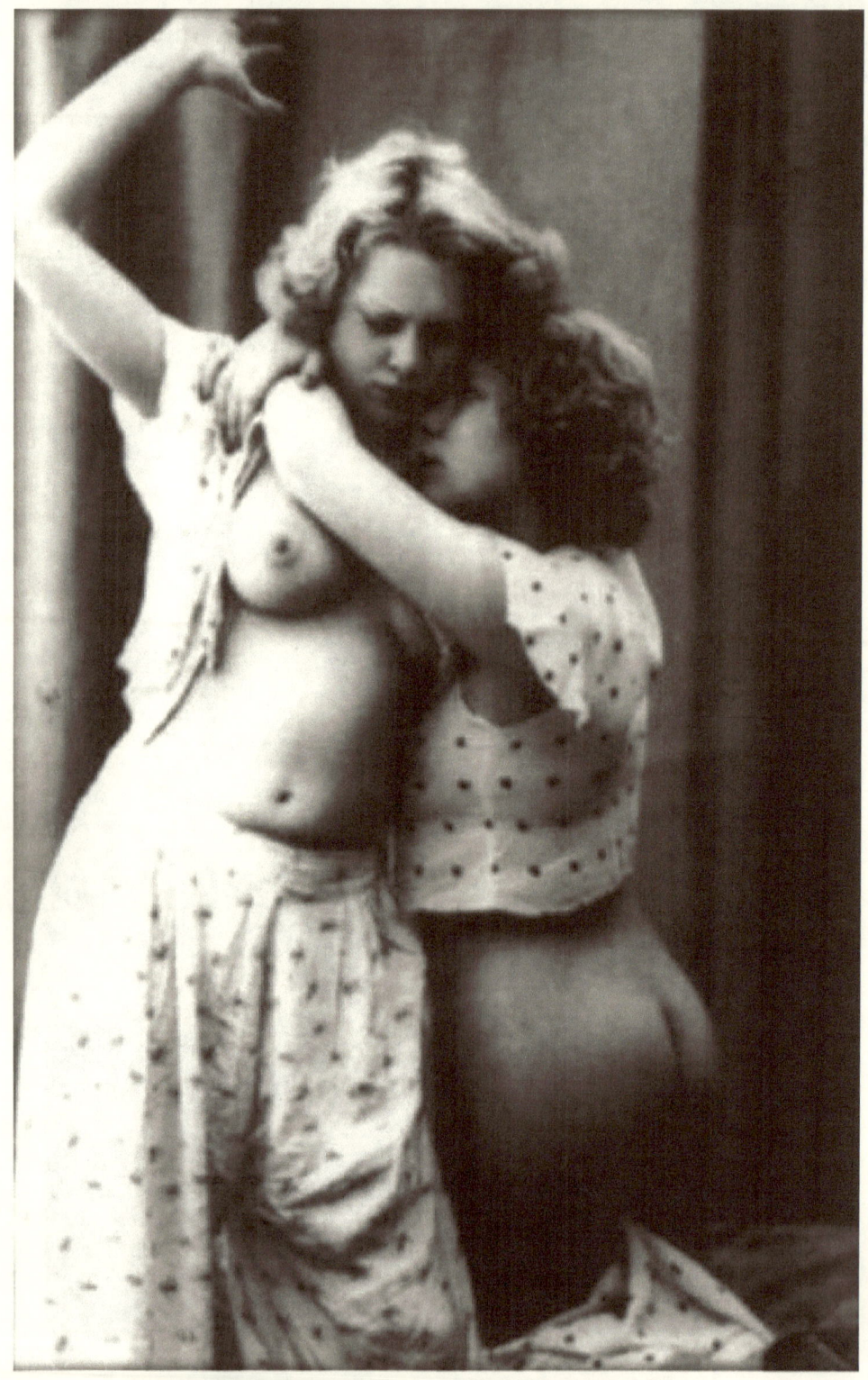

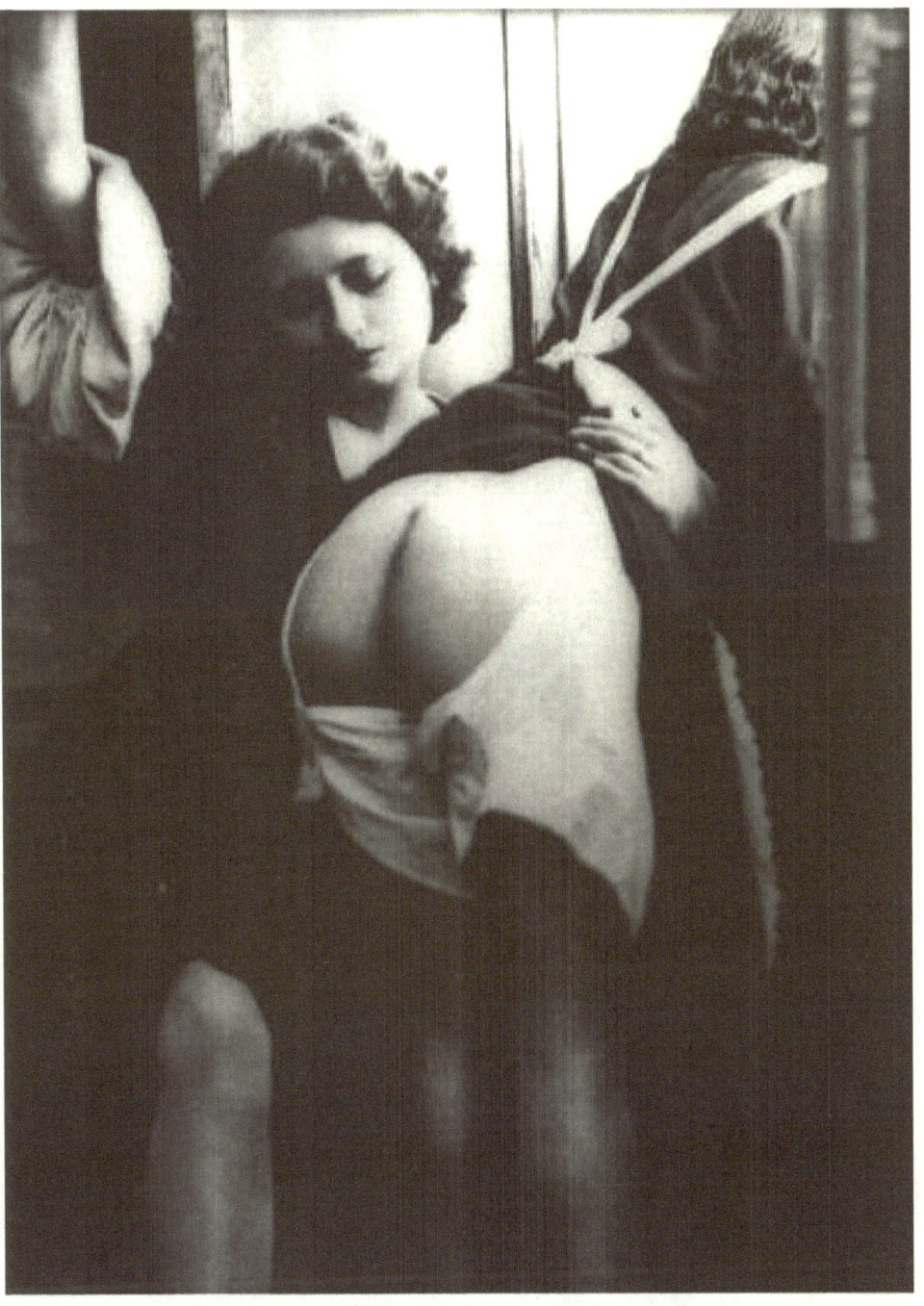

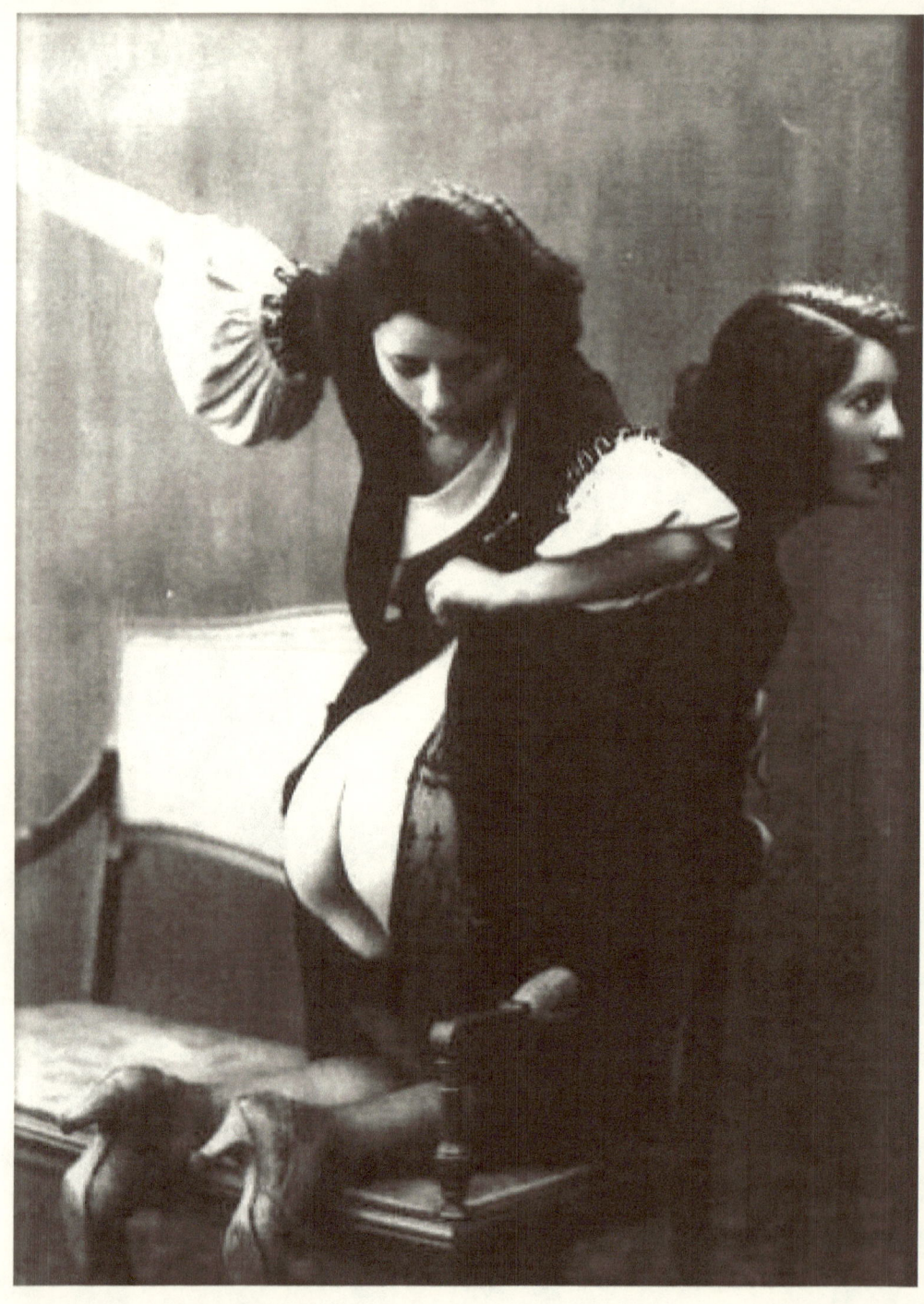

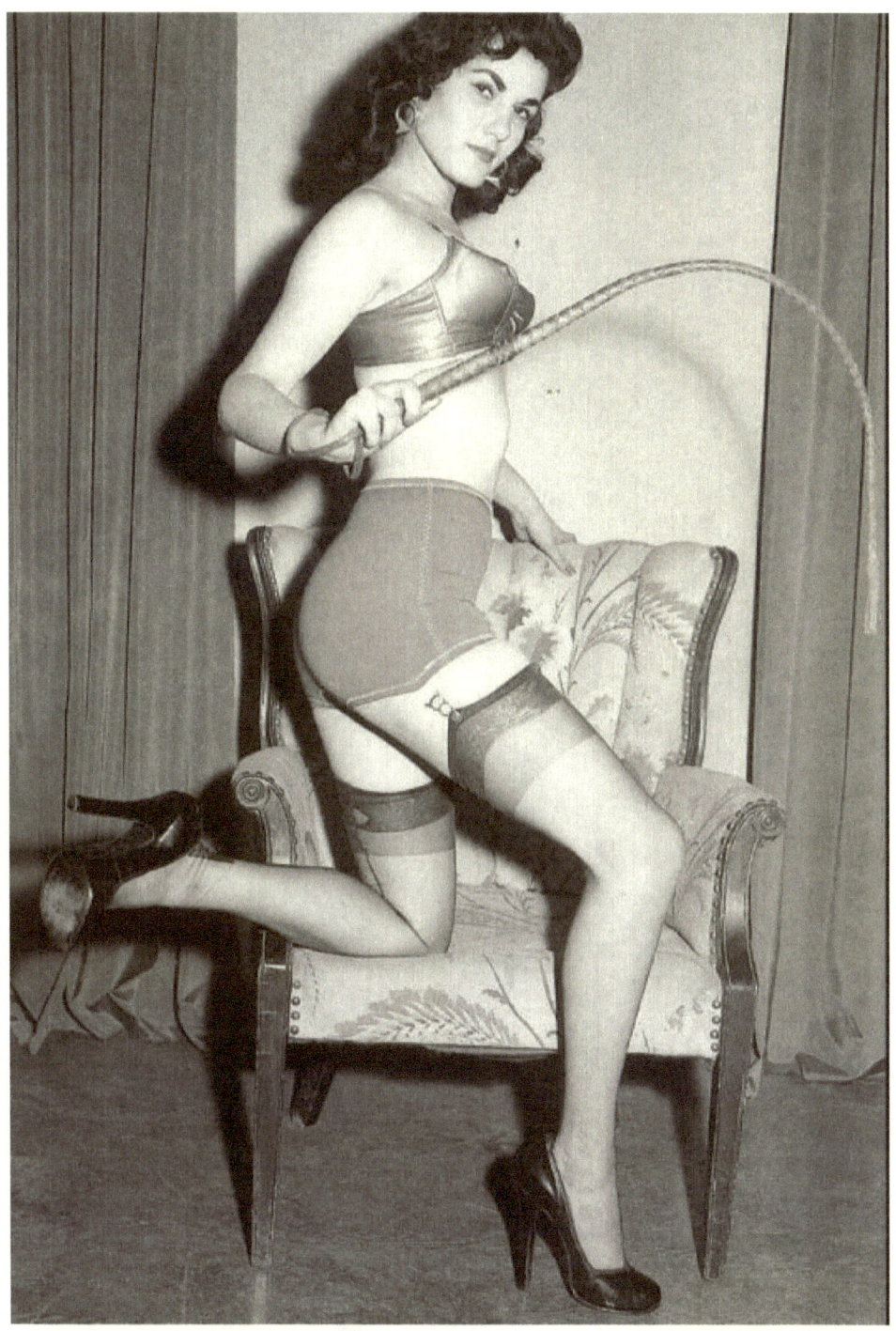

La Ceinture d'Or.

Tombé sur deux Épaules

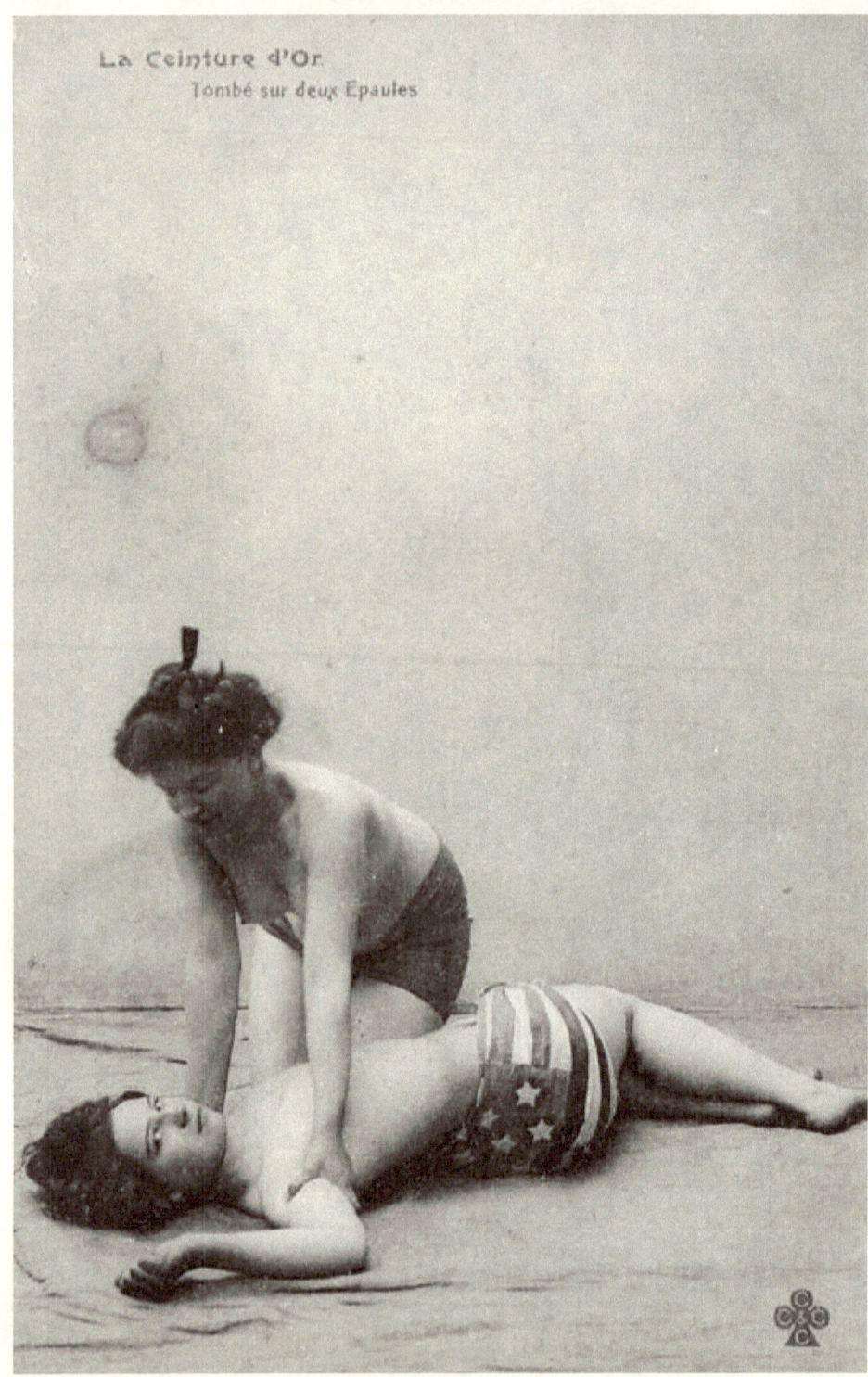

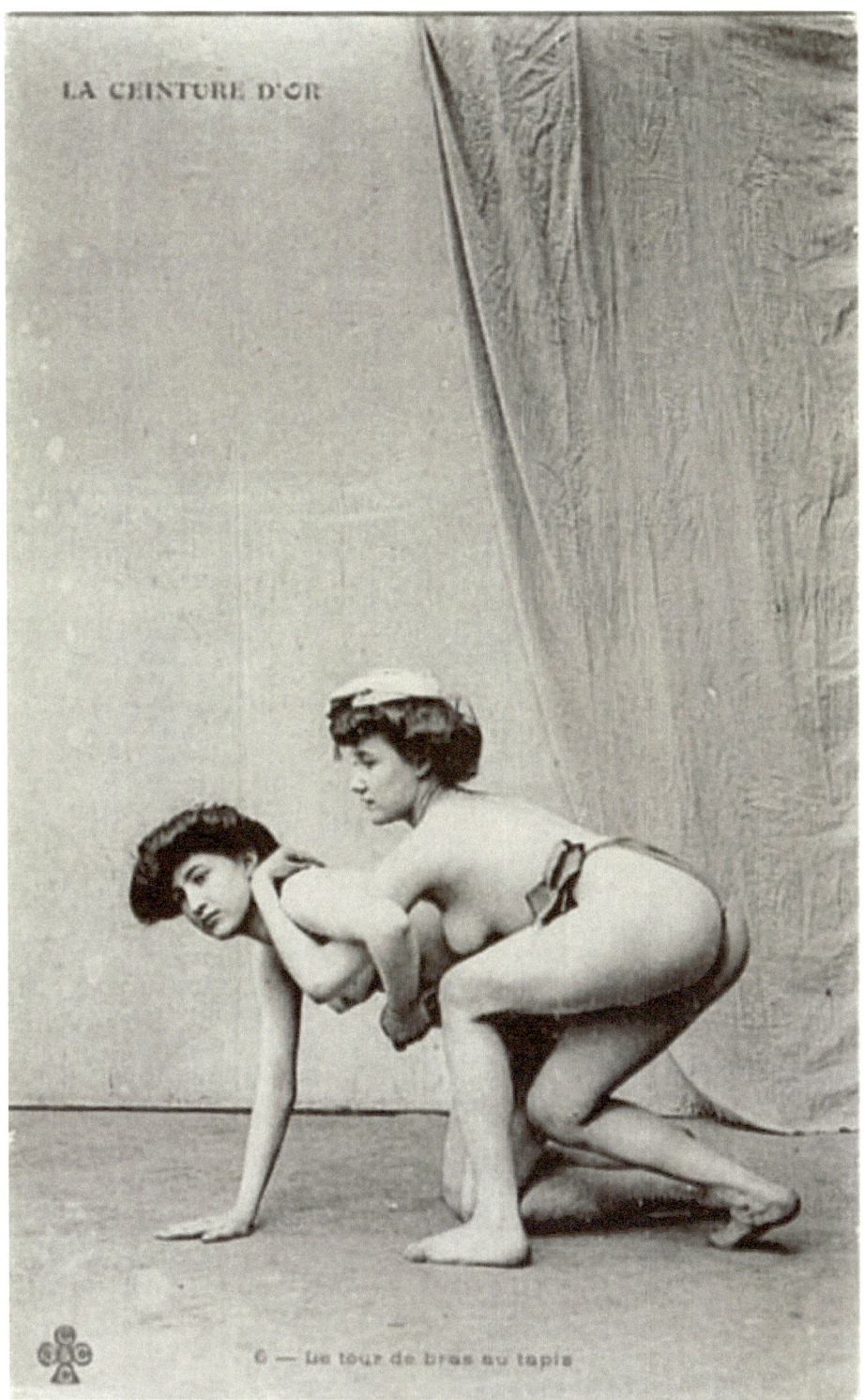

LA CEINTURE D'OR

6 — Le tour de bras au tapis

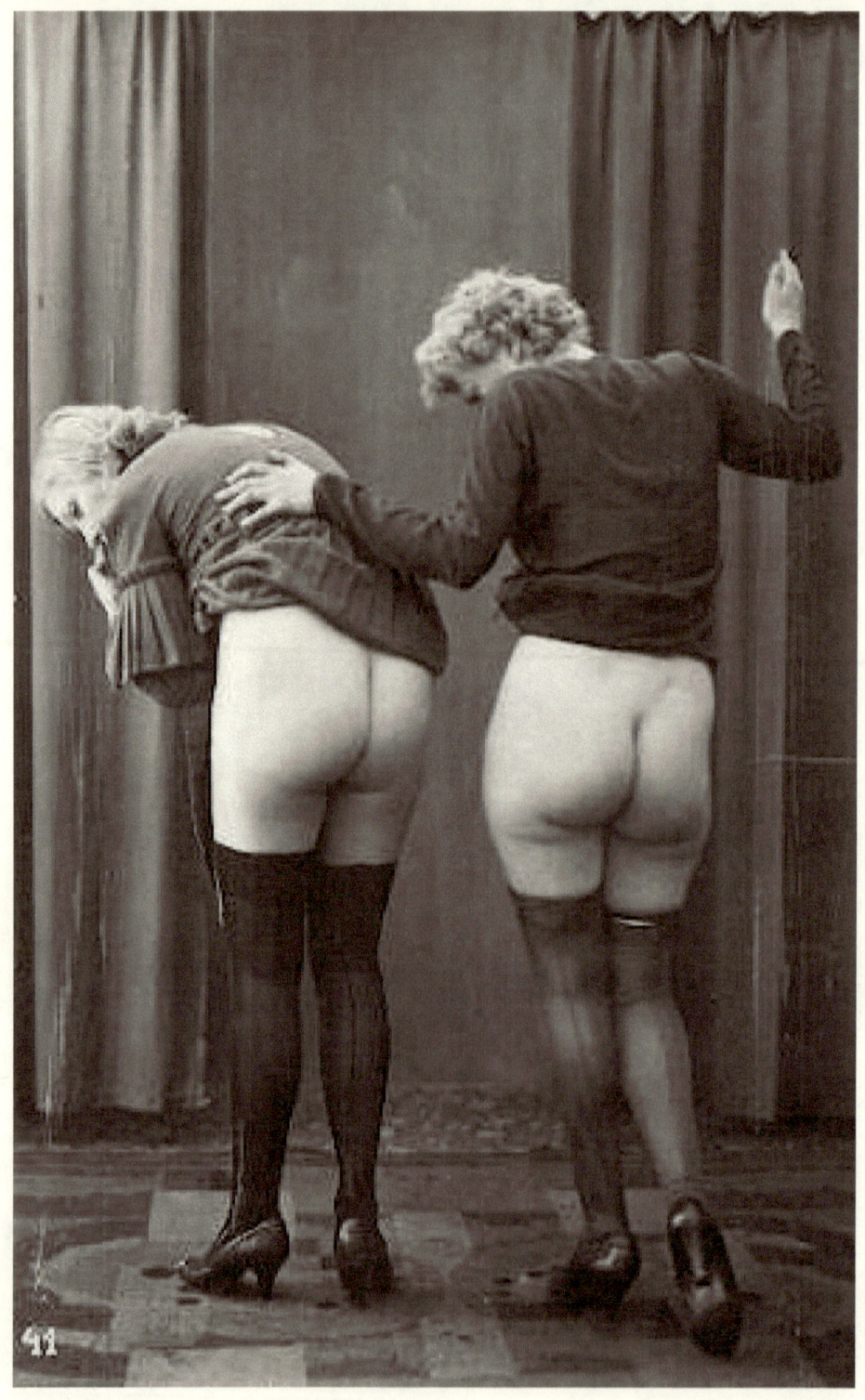

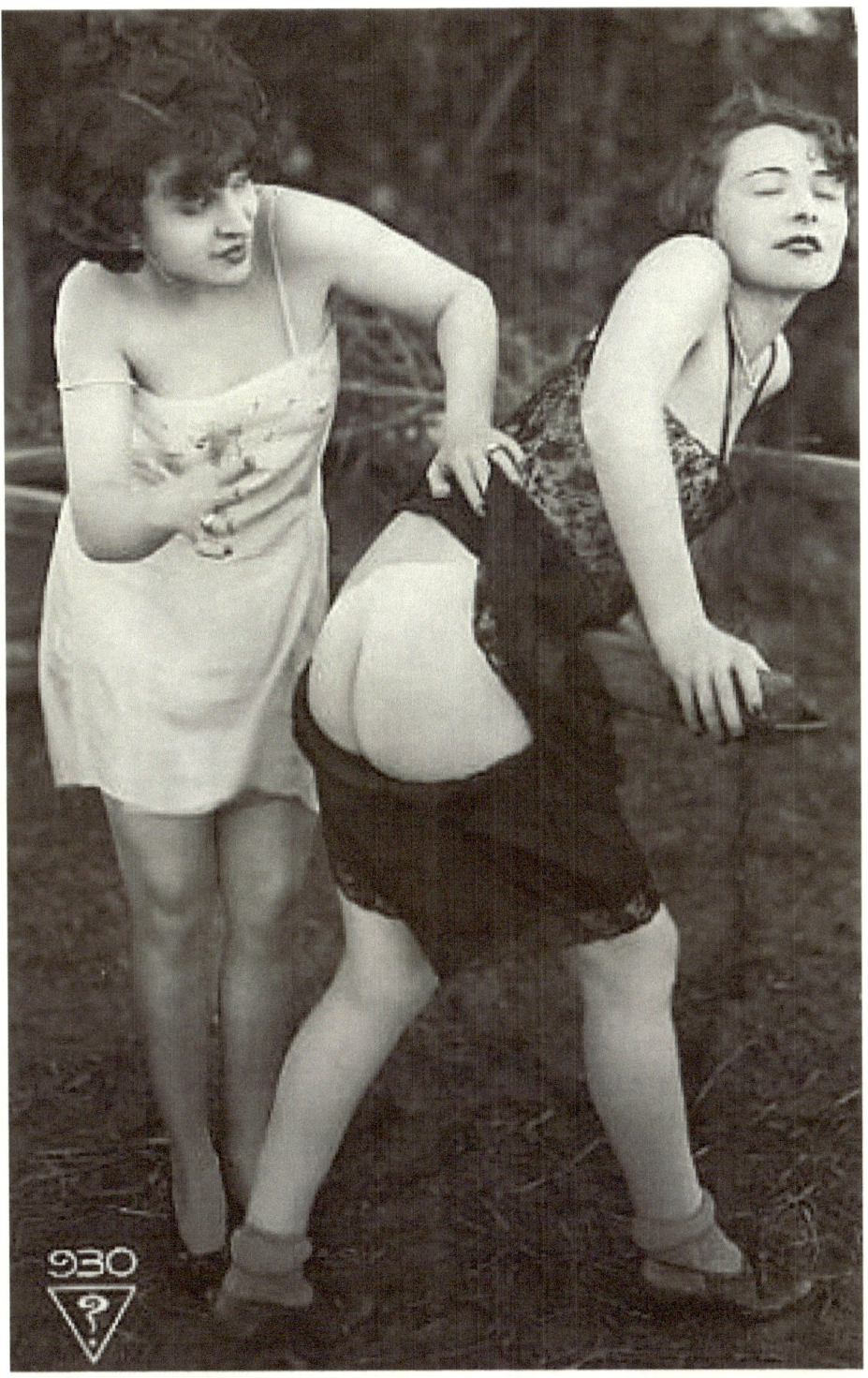

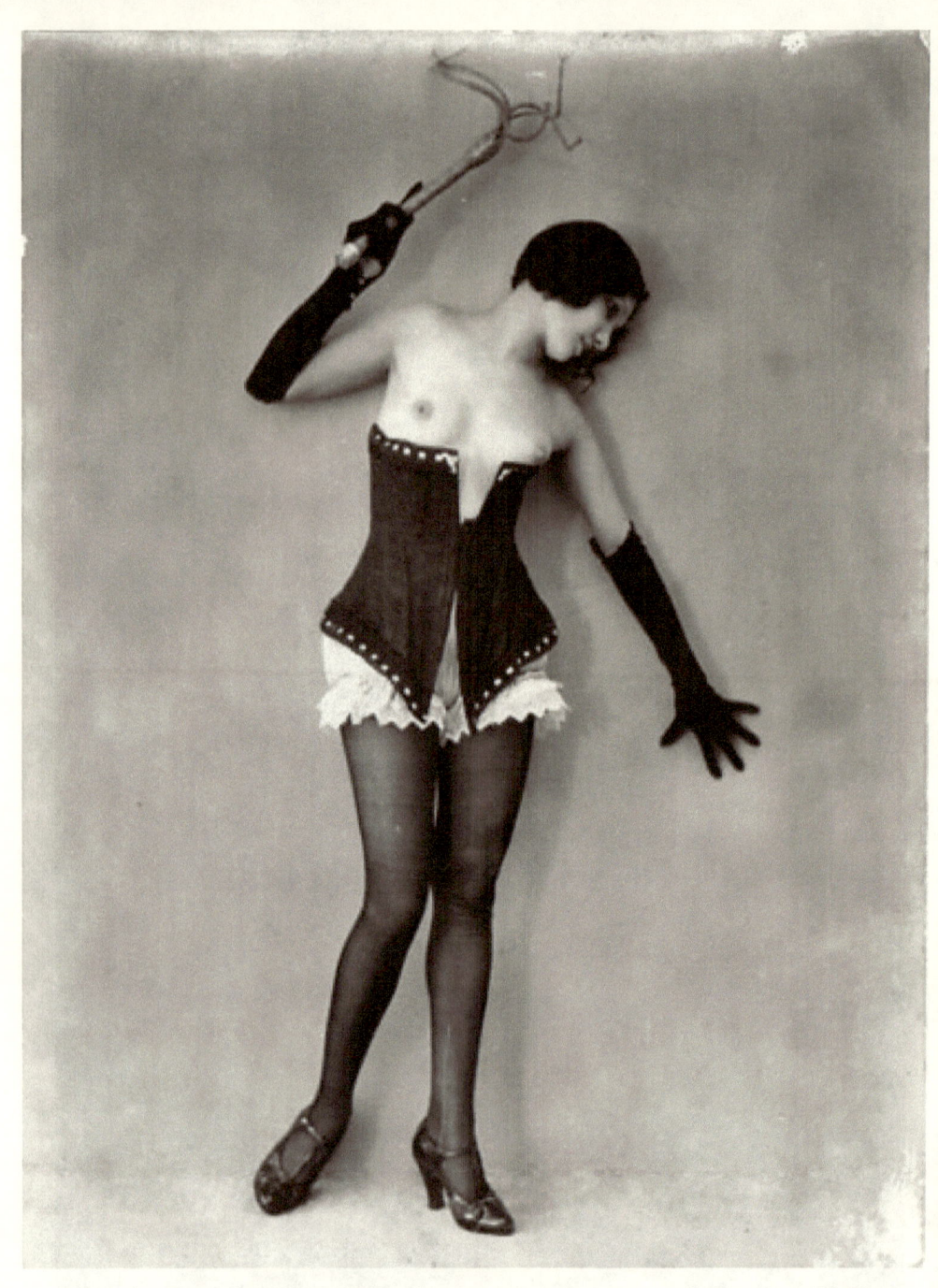

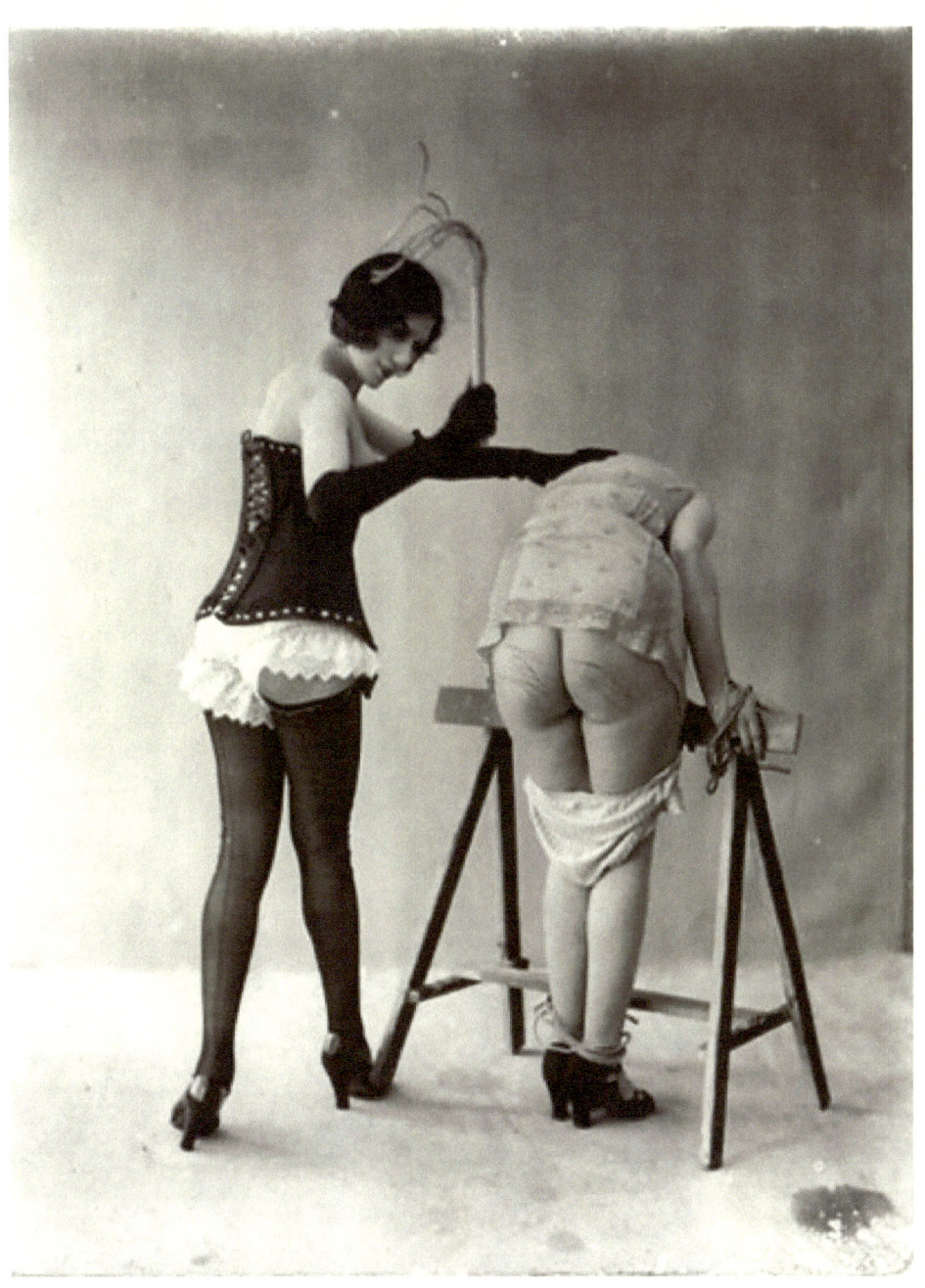

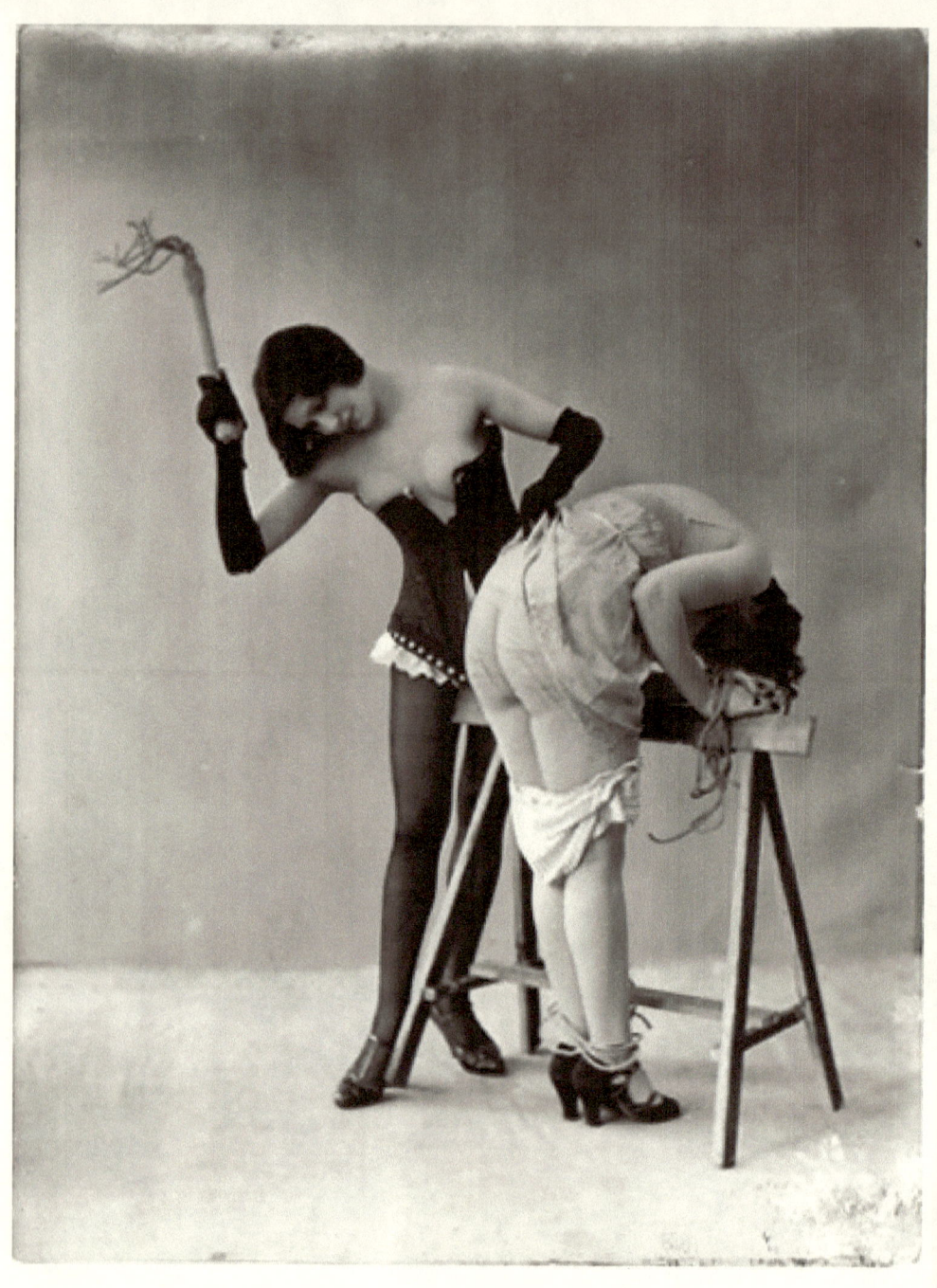

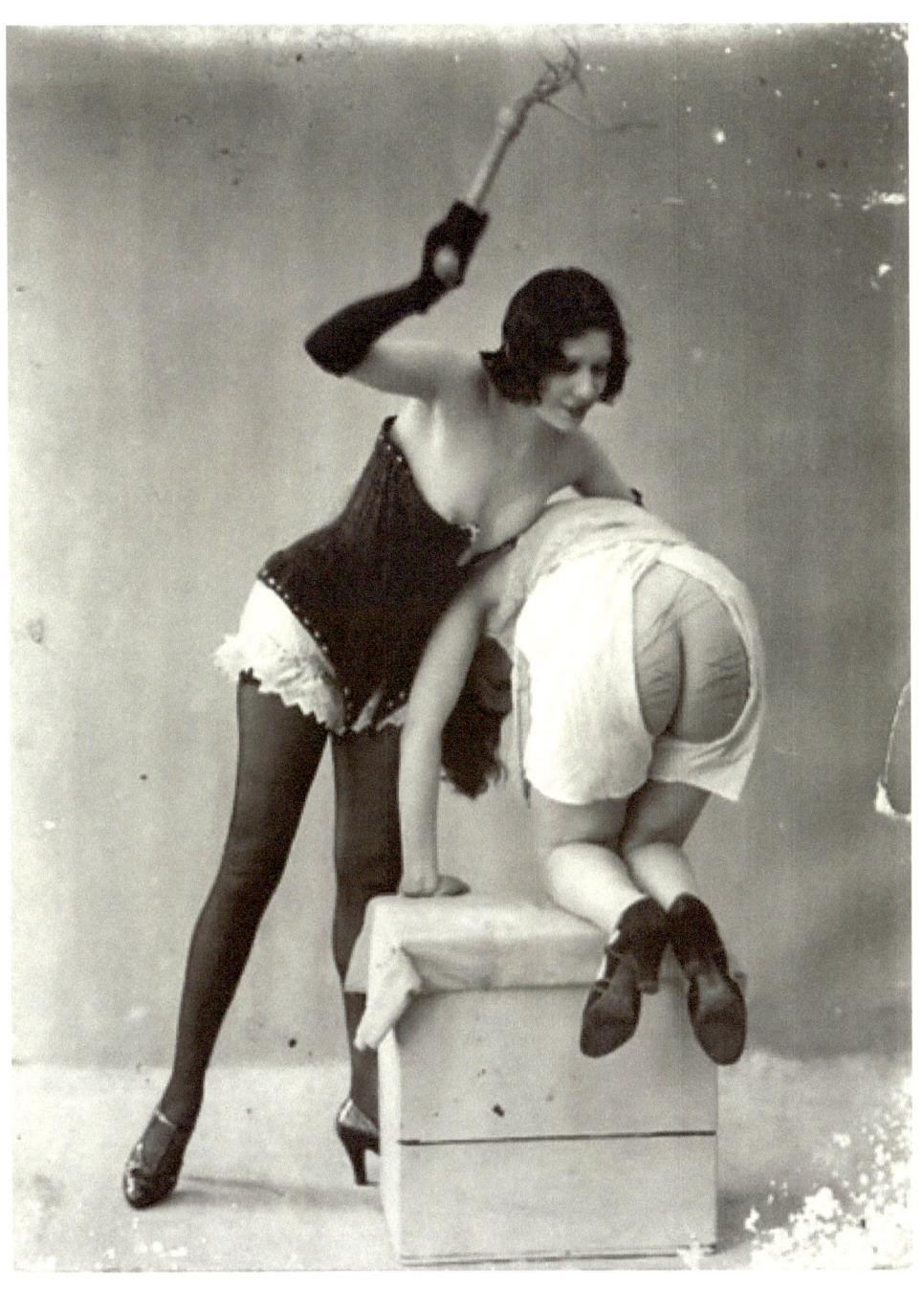

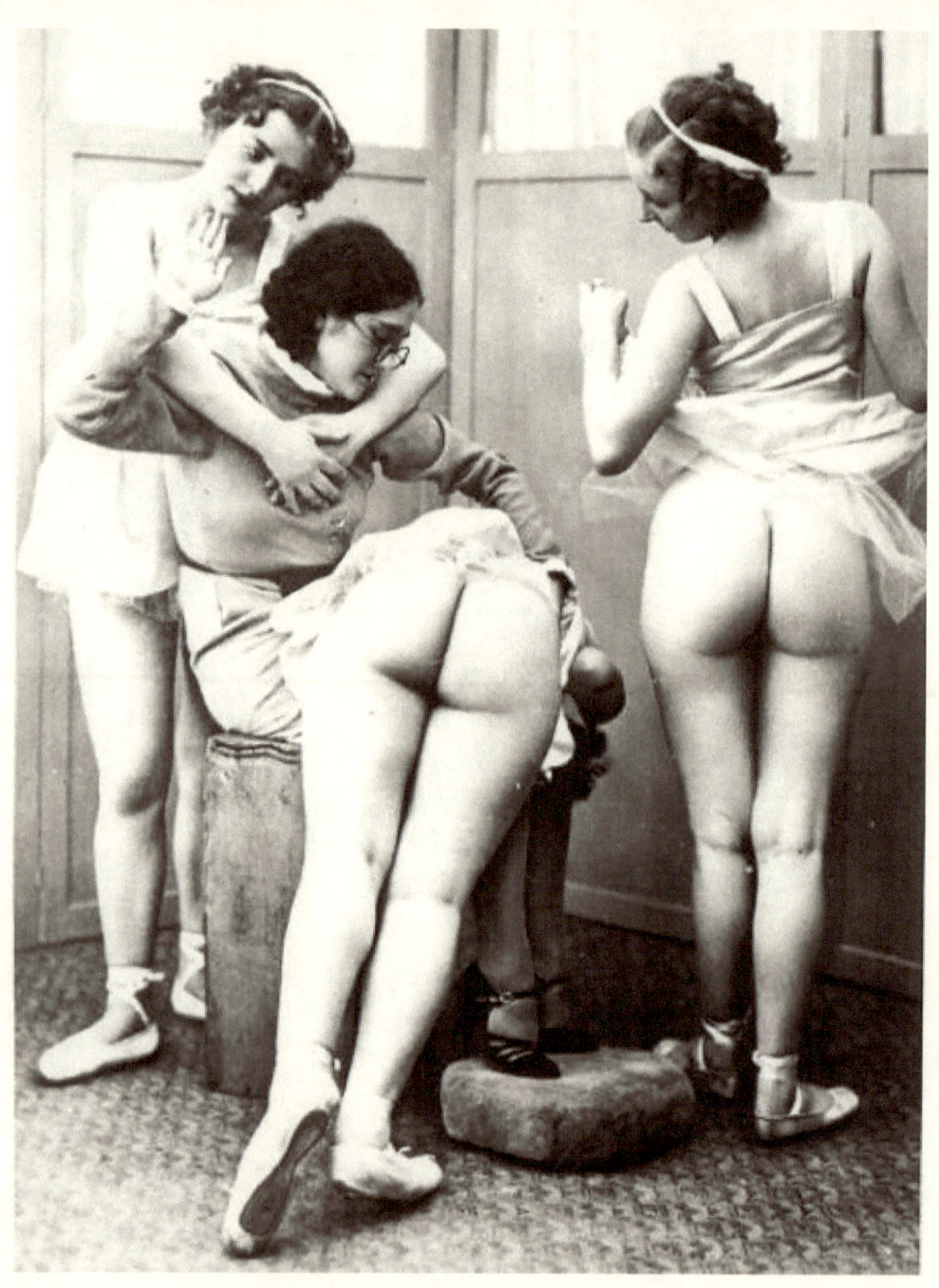

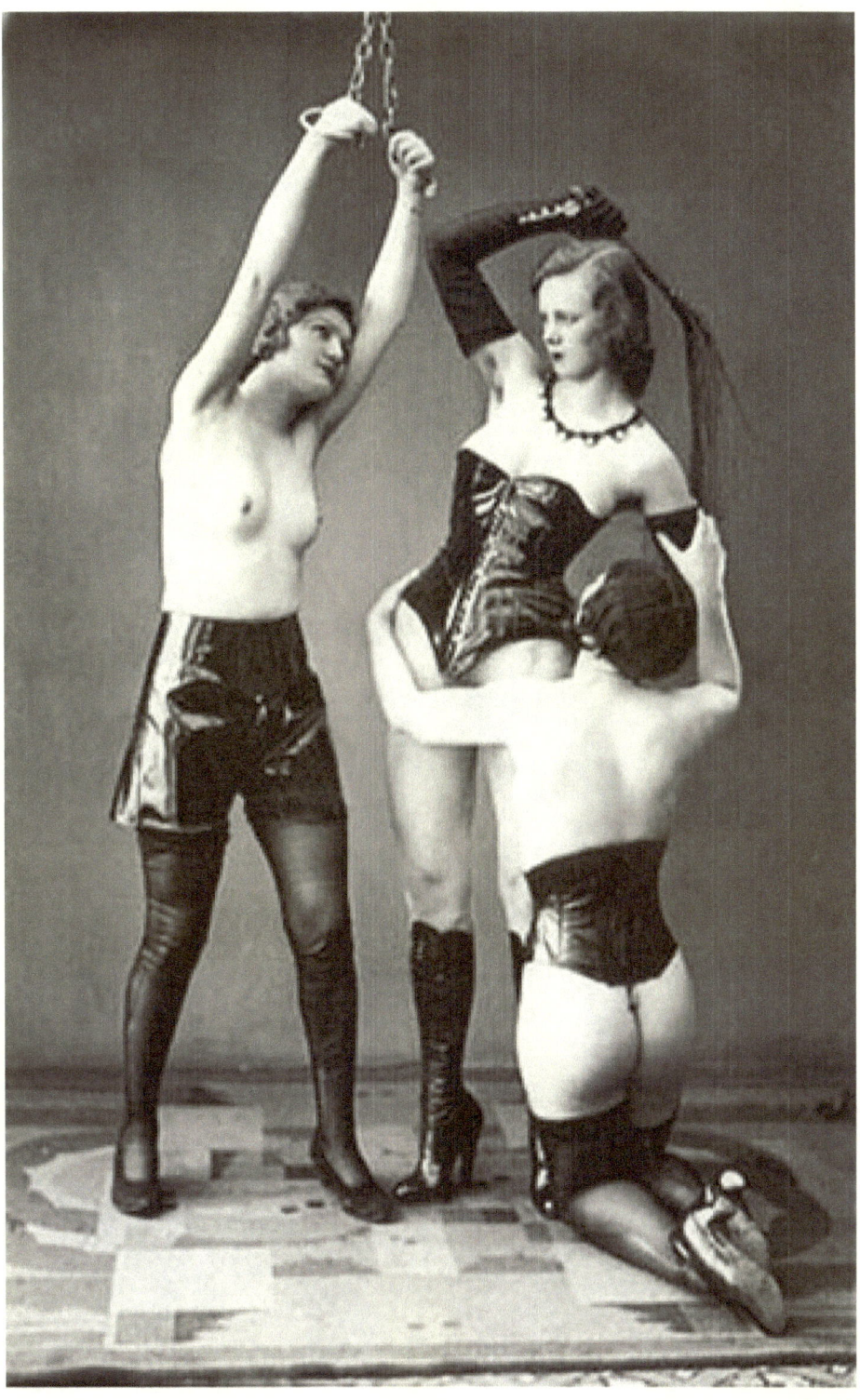

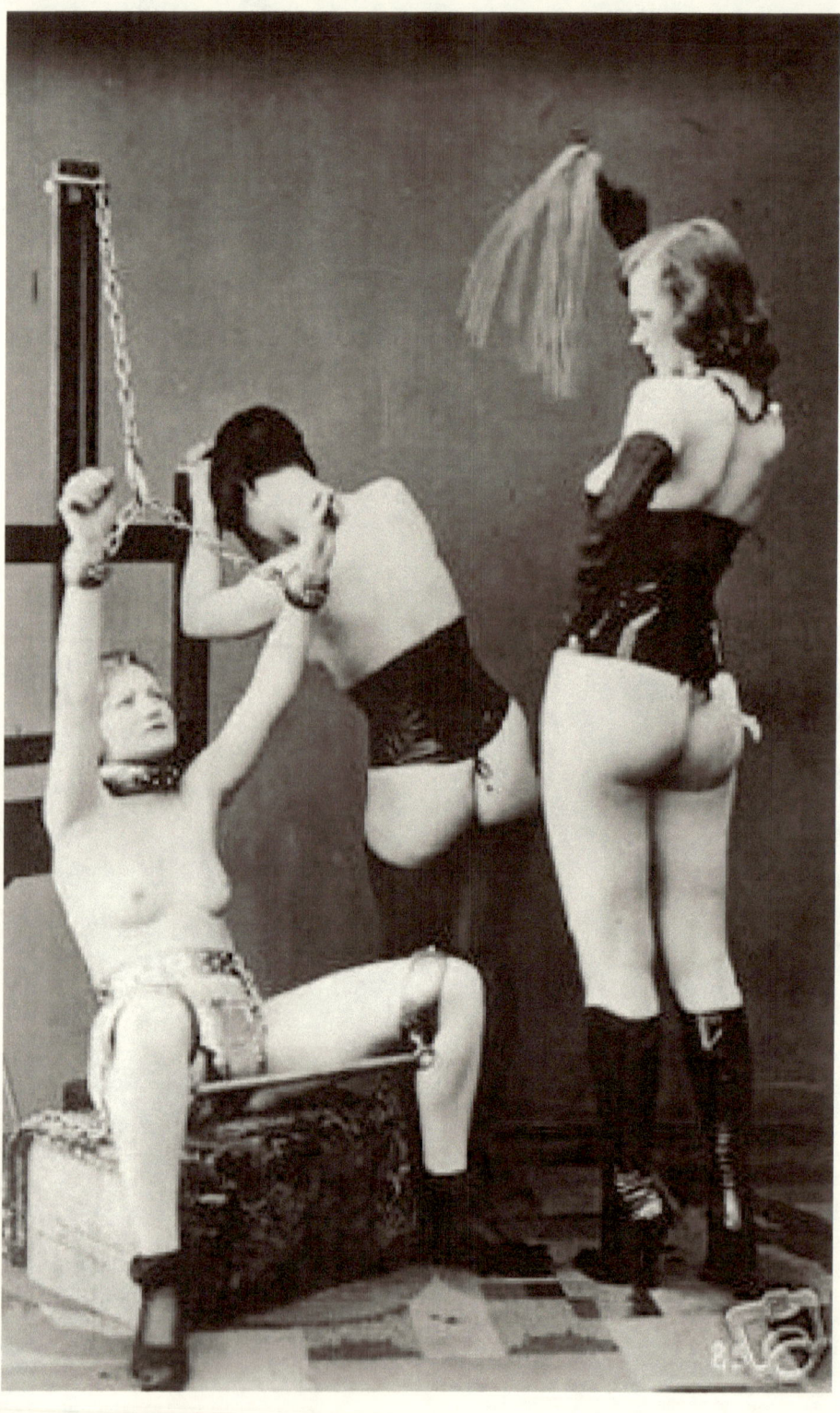

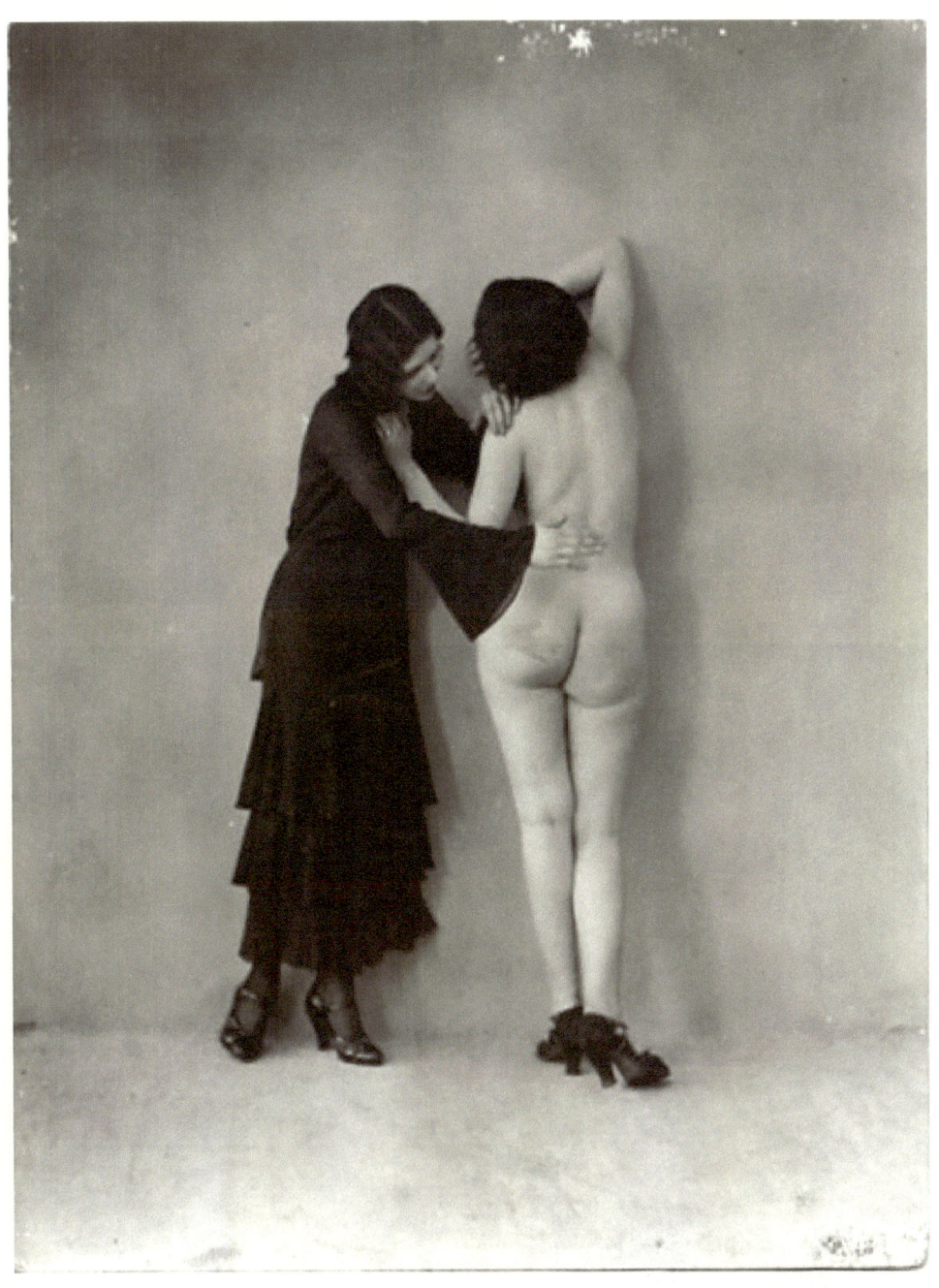

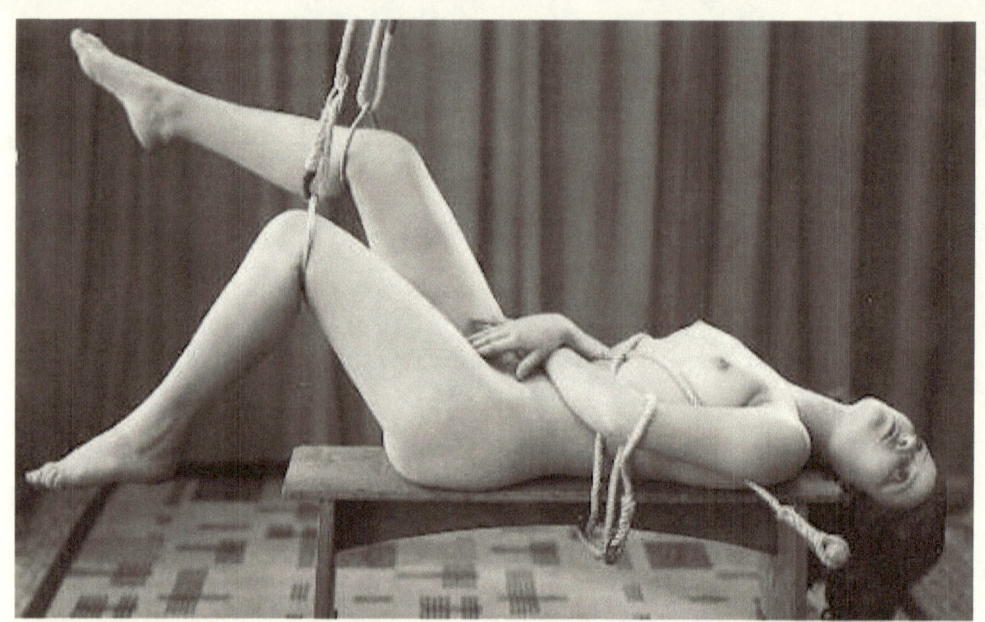

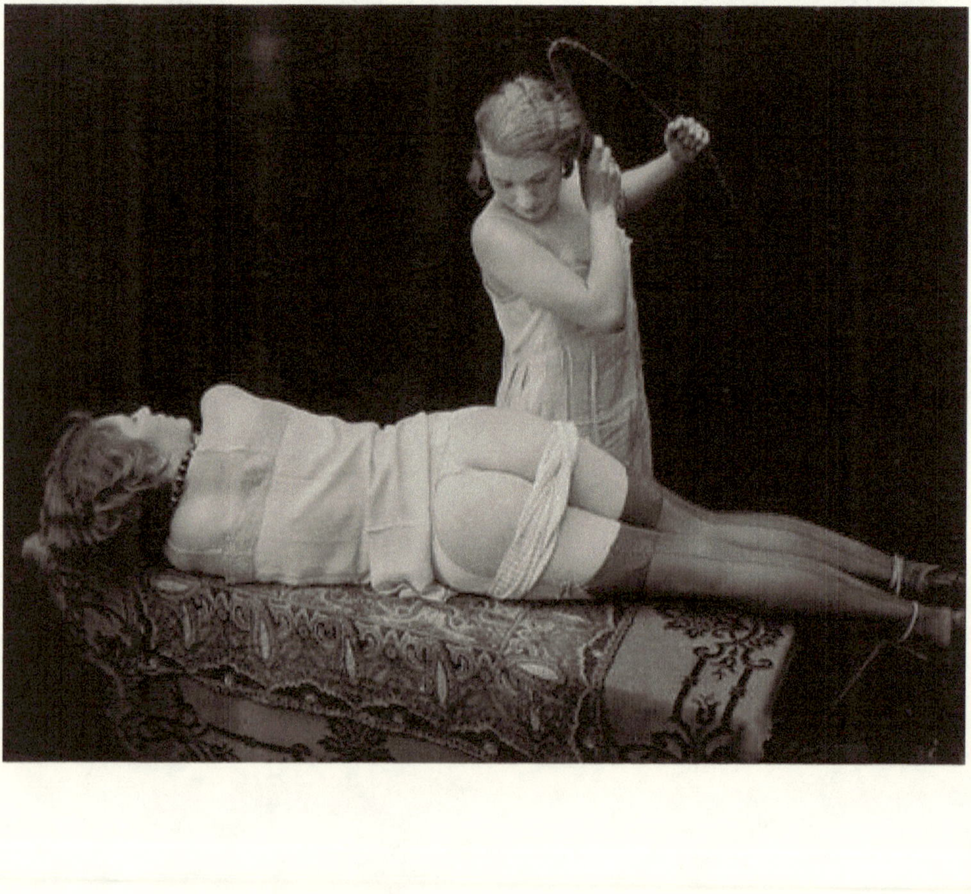

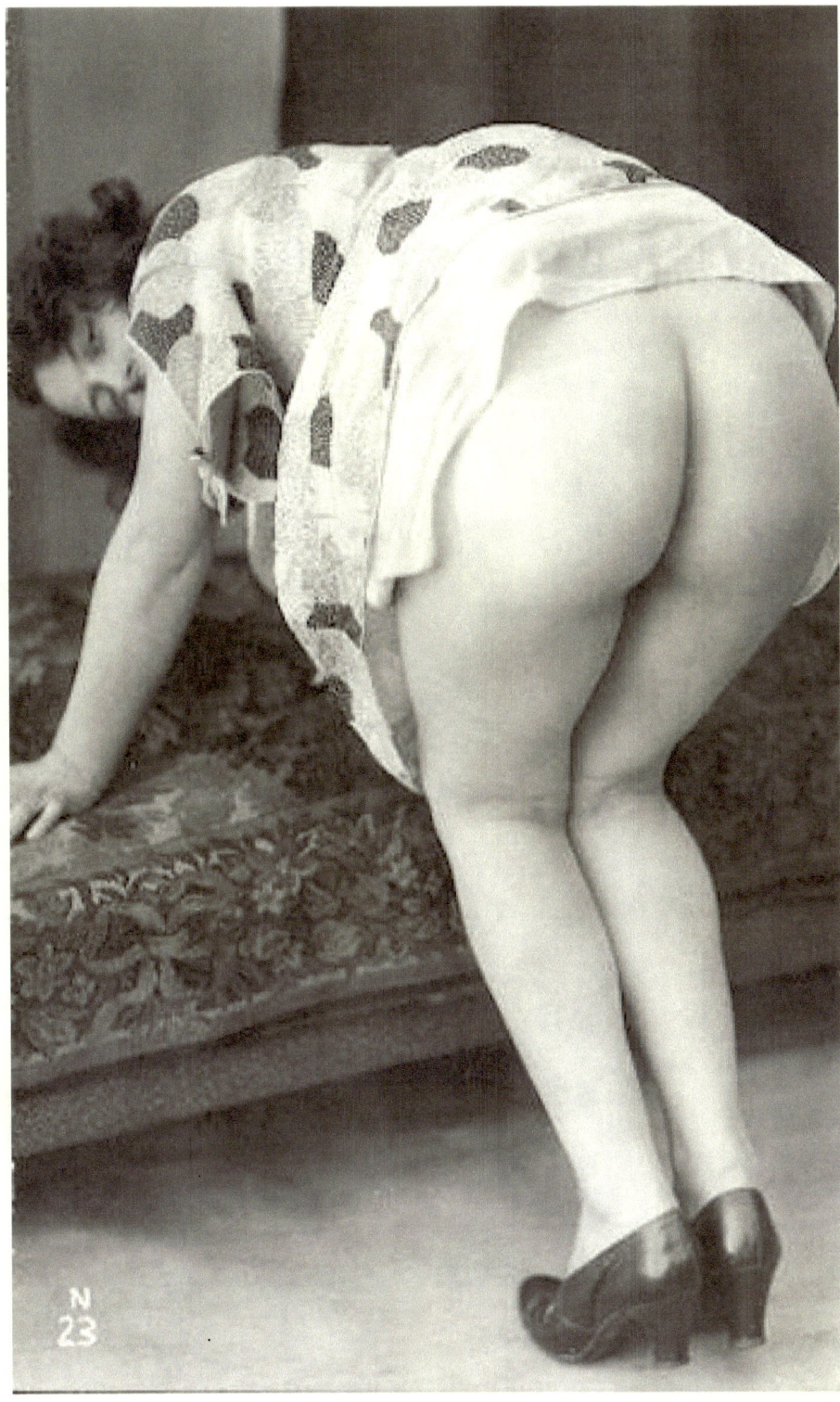

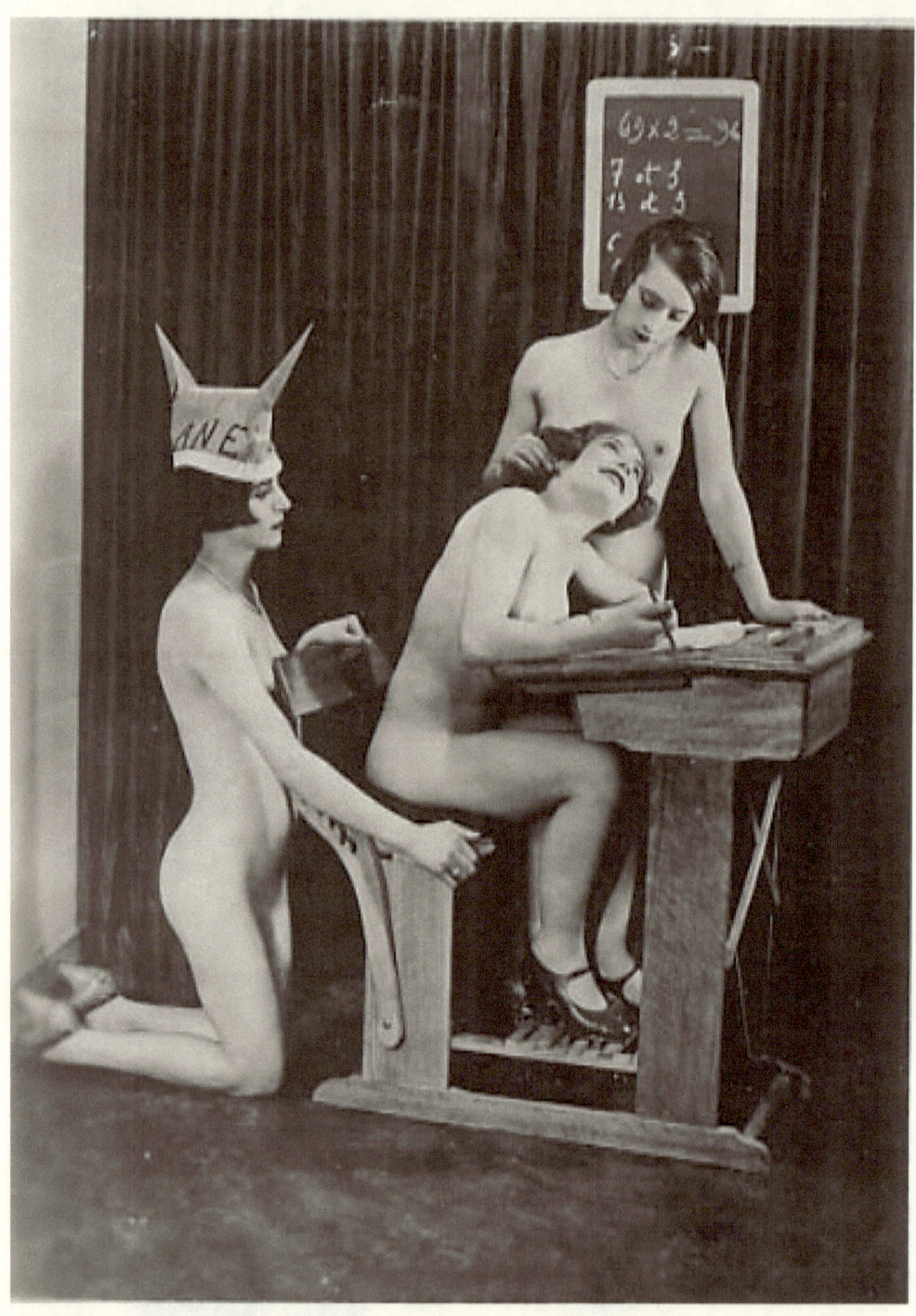

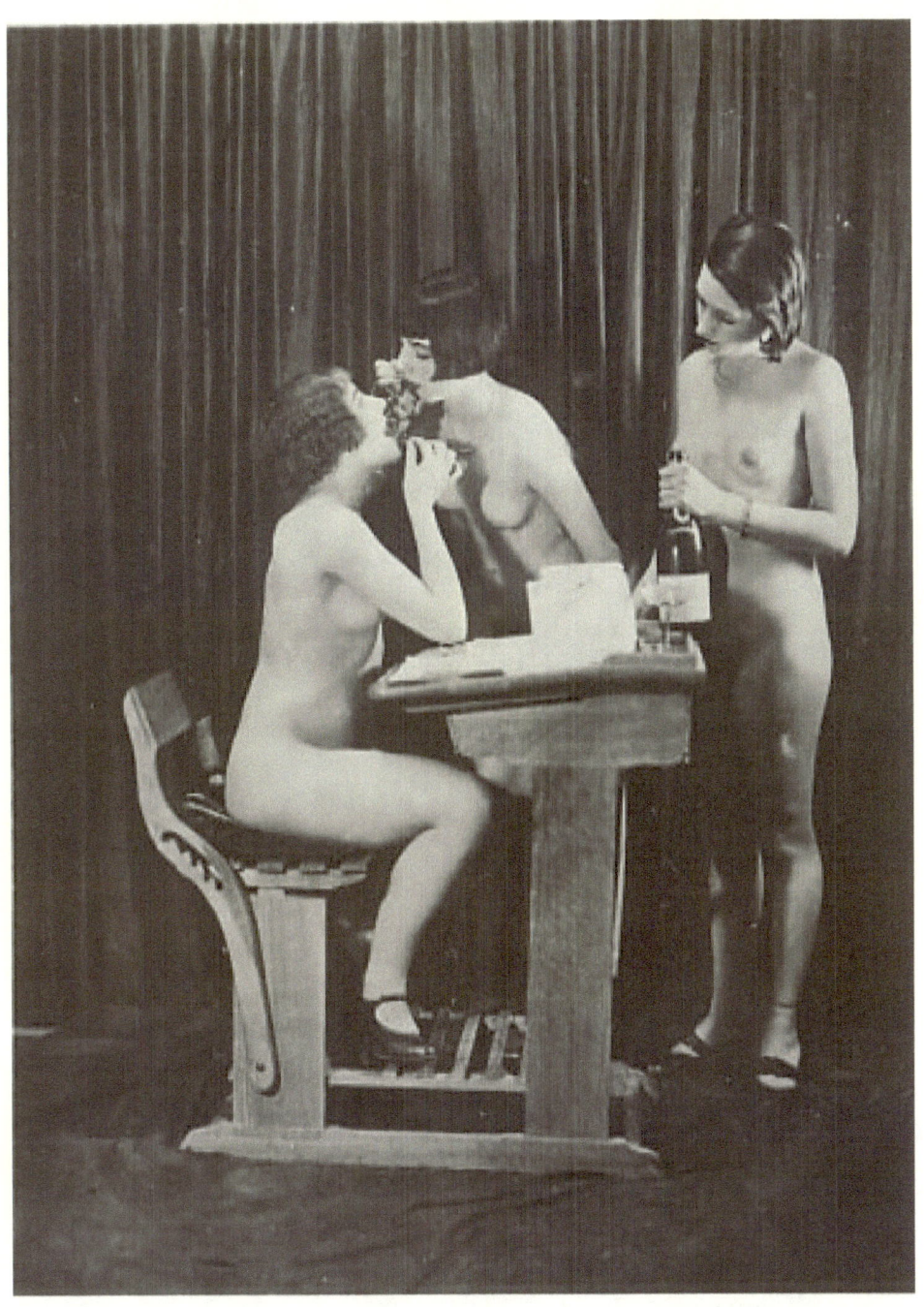

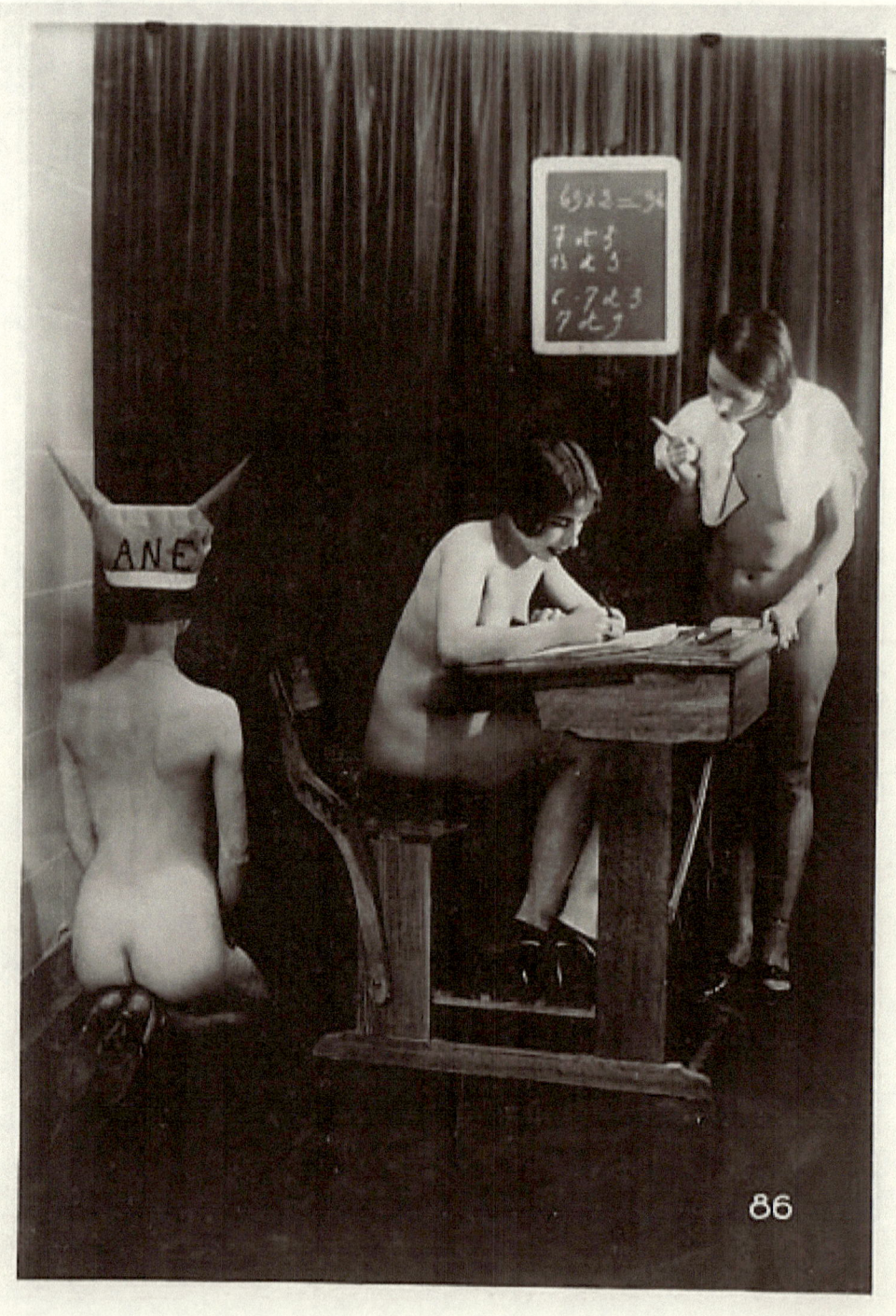

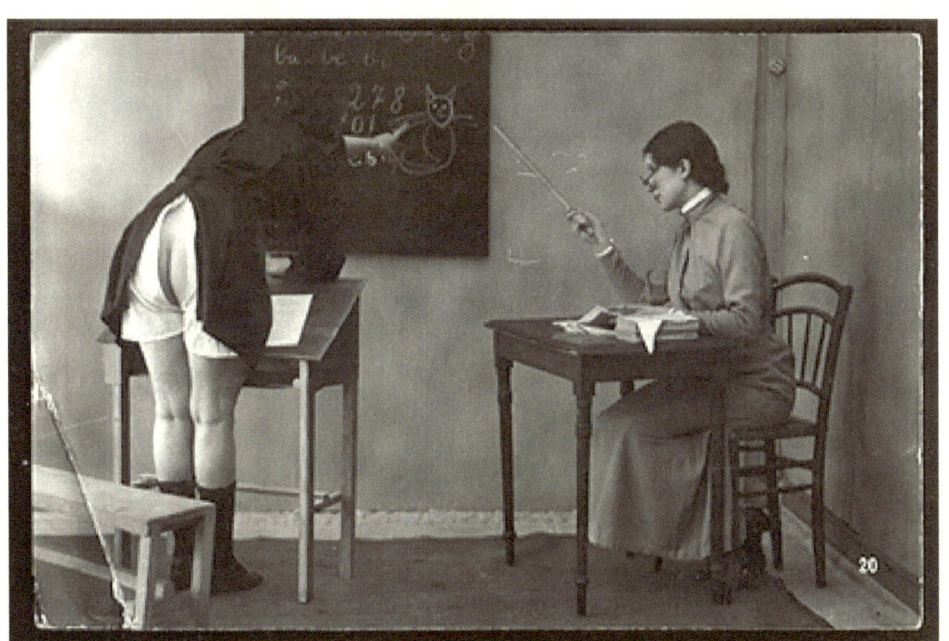

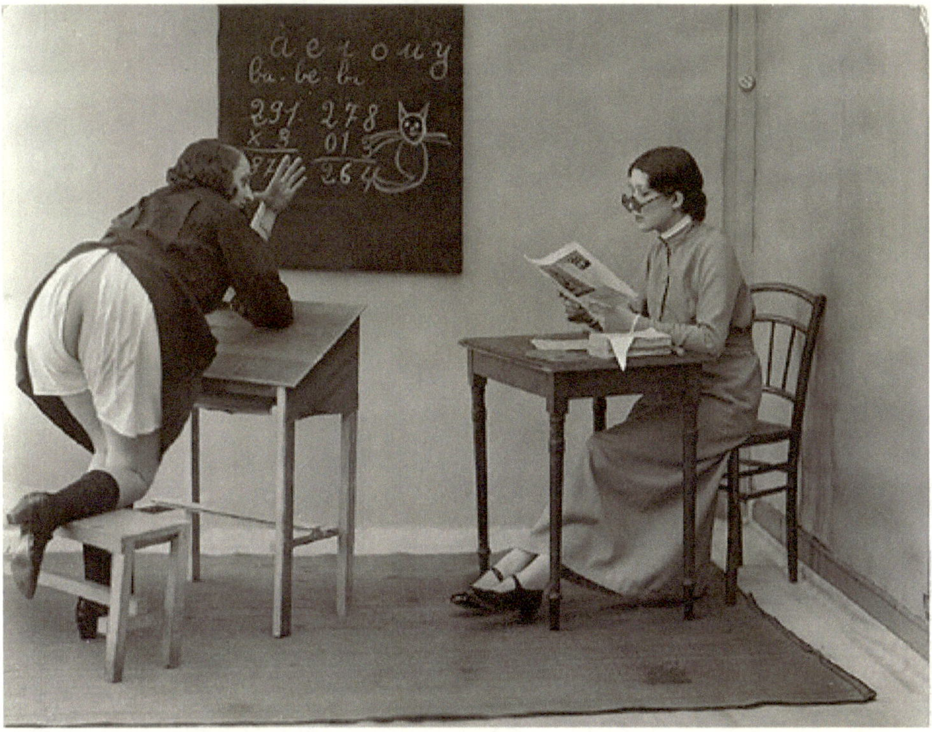

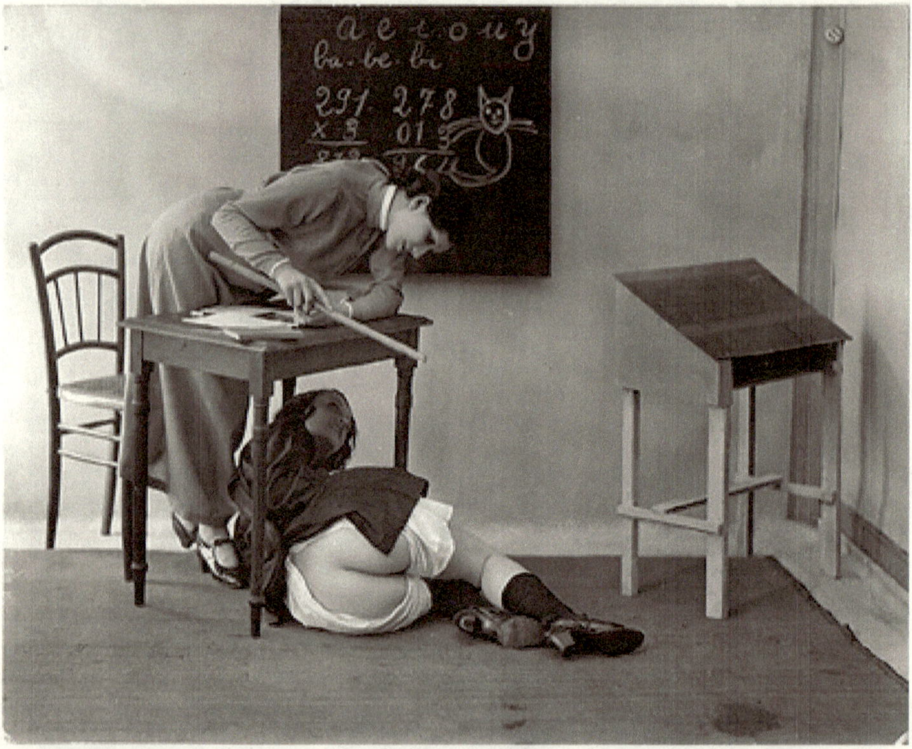
a e i o u y
ba . be . bi
291 . 278

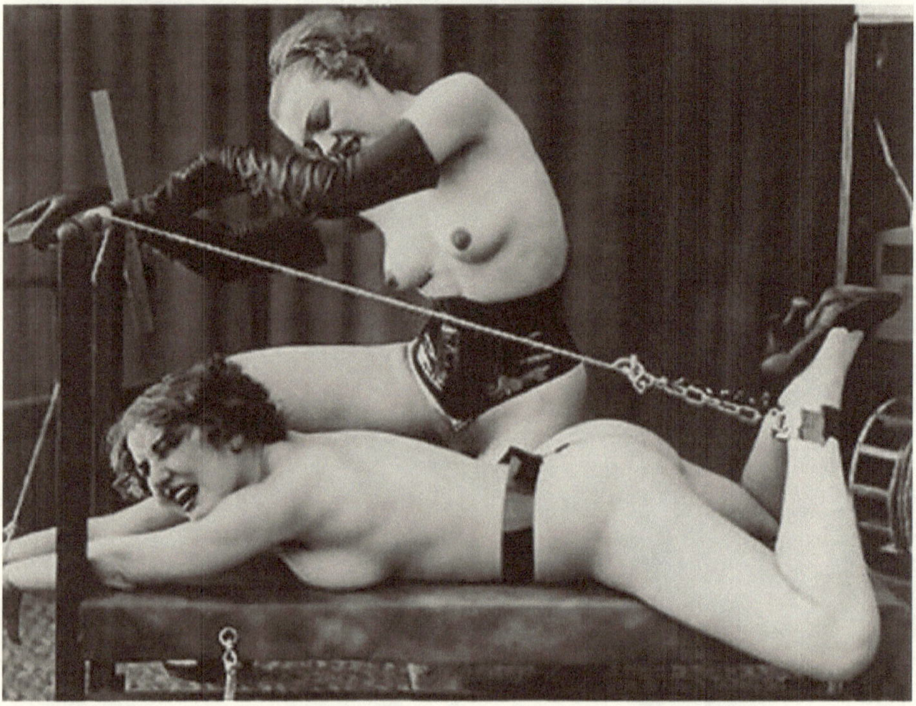

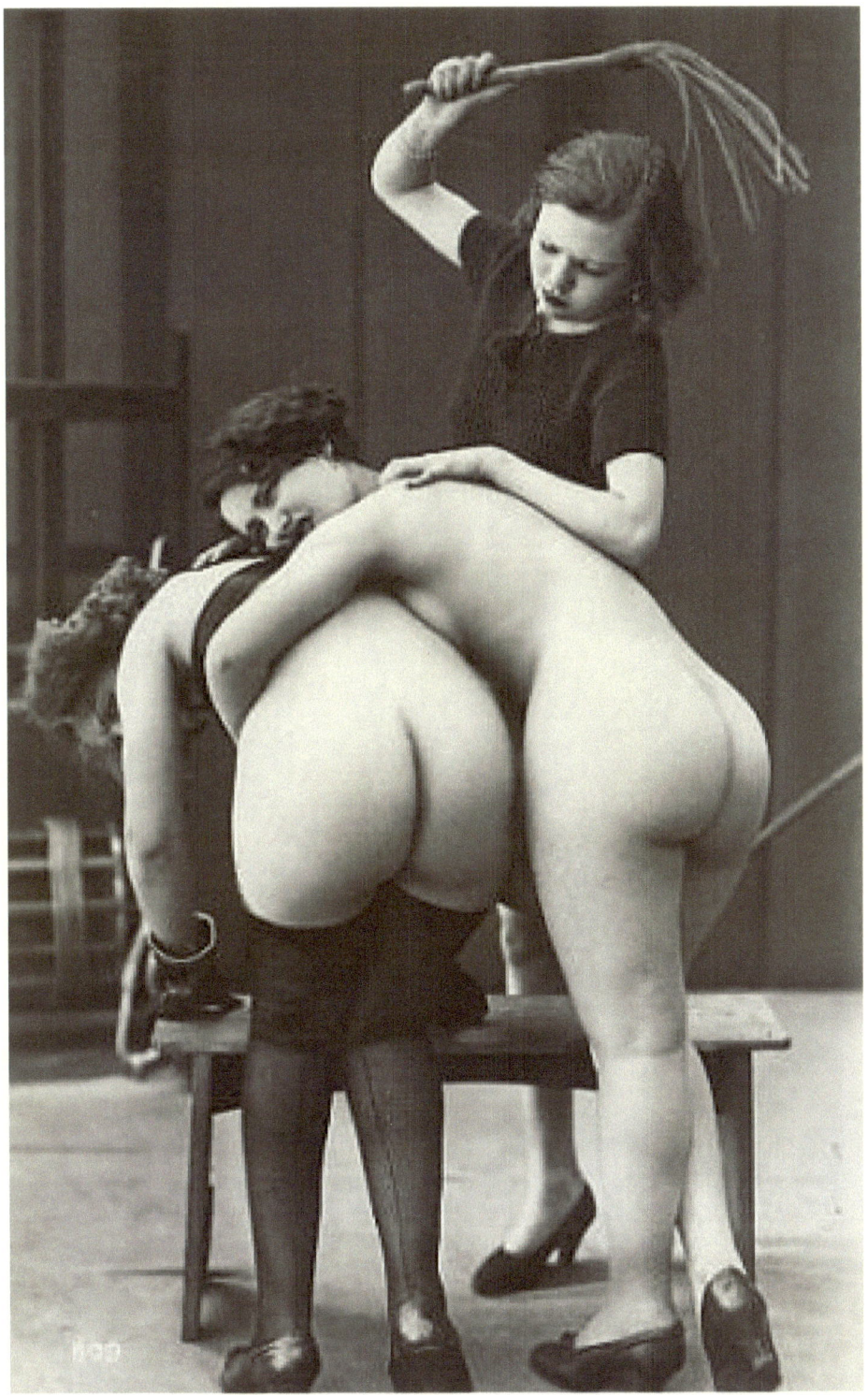

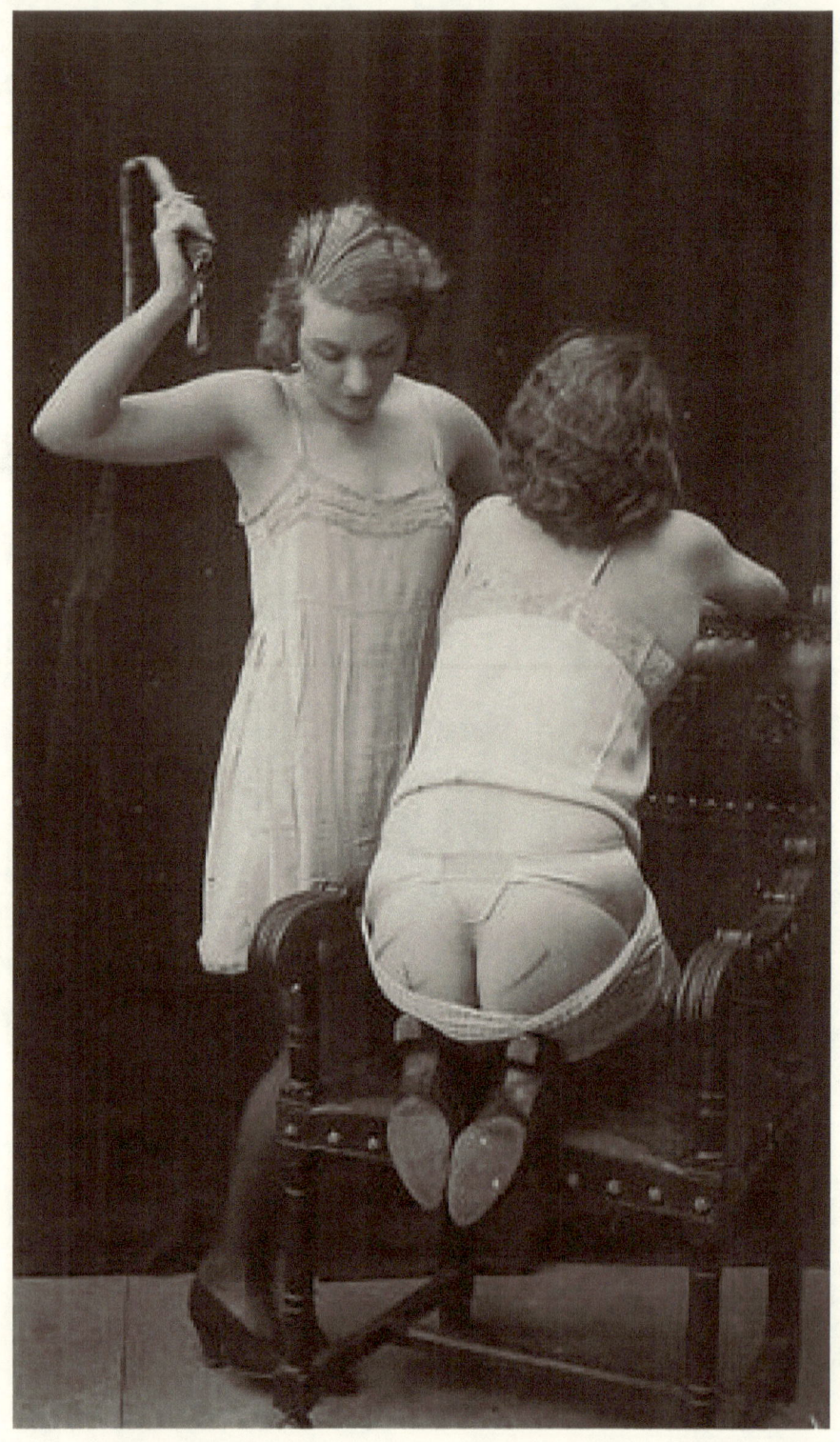

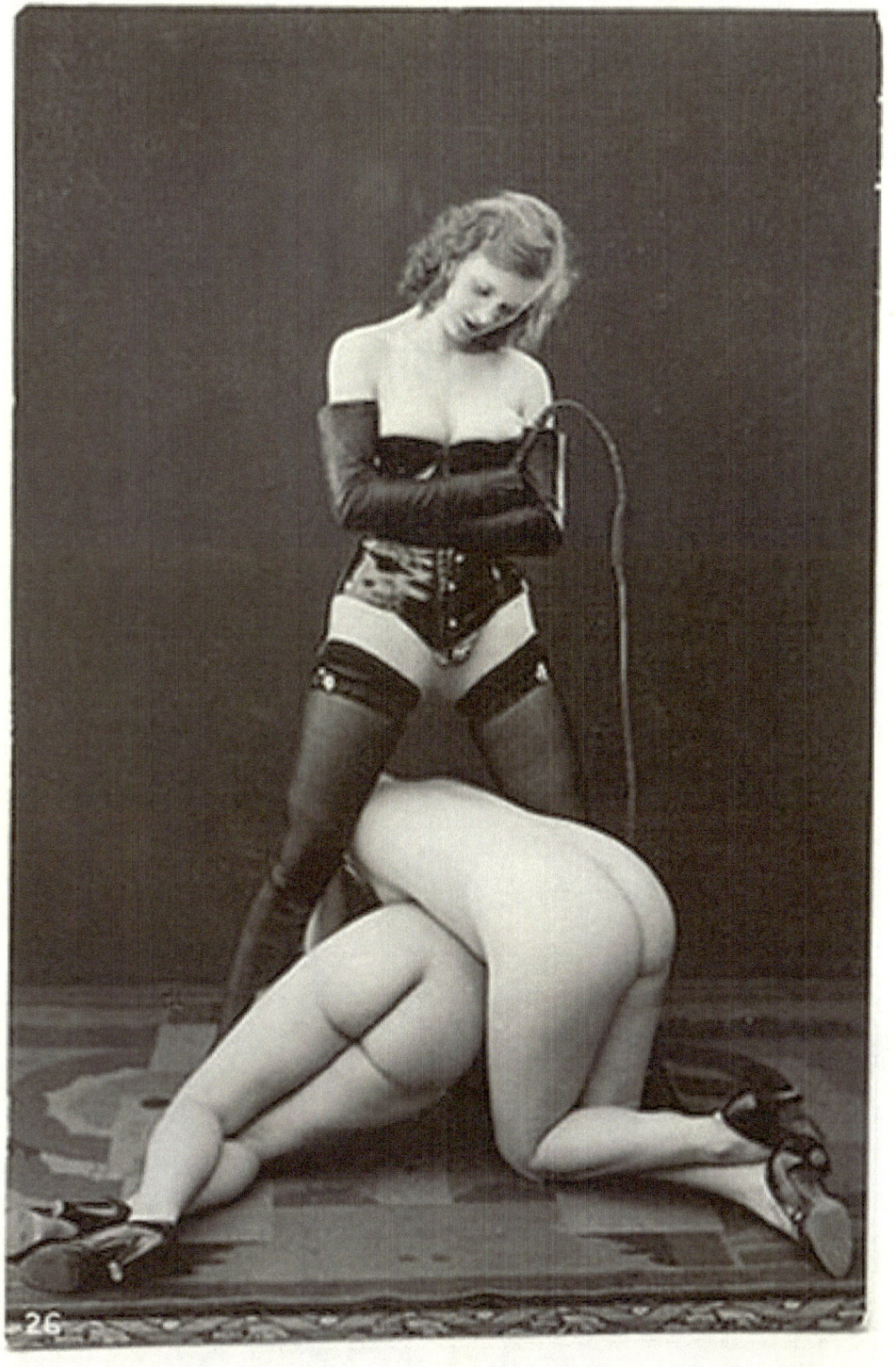

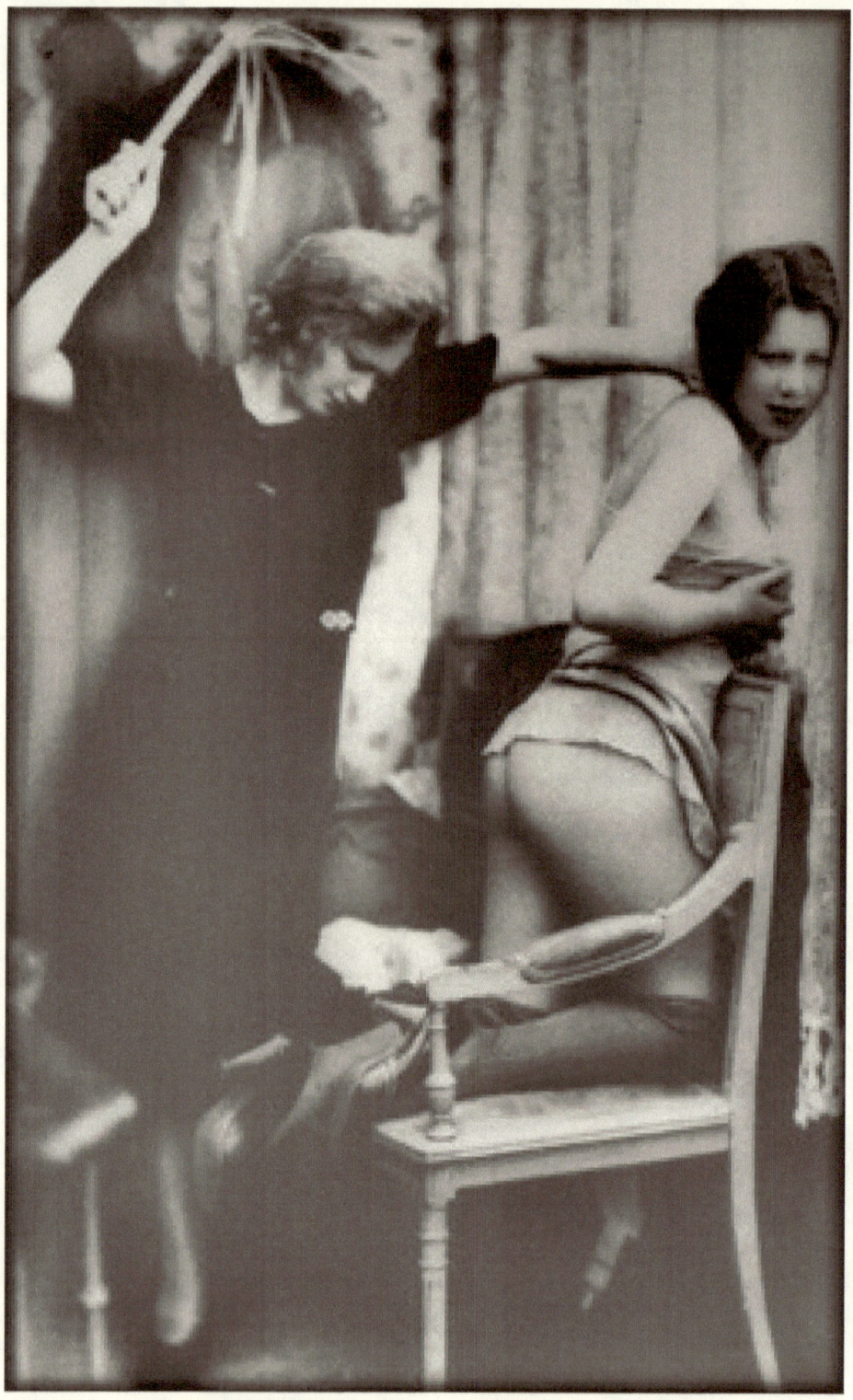

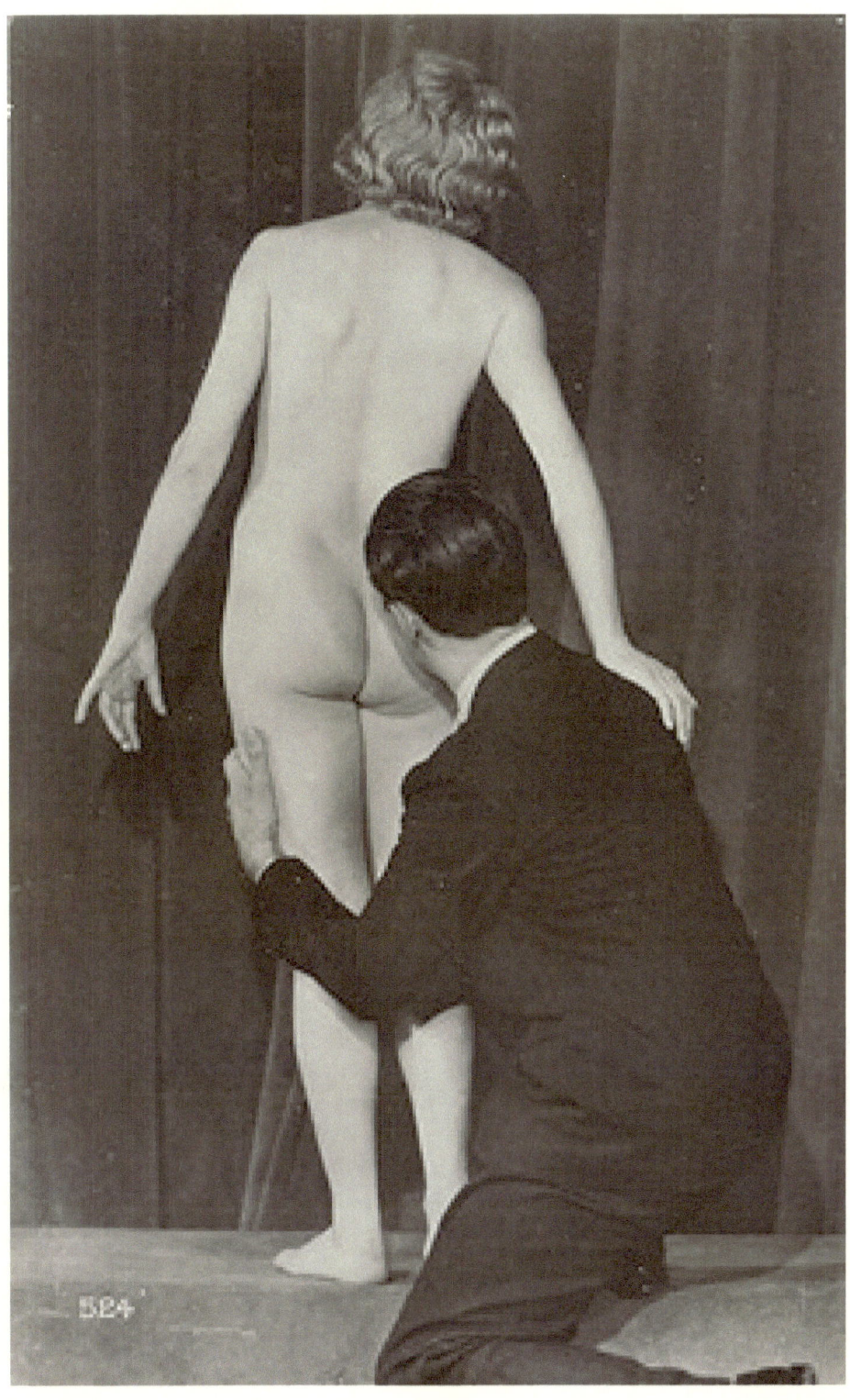

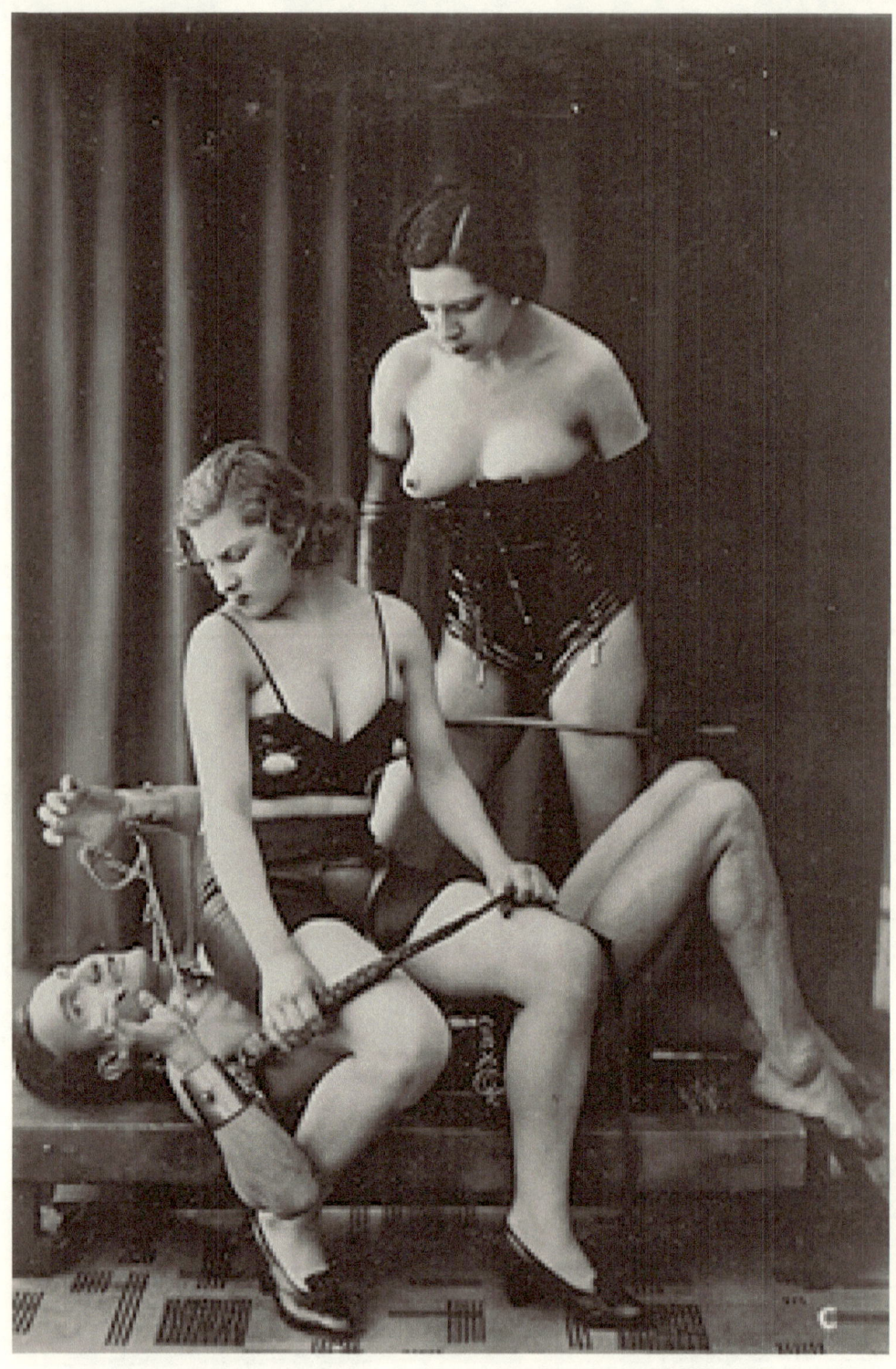

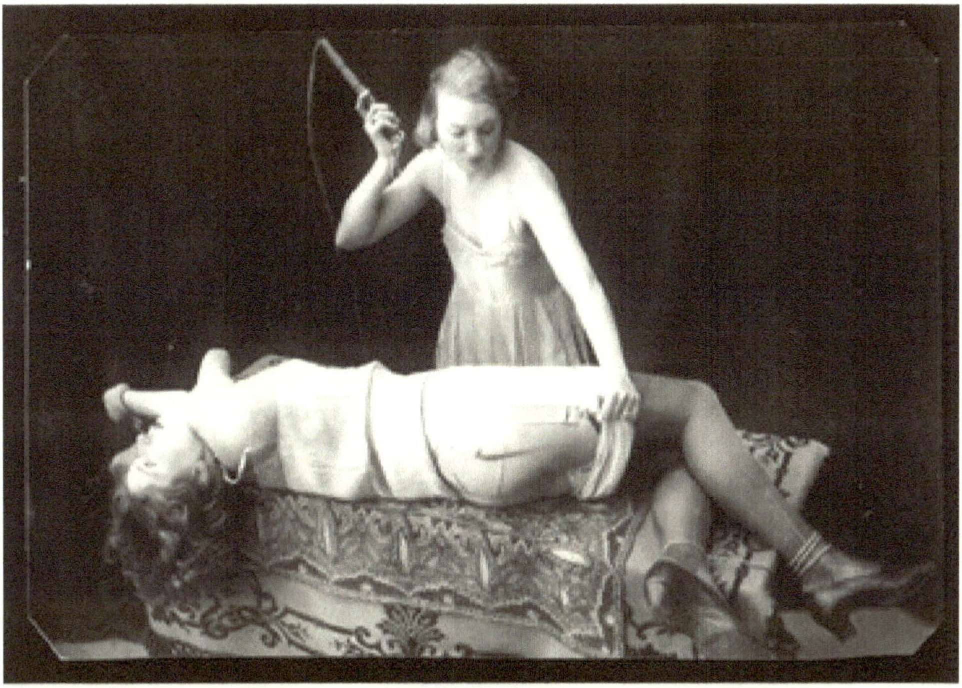

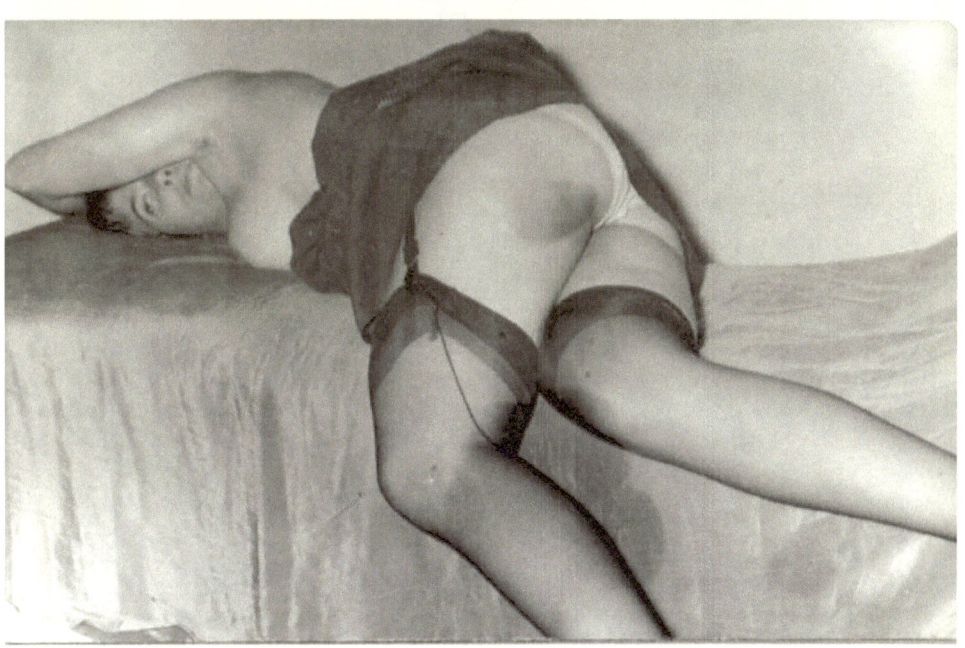

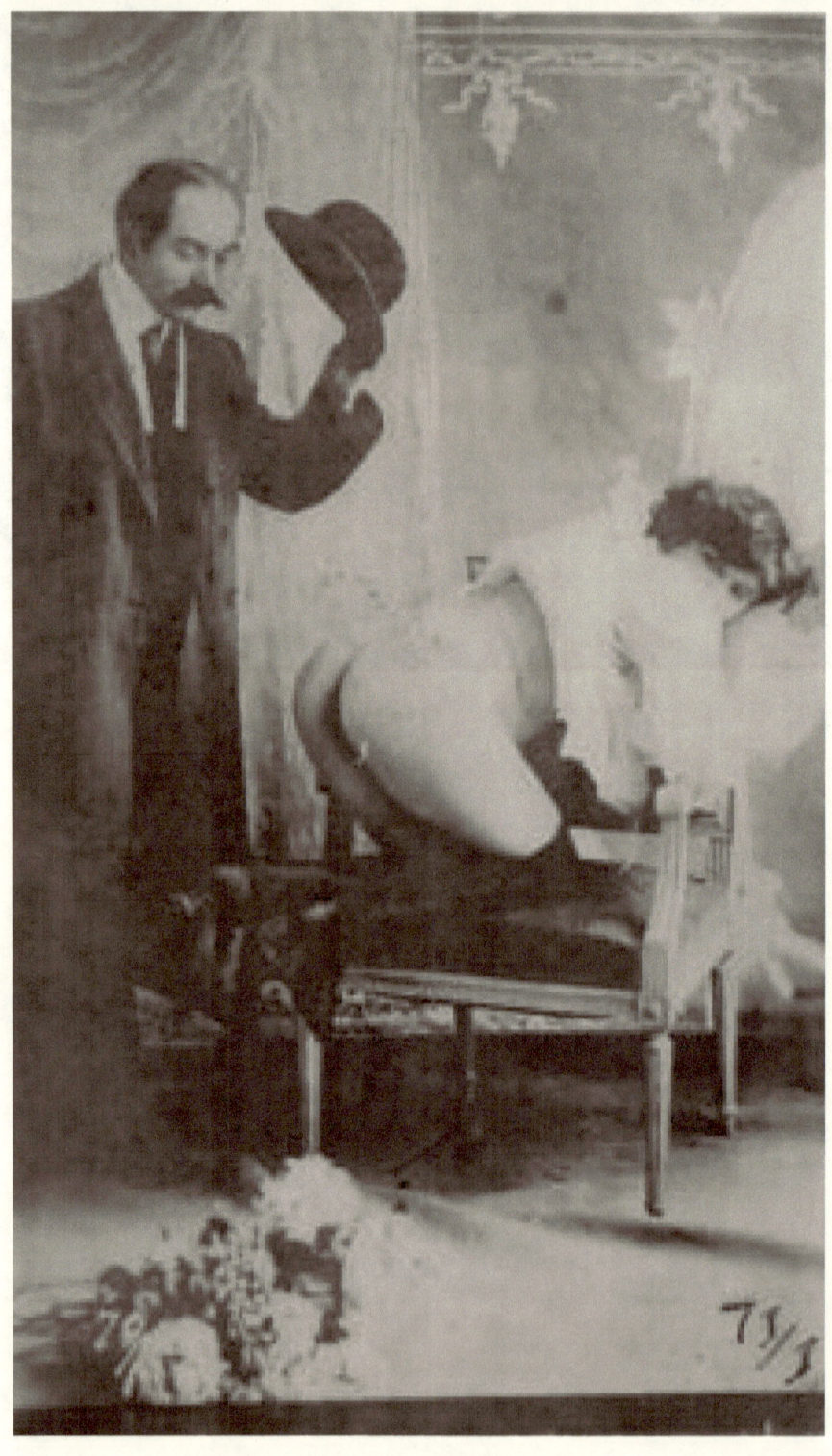

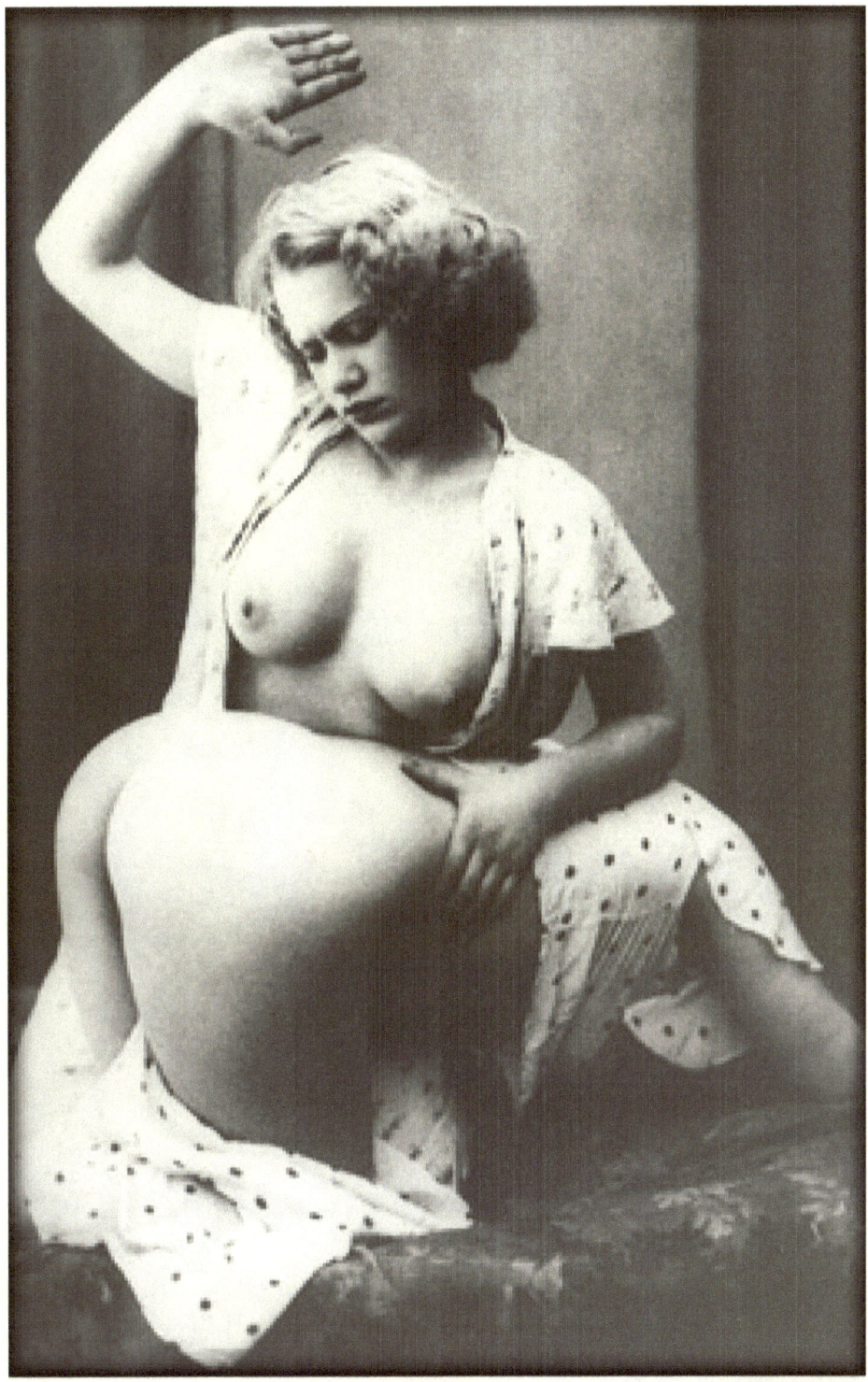

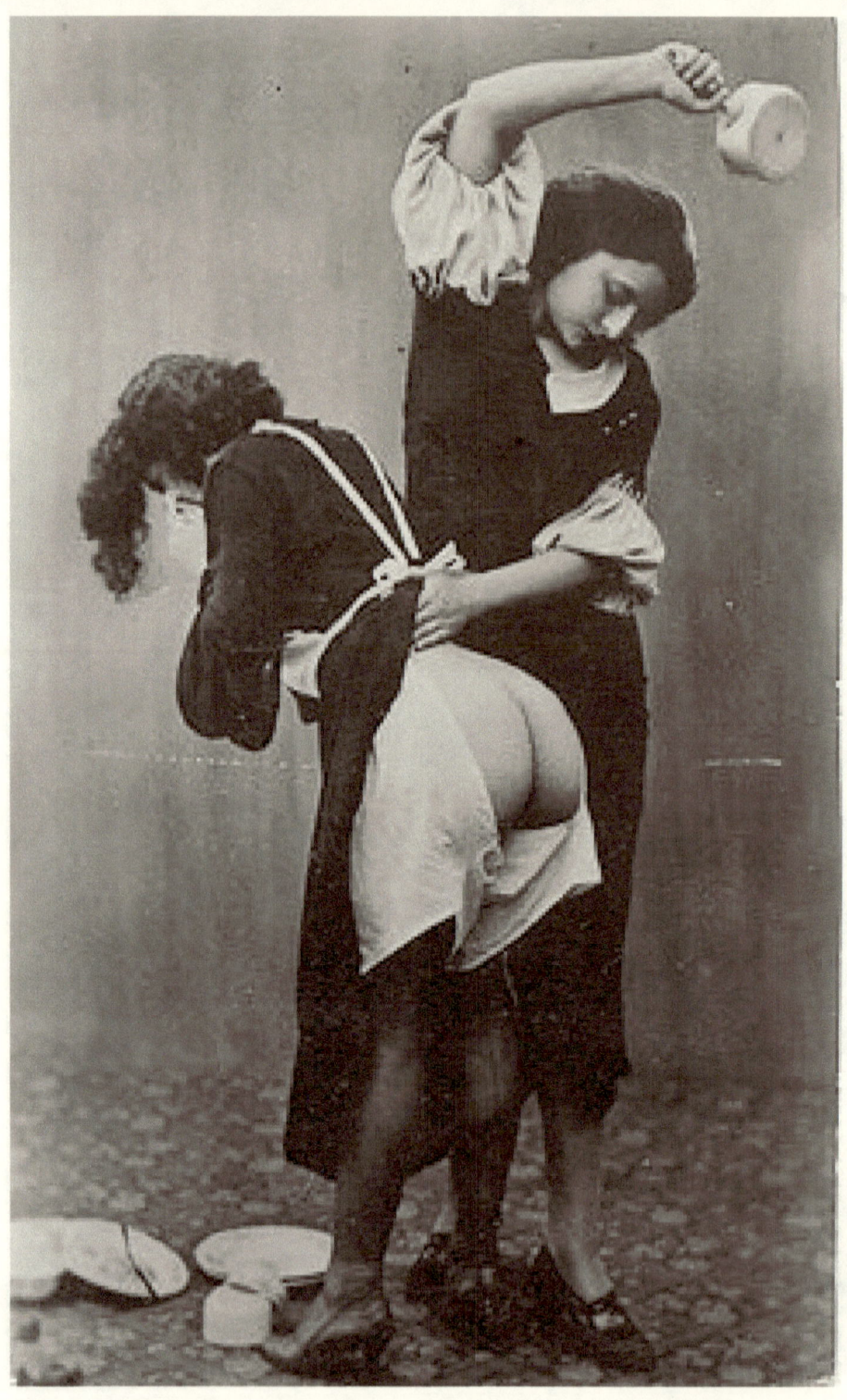

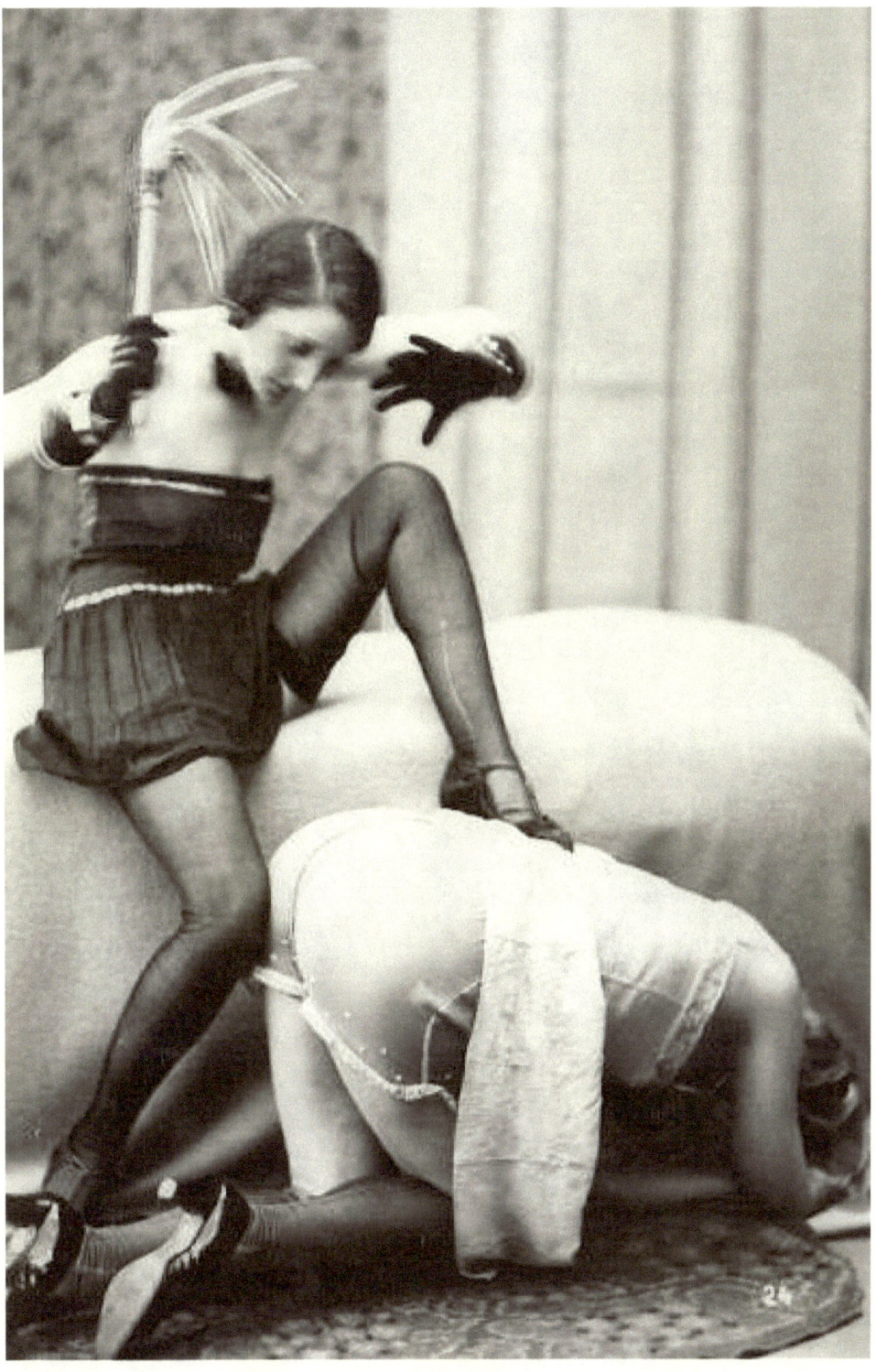

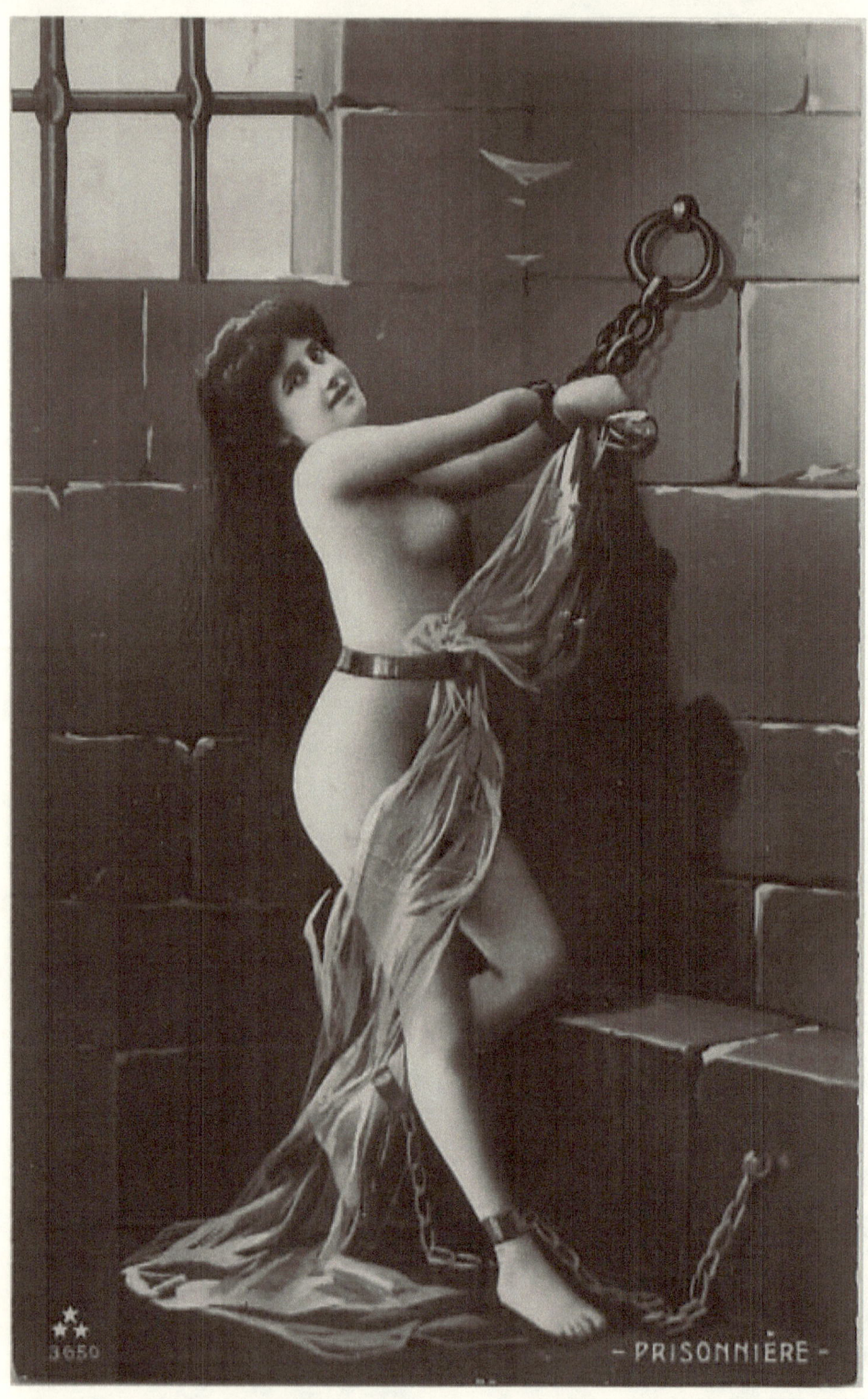

- PRISONNIÈRE -

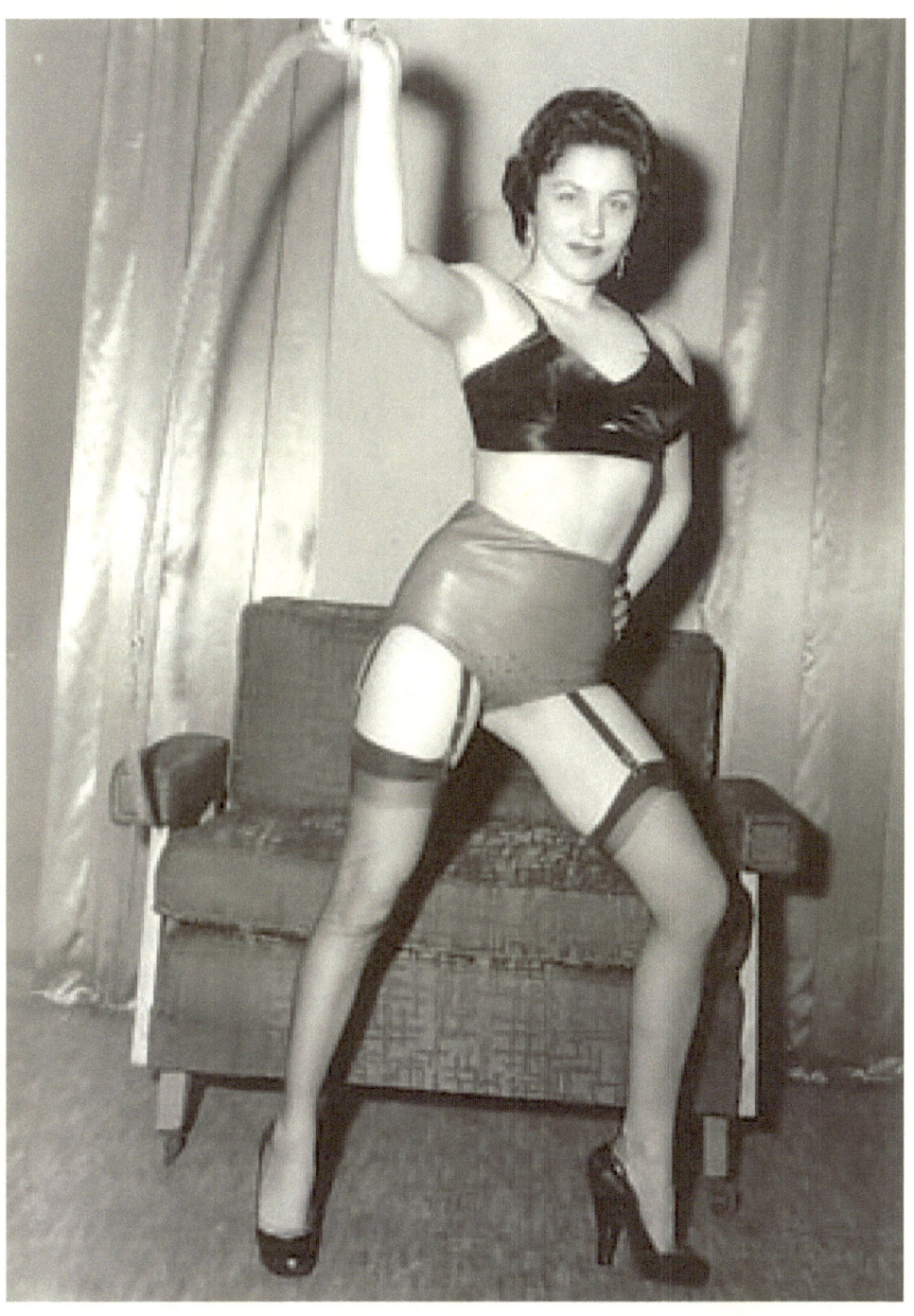

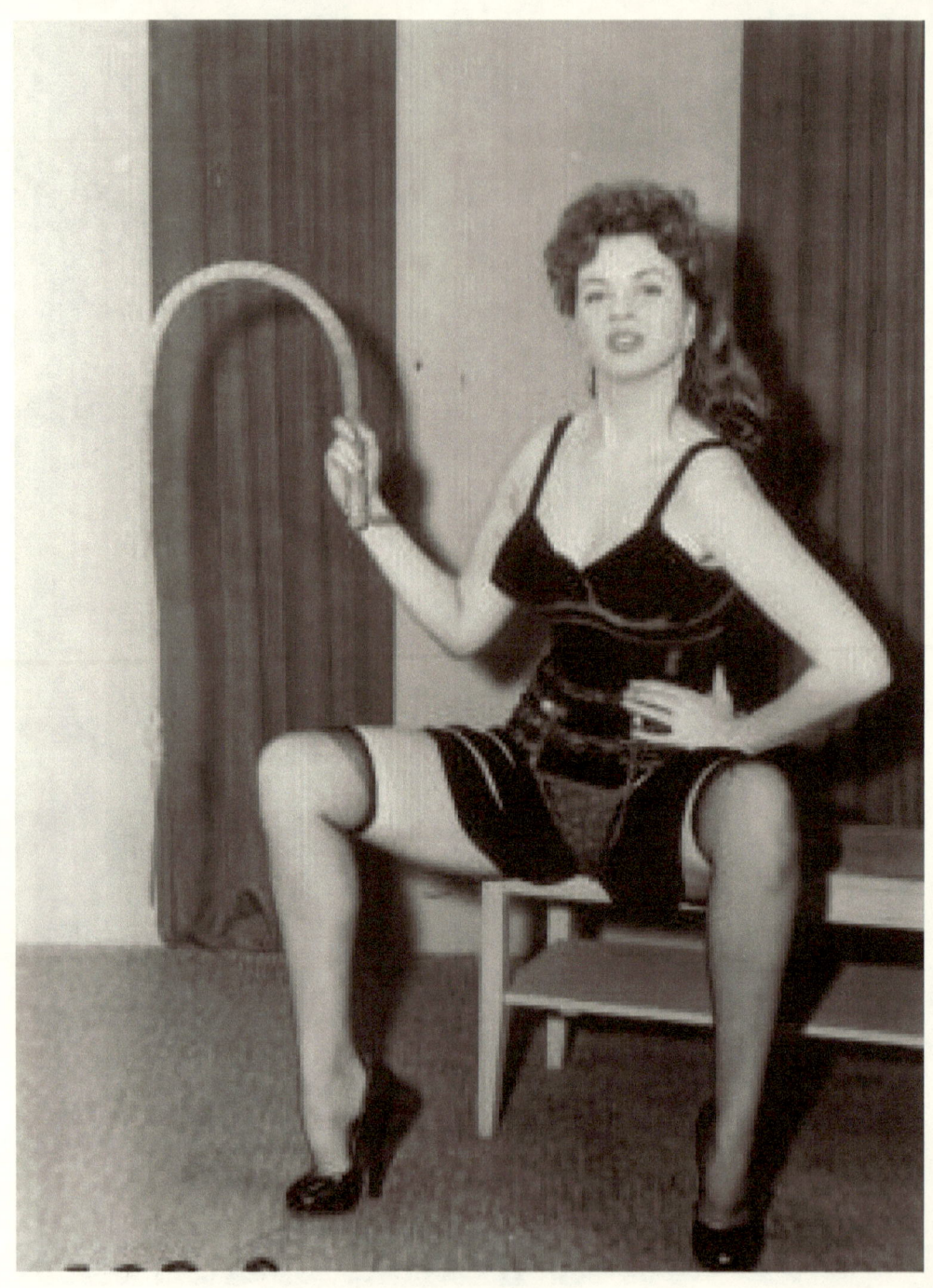

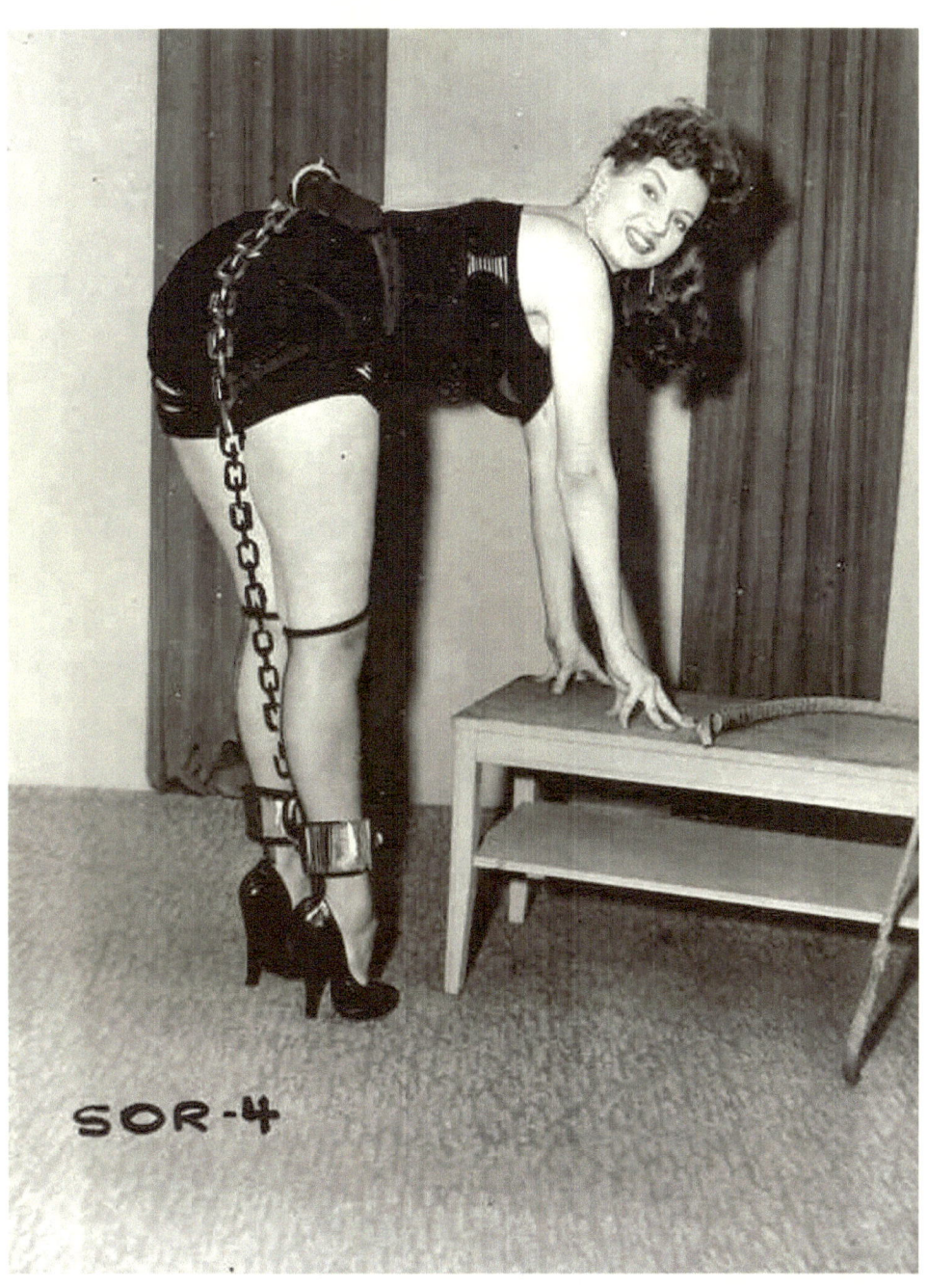

SOR-4

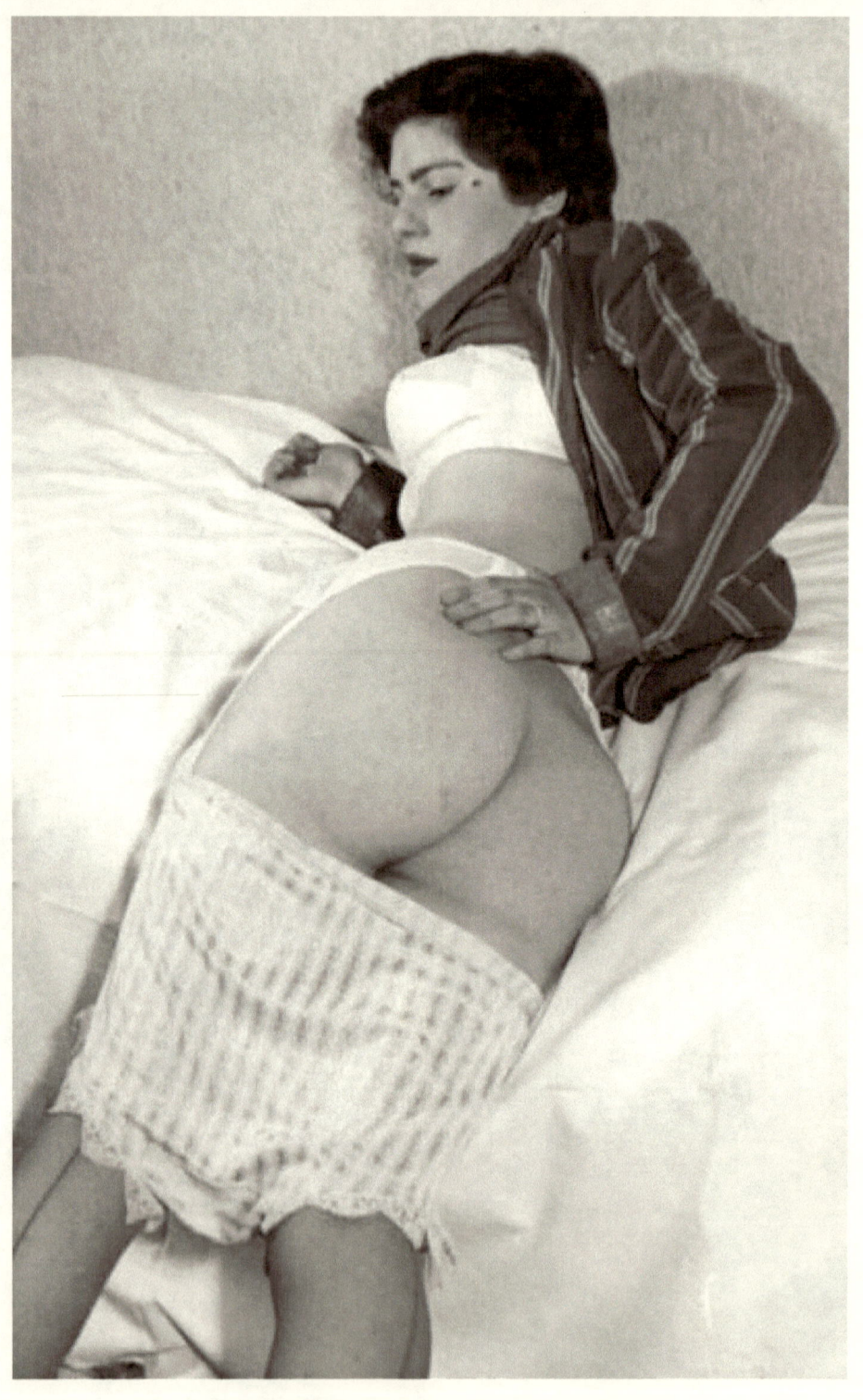

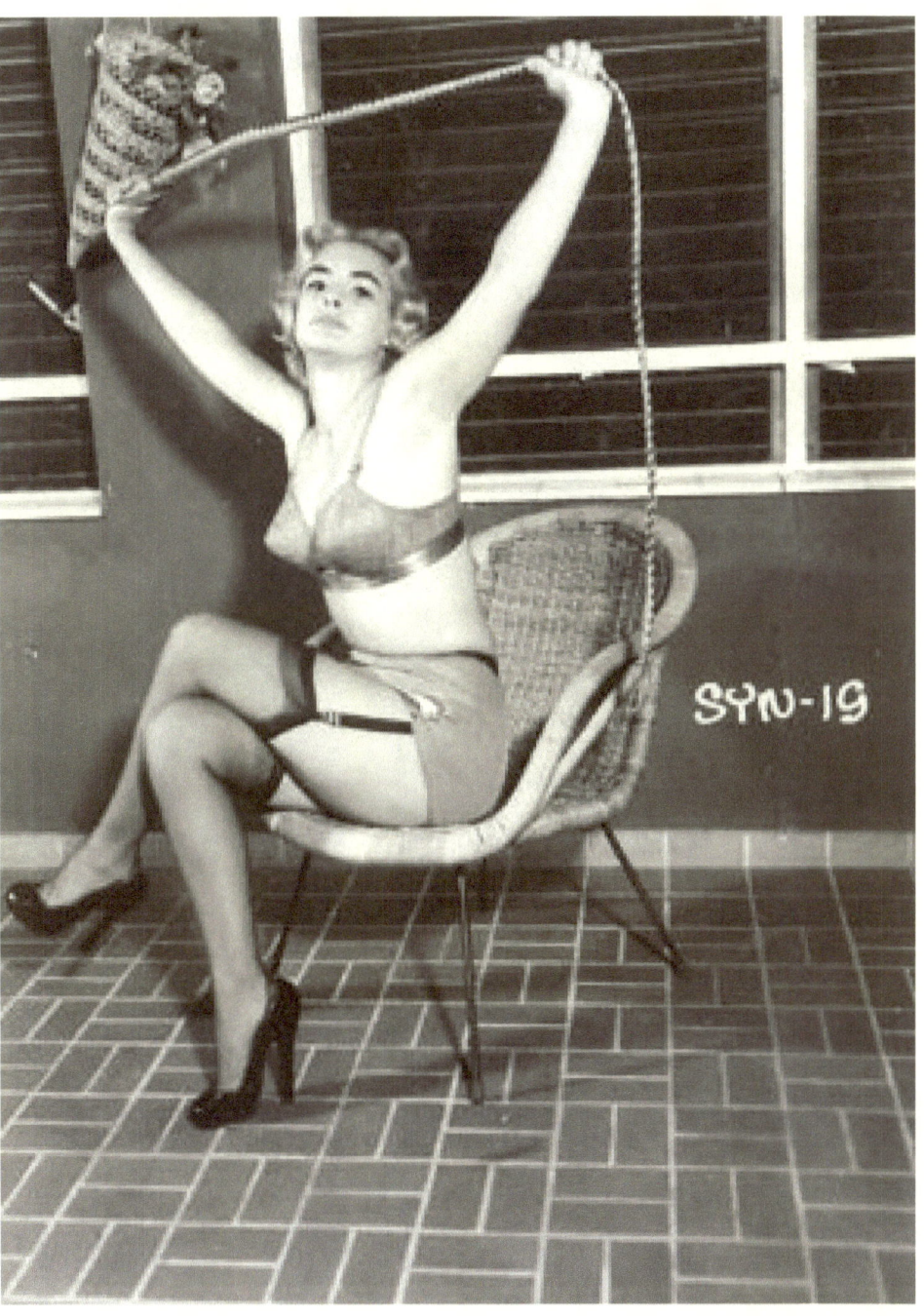

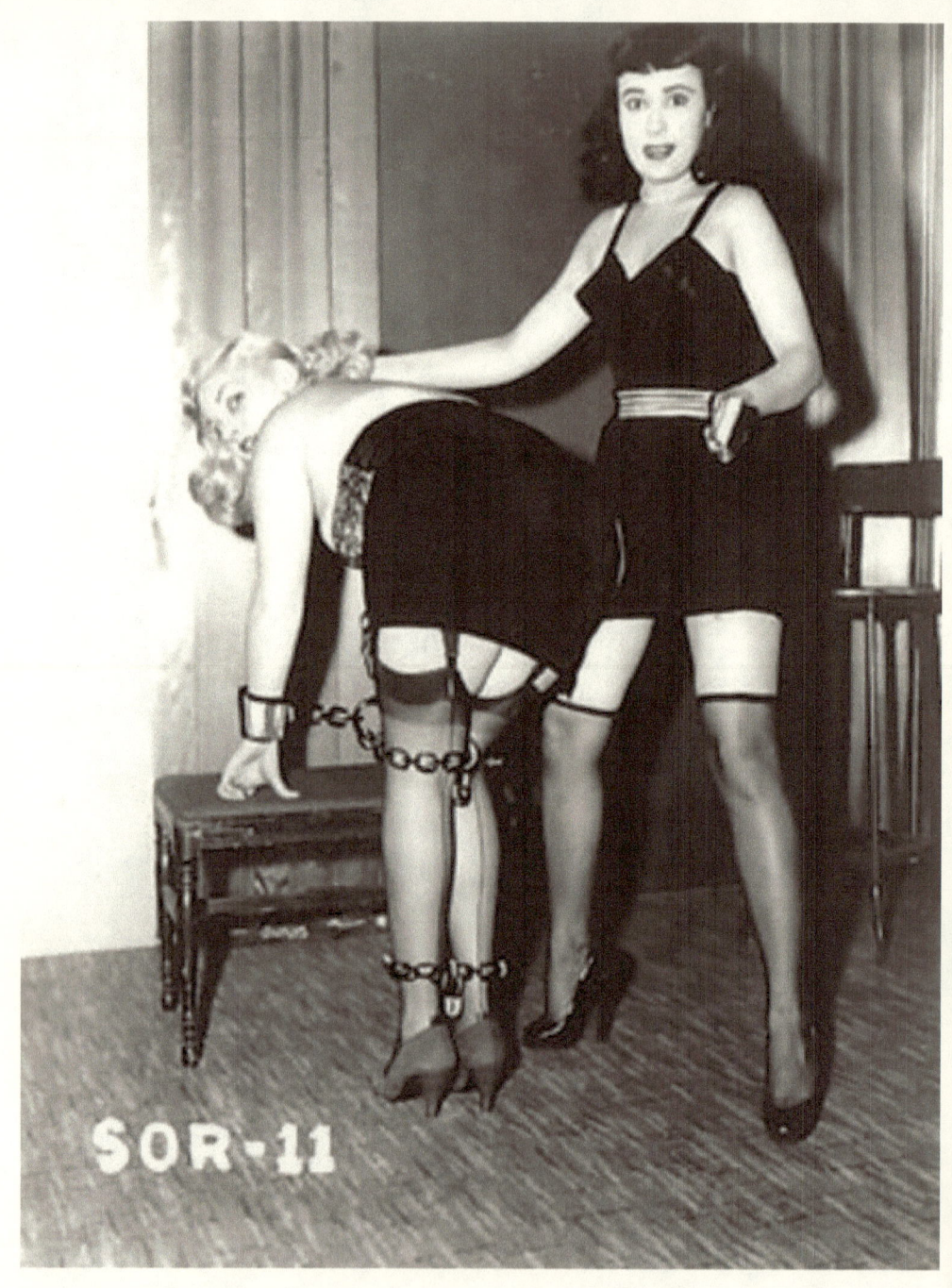

SOR-11

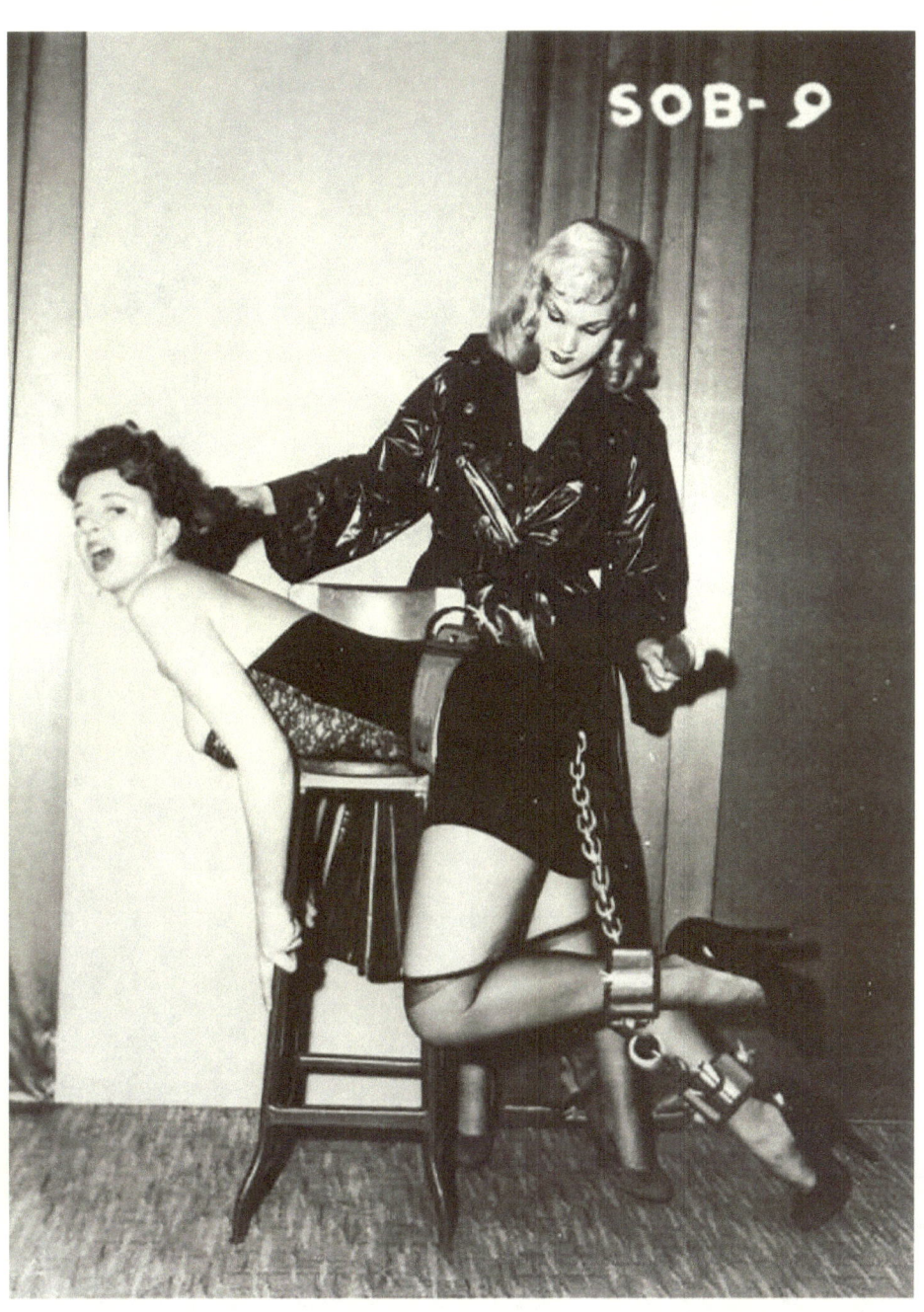

SOB-9

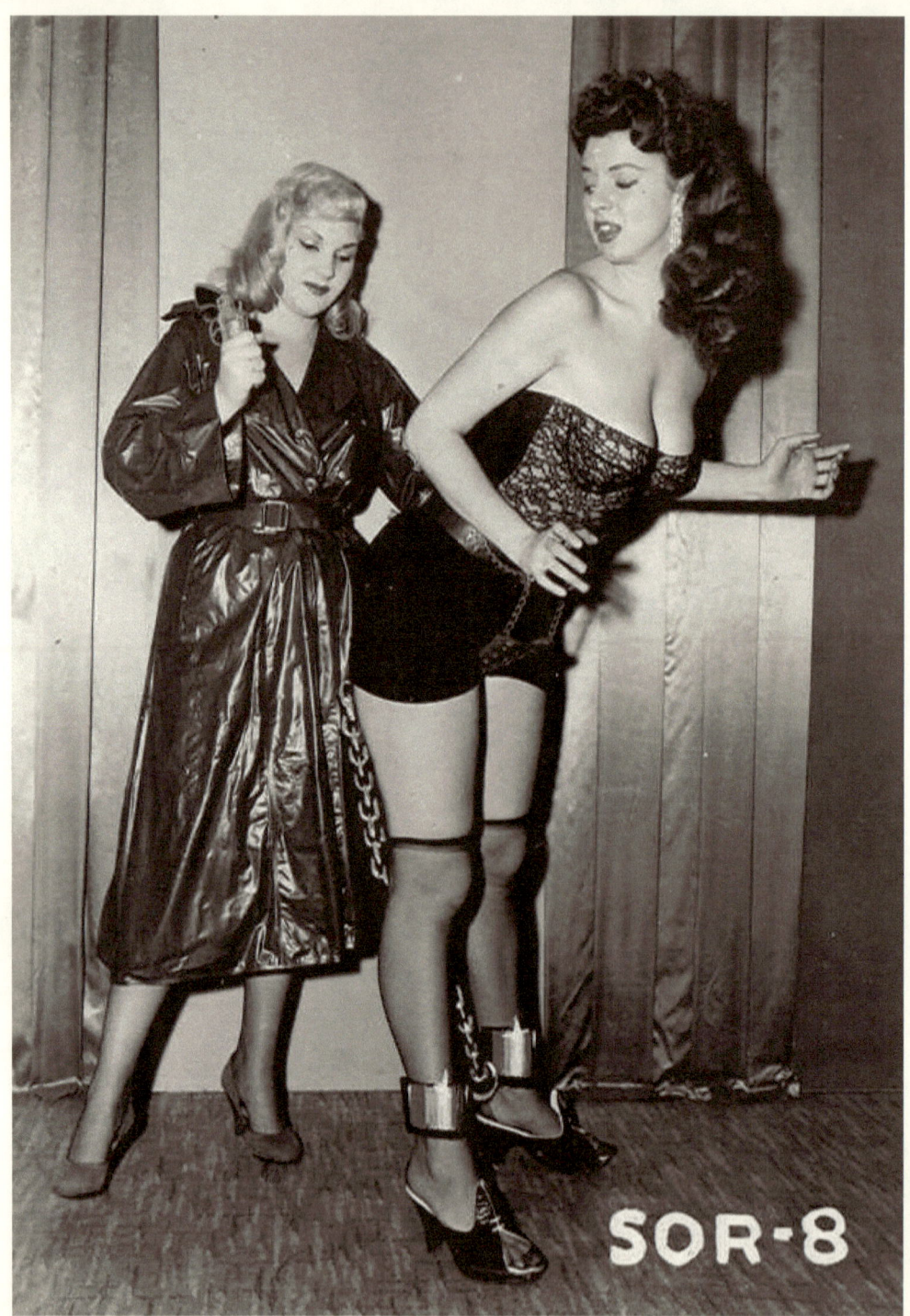

SOR-8

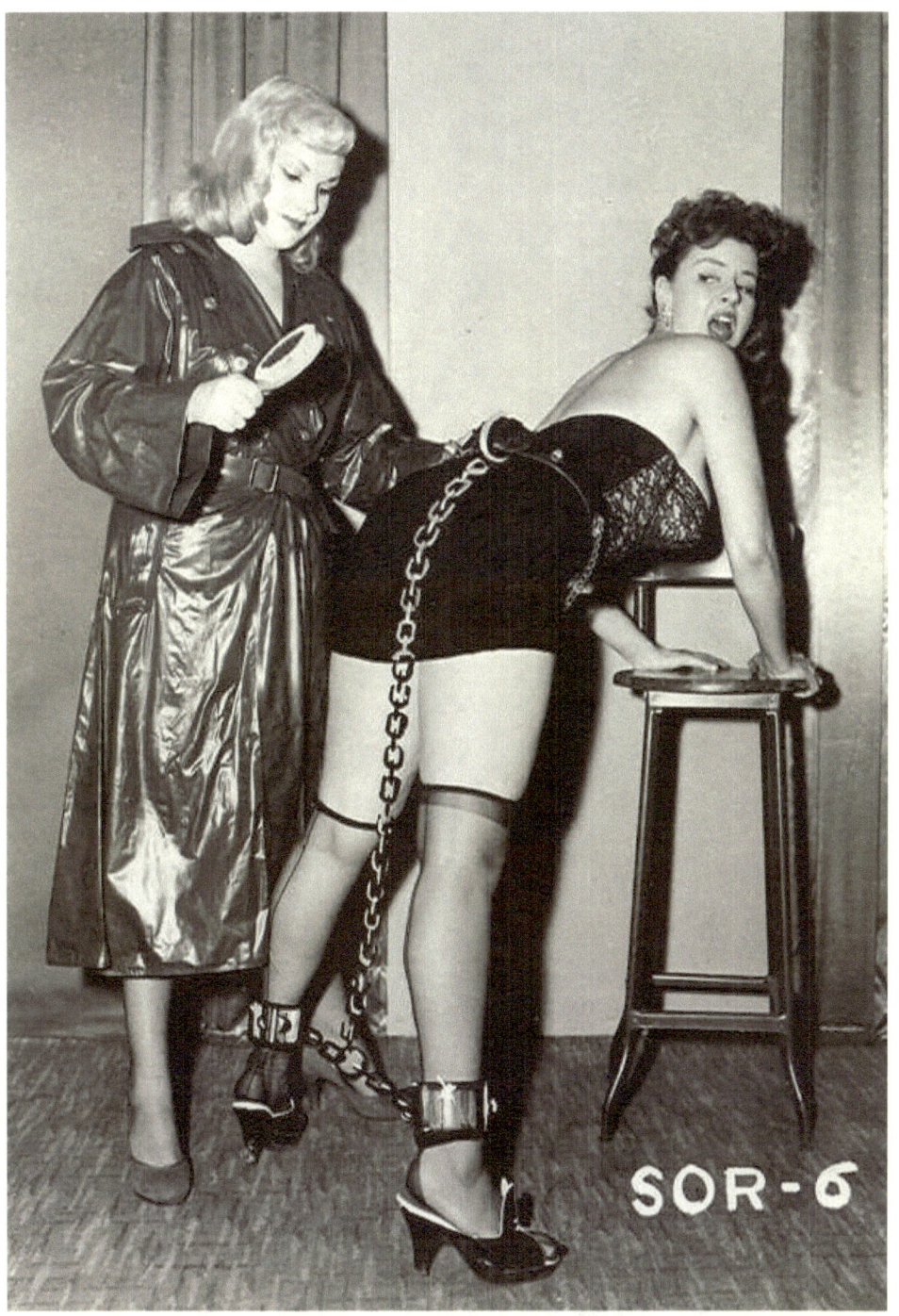

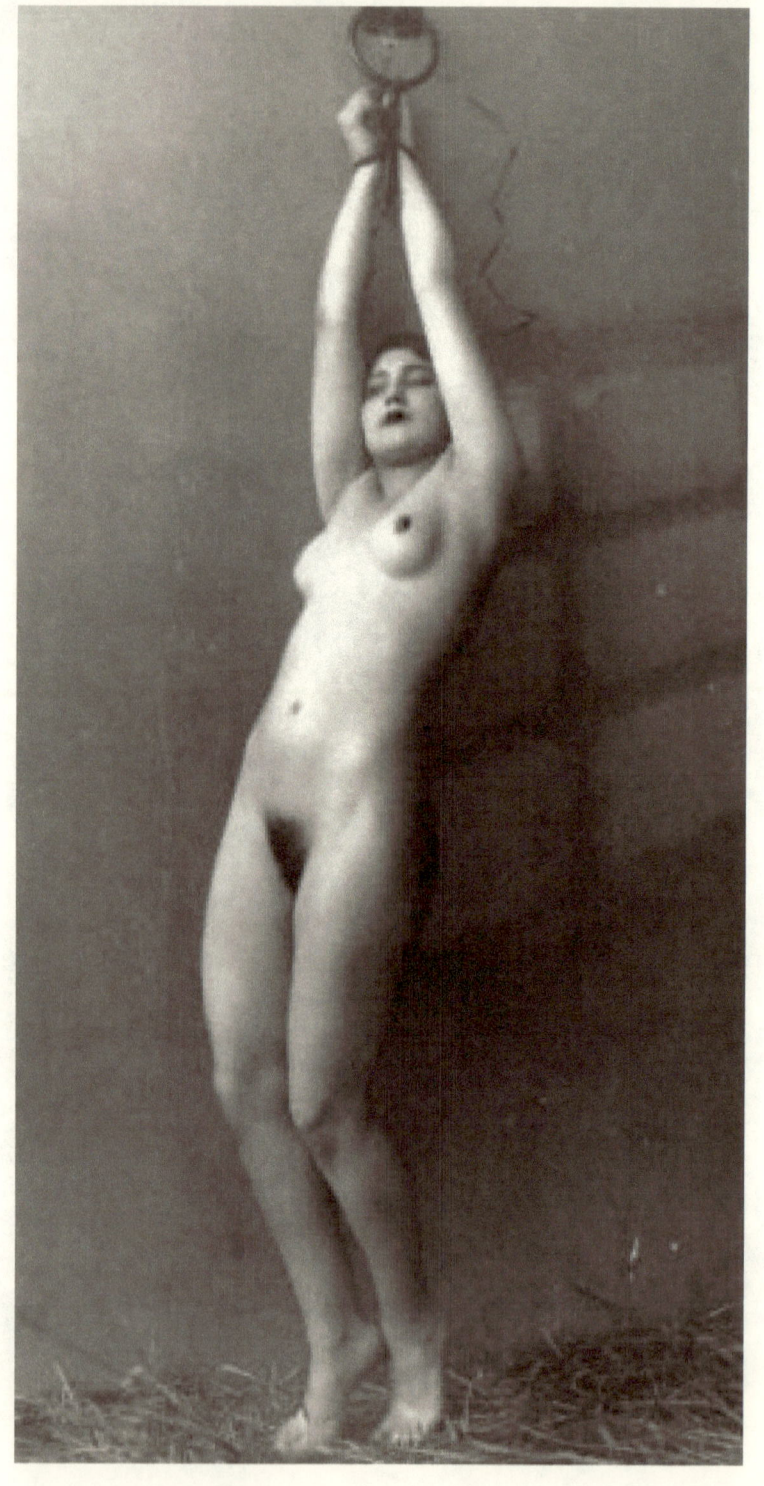

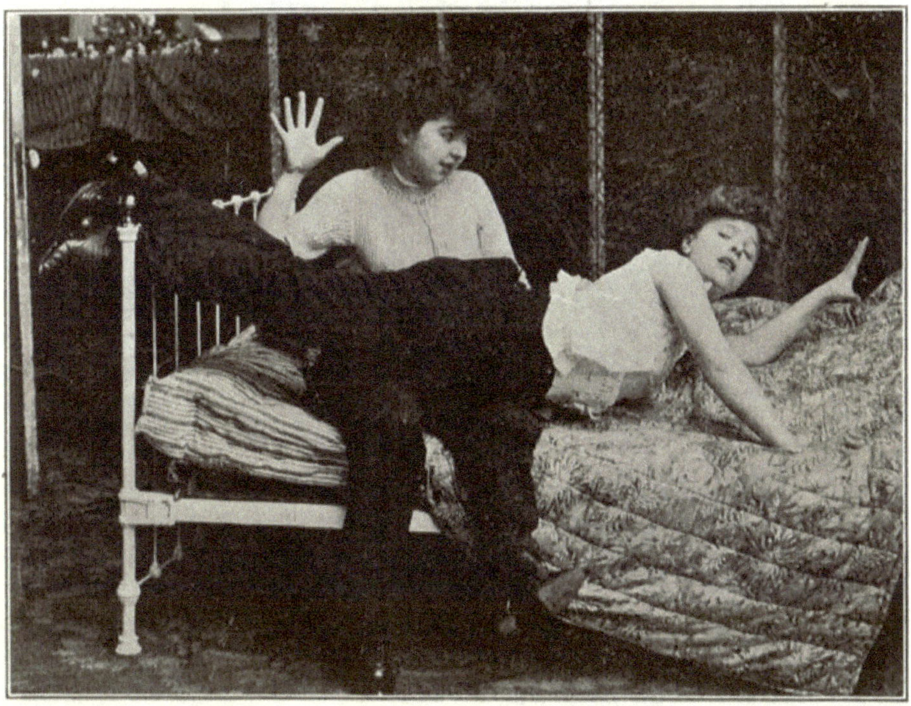

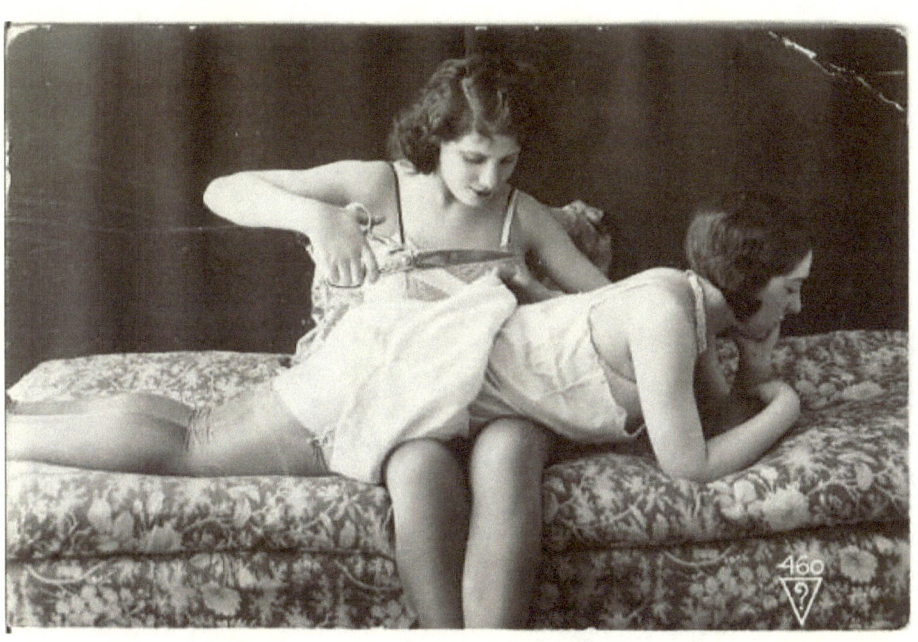

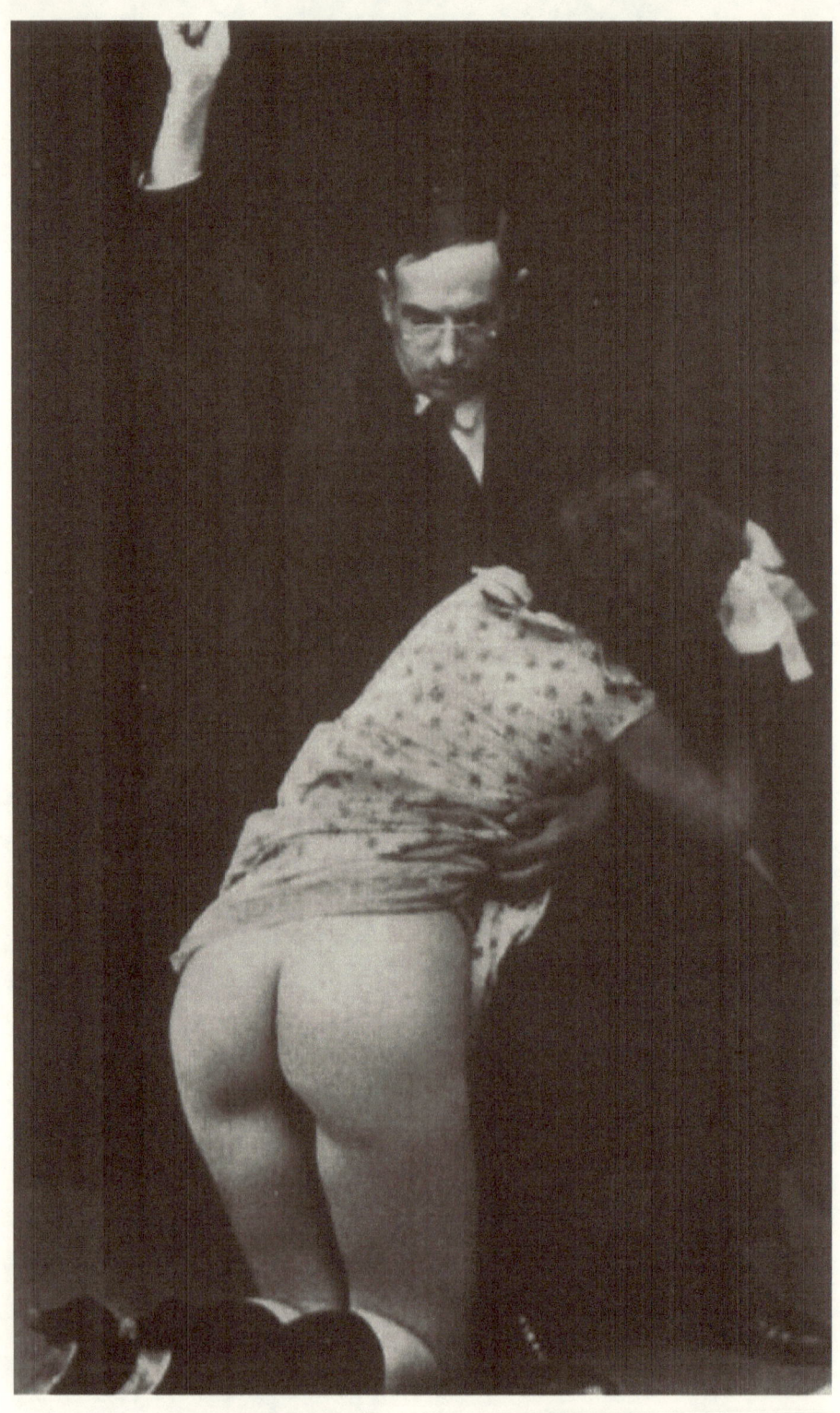

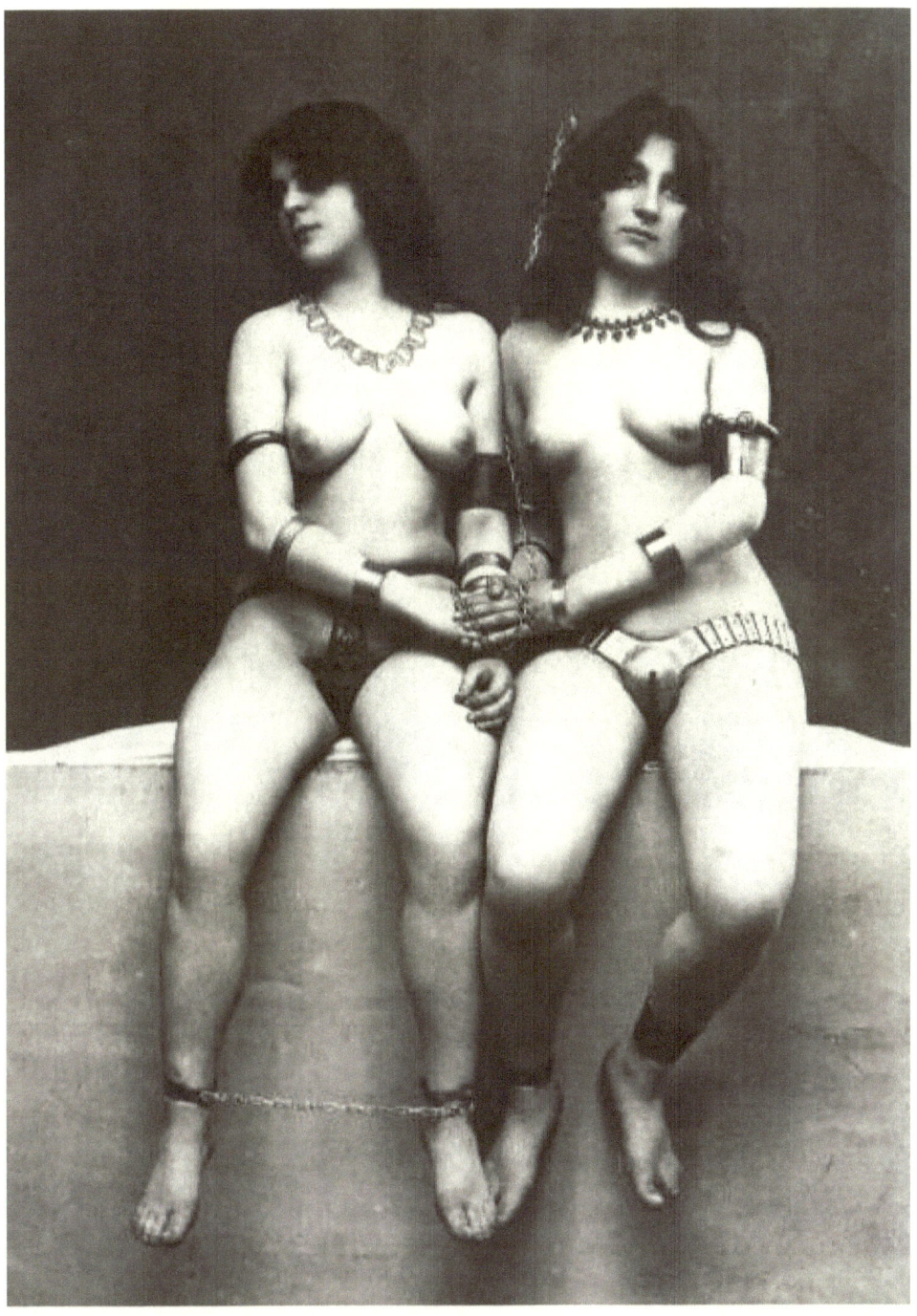

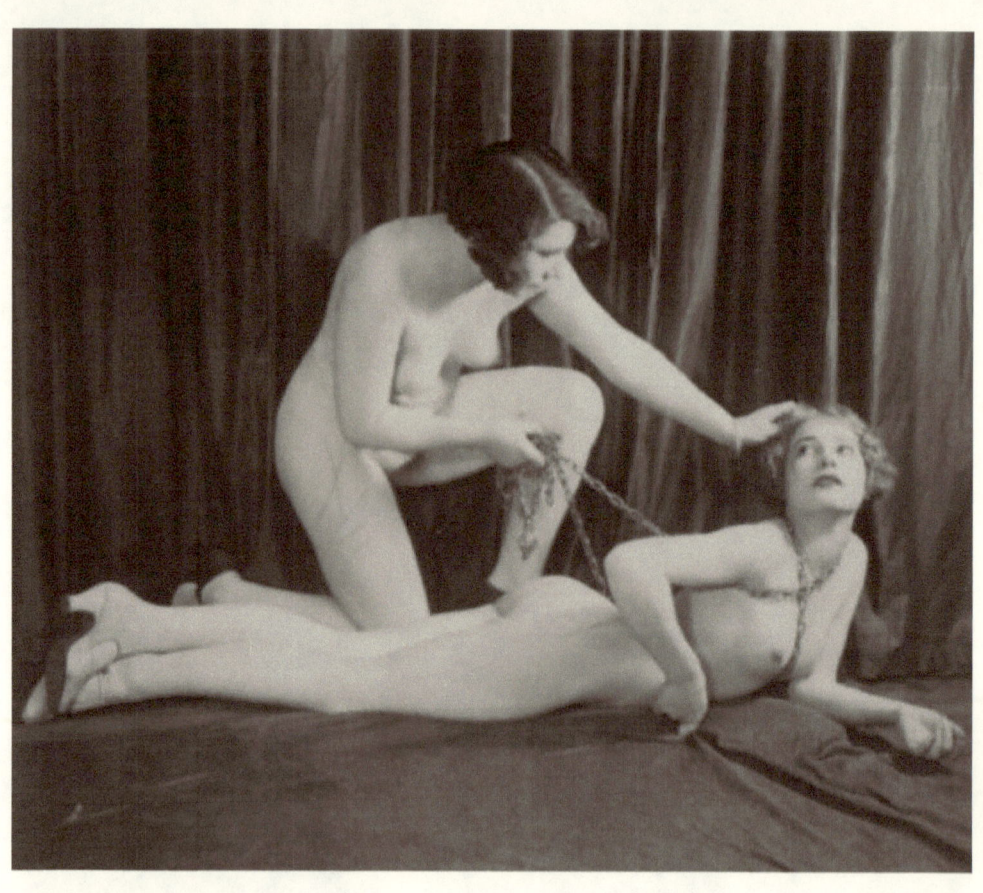

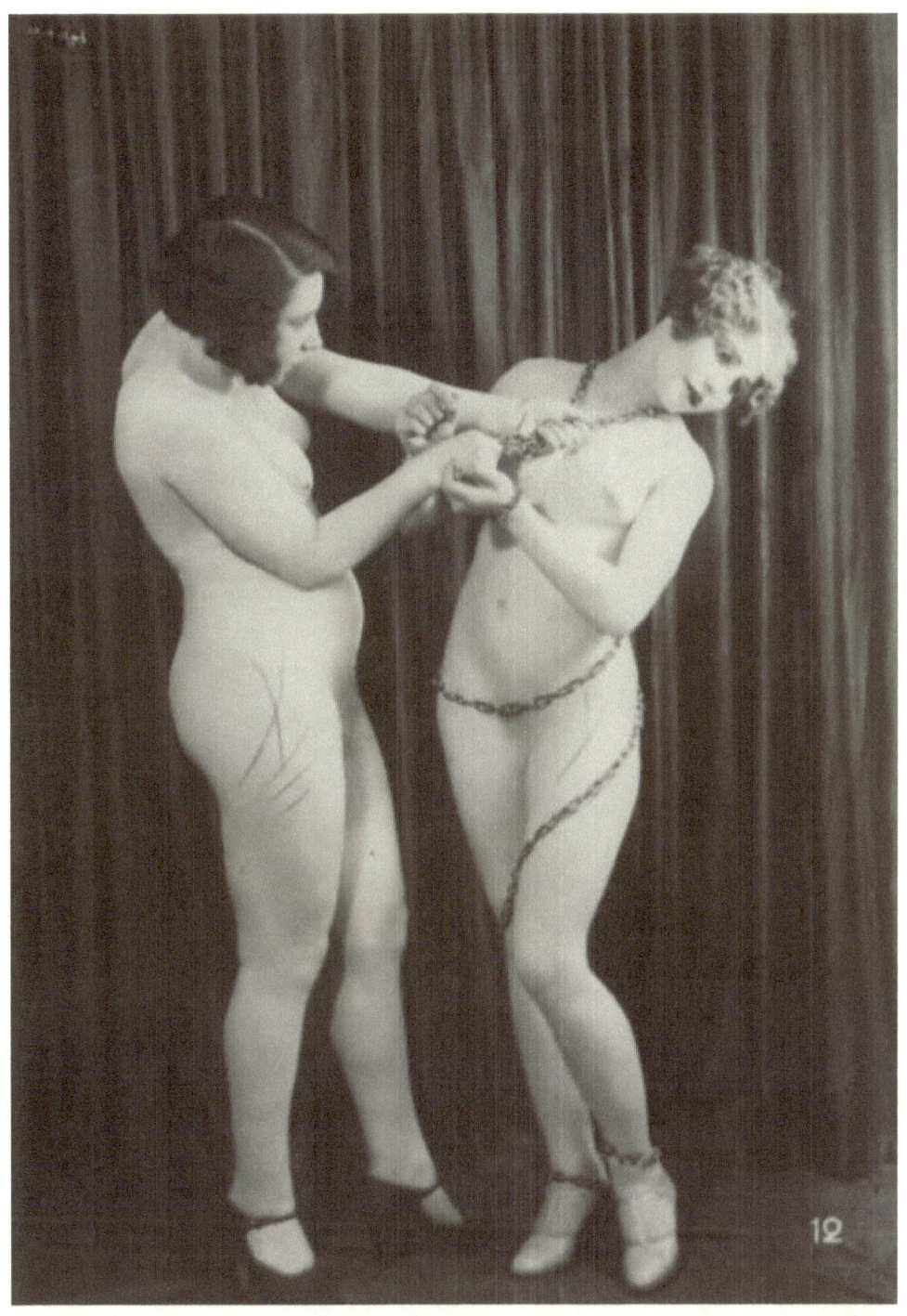

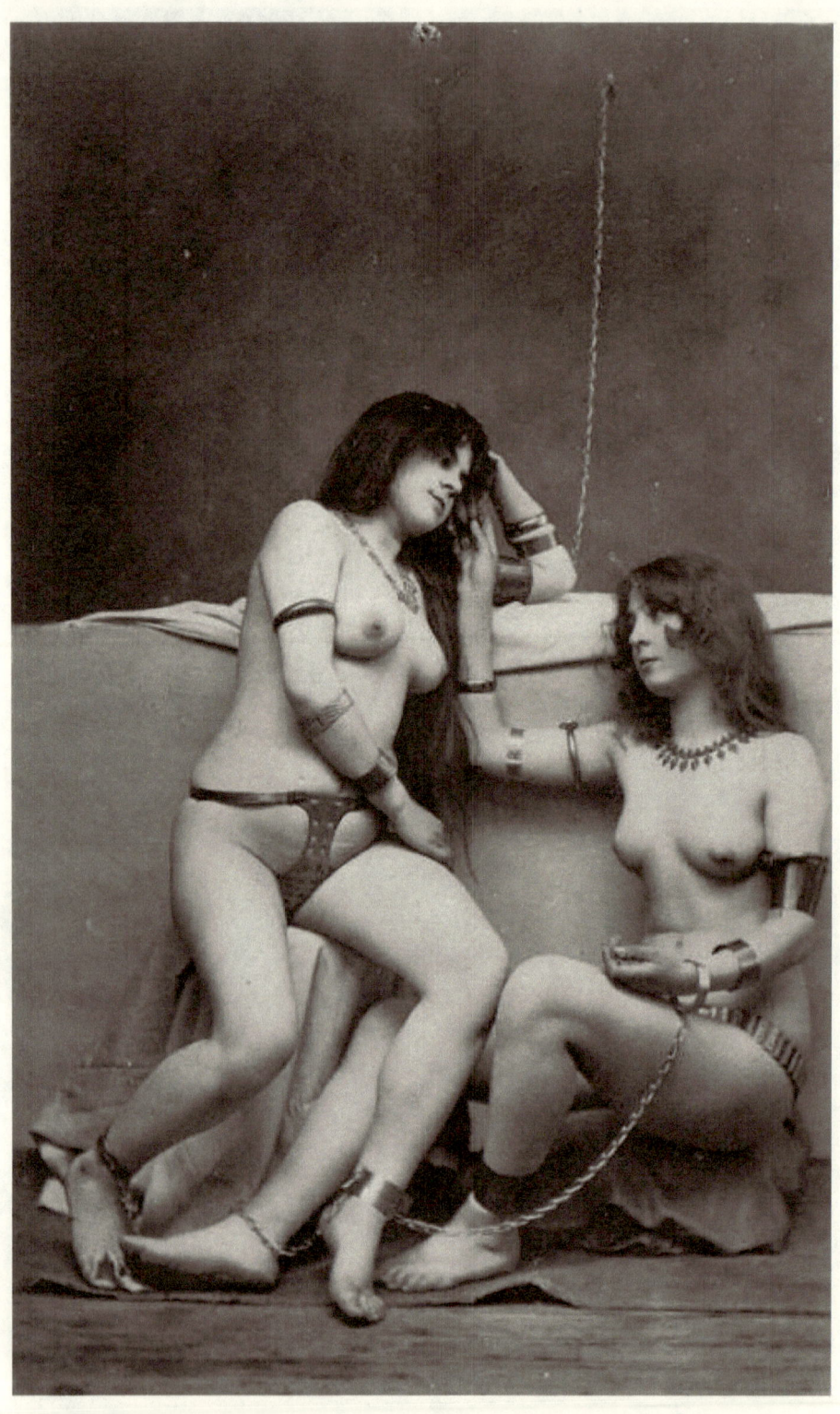

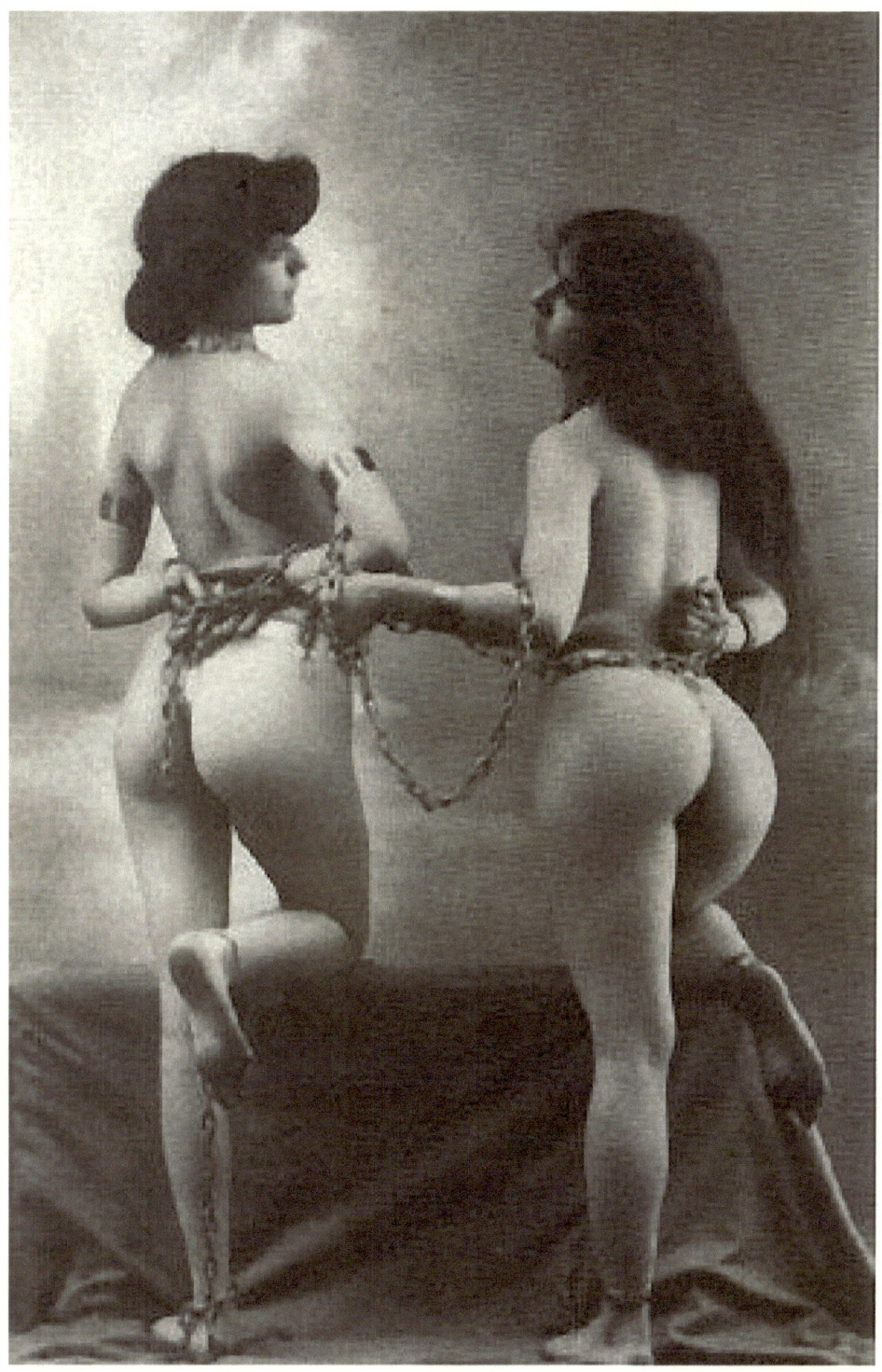

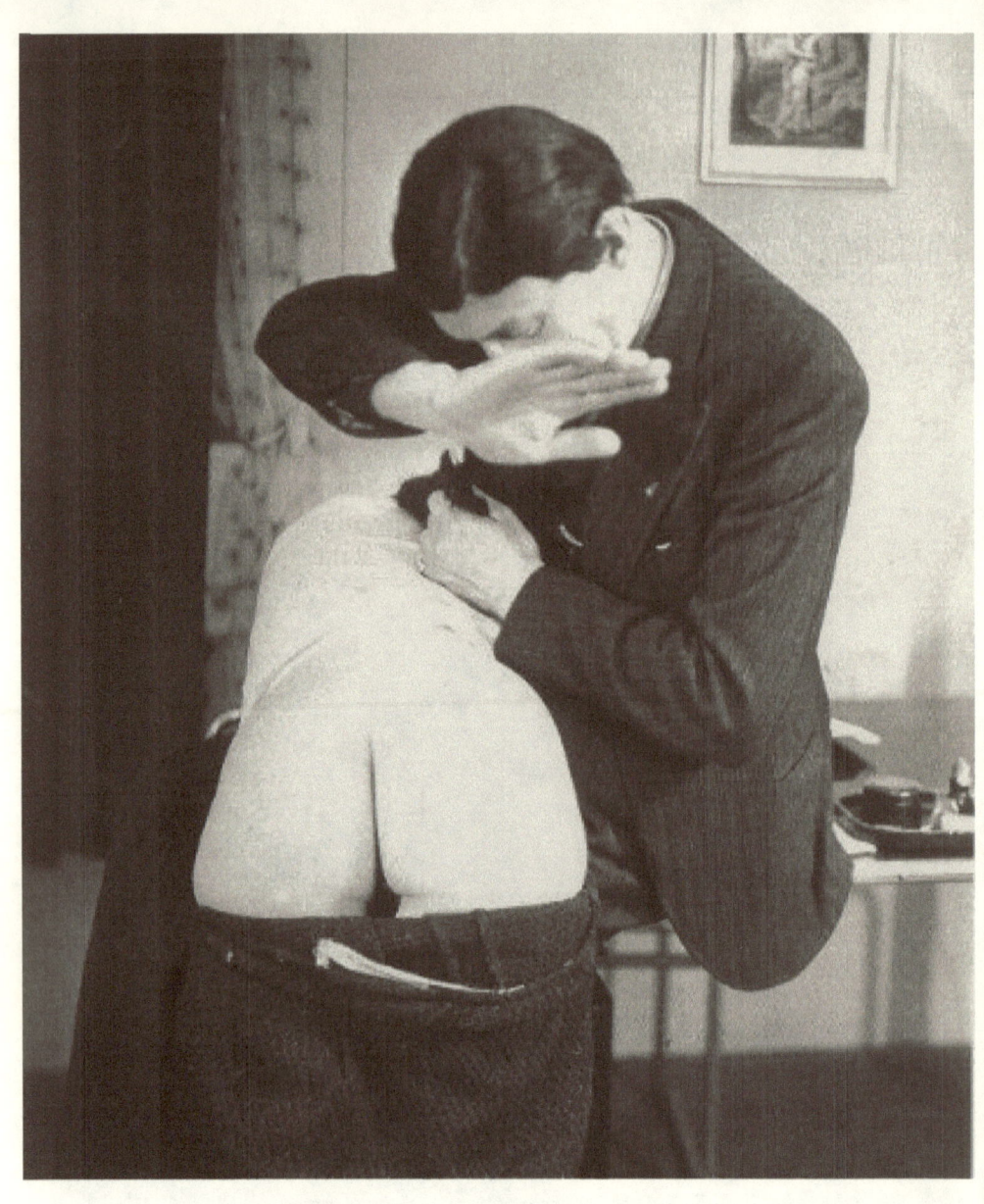

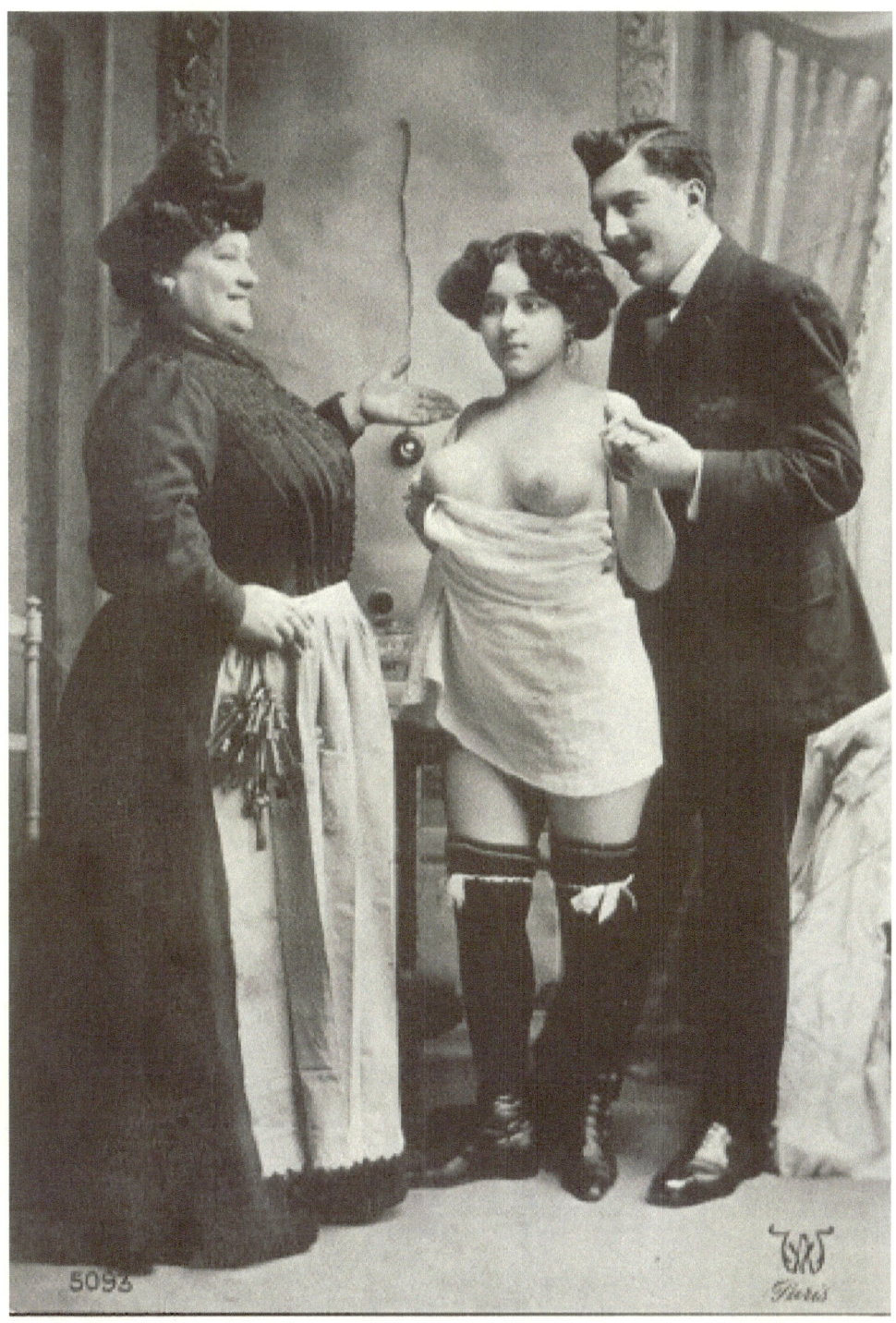

5093

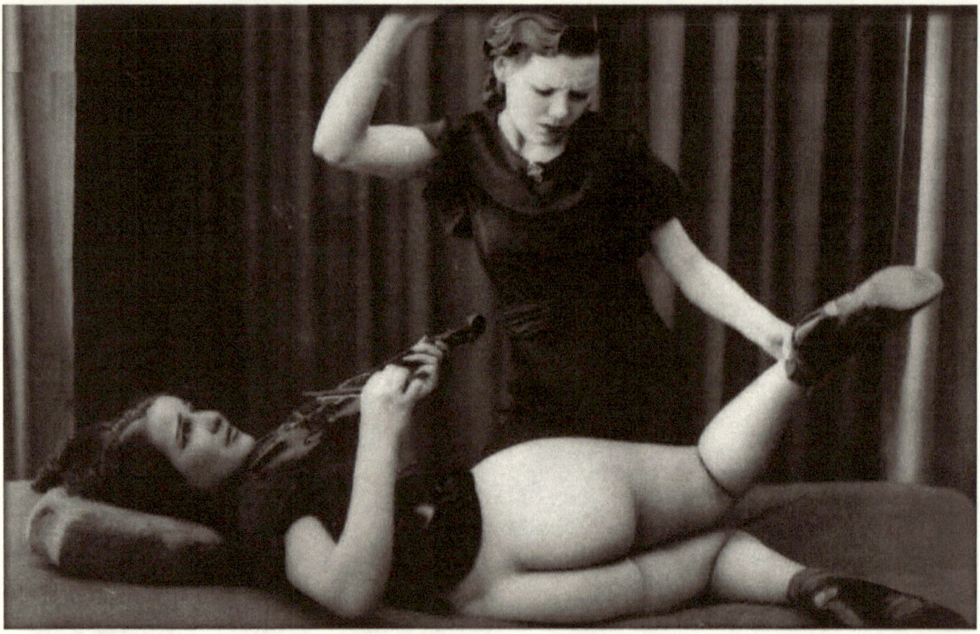

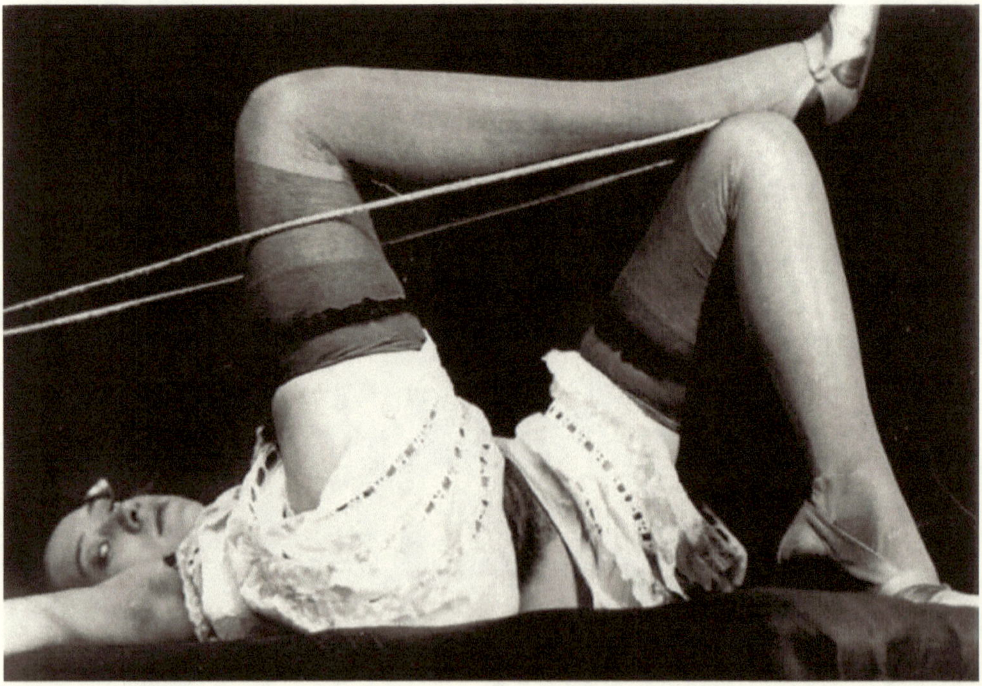

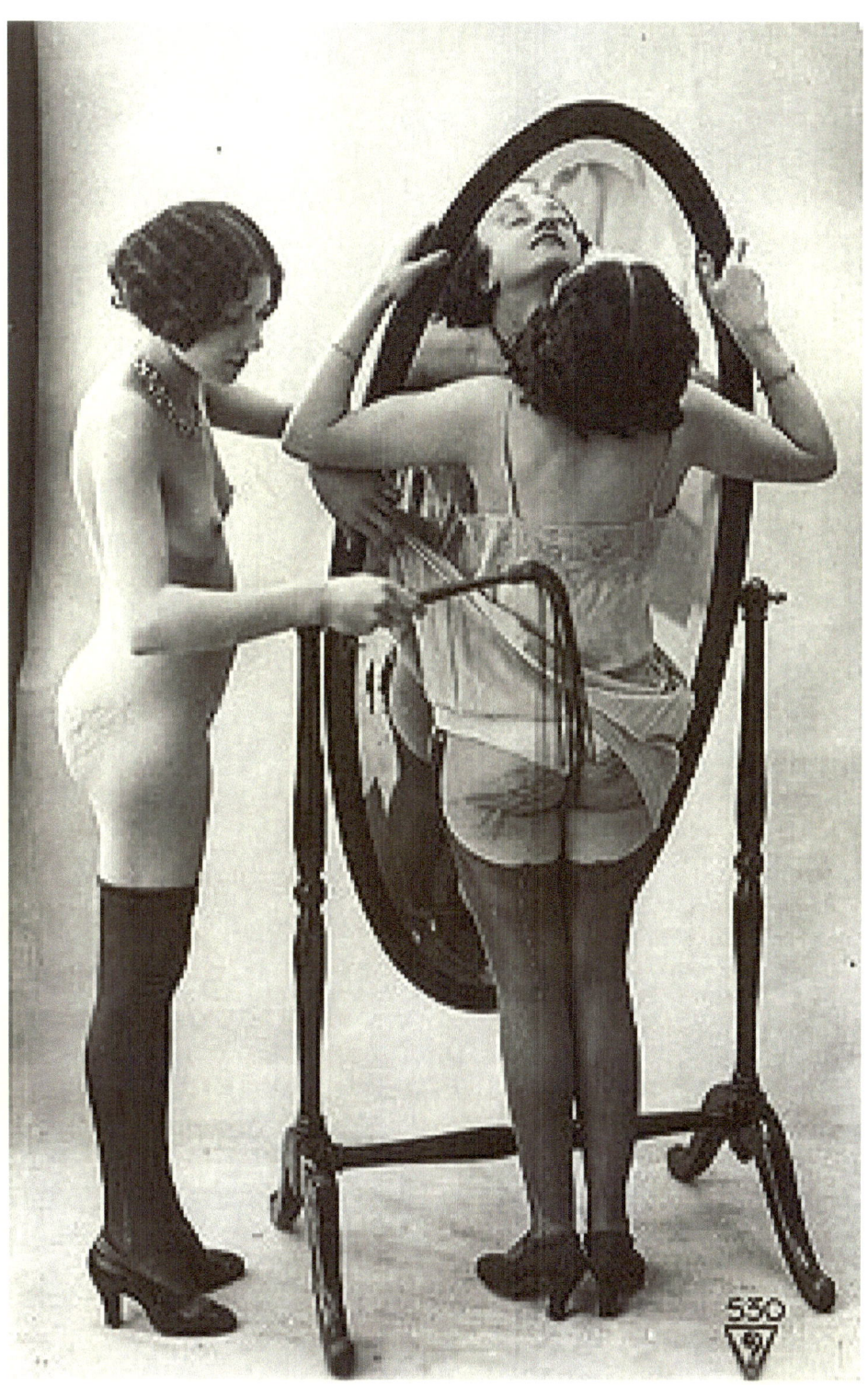

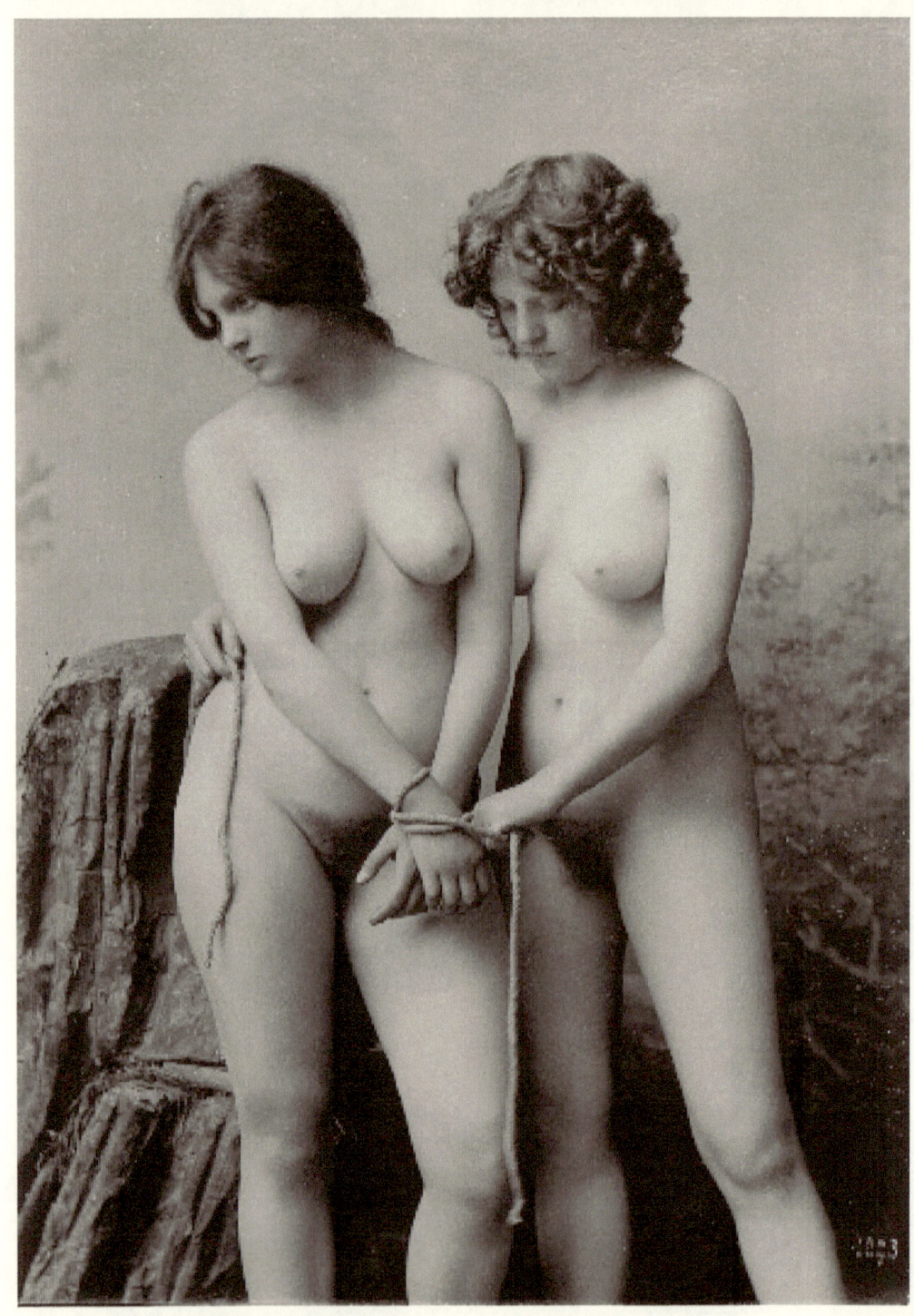

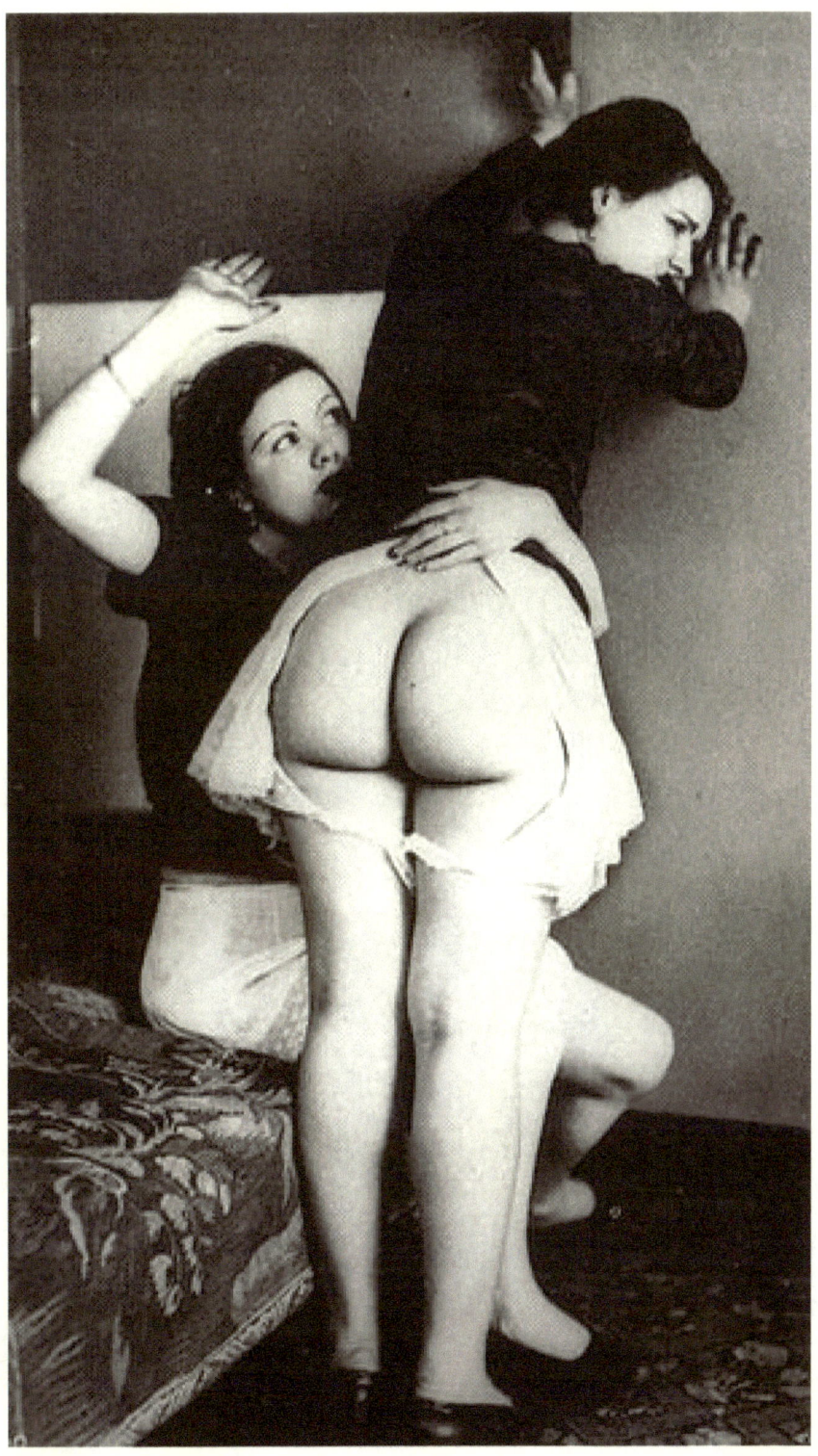

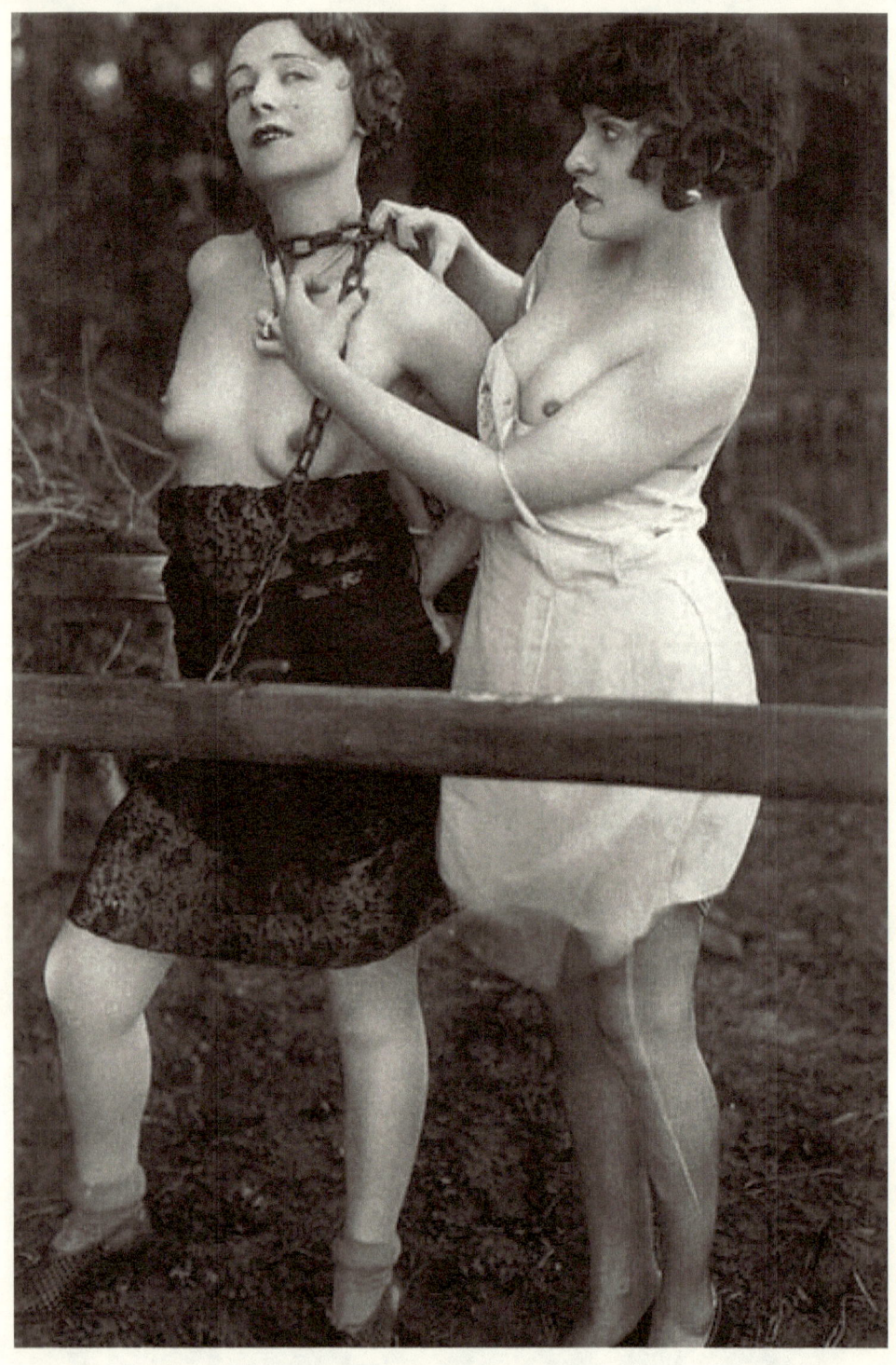

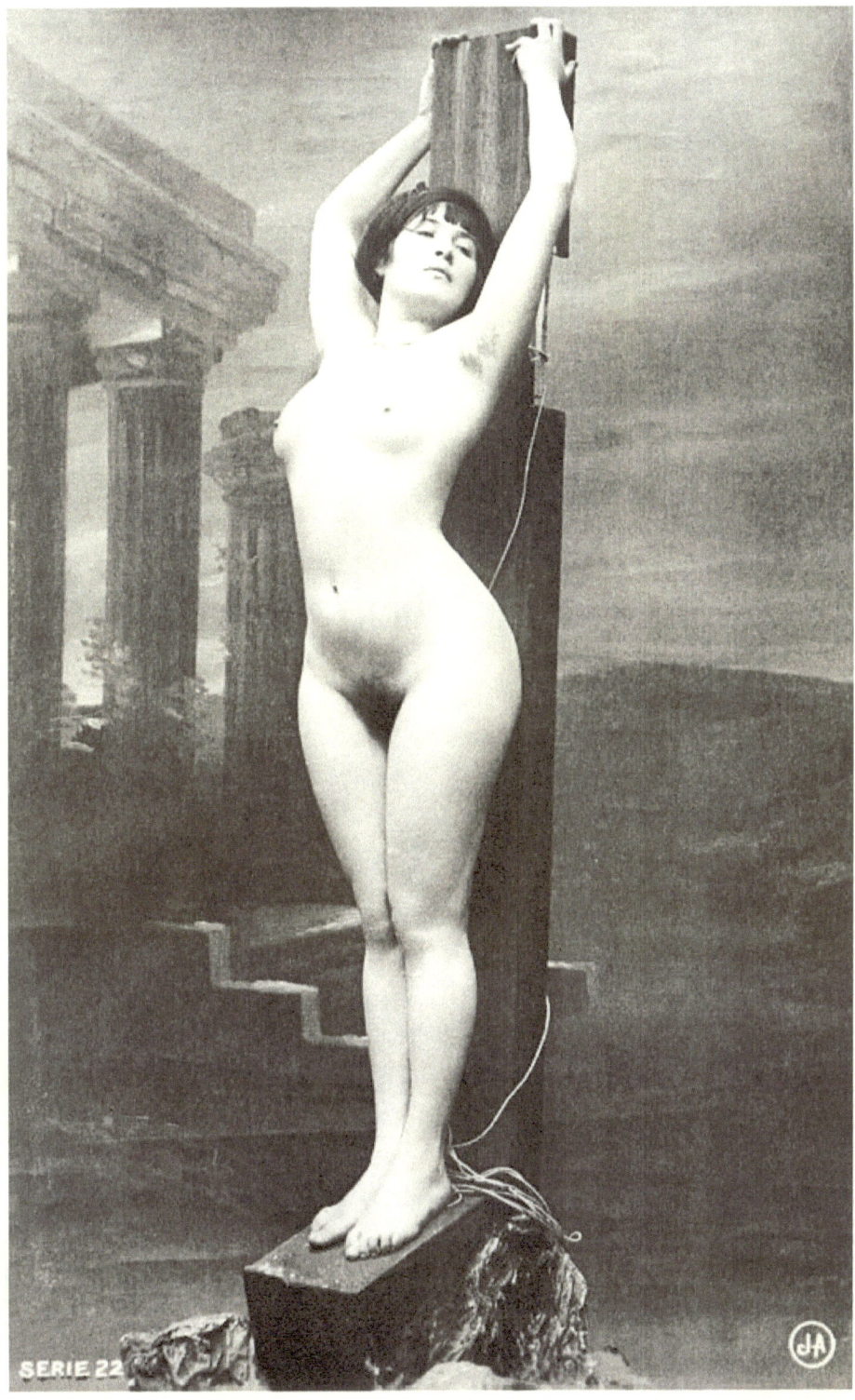

SERIE 22

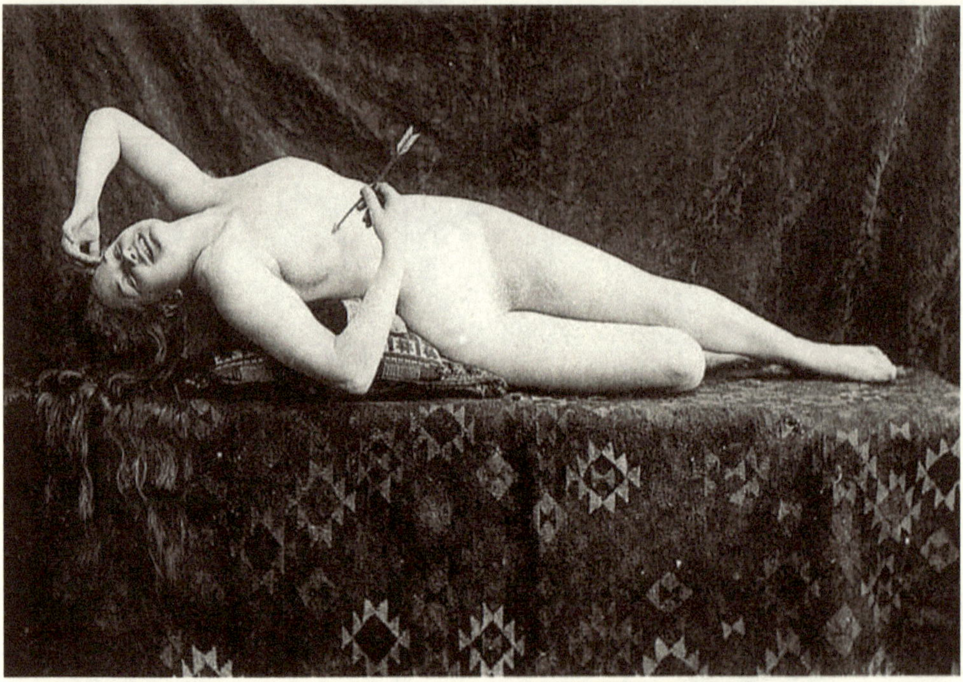

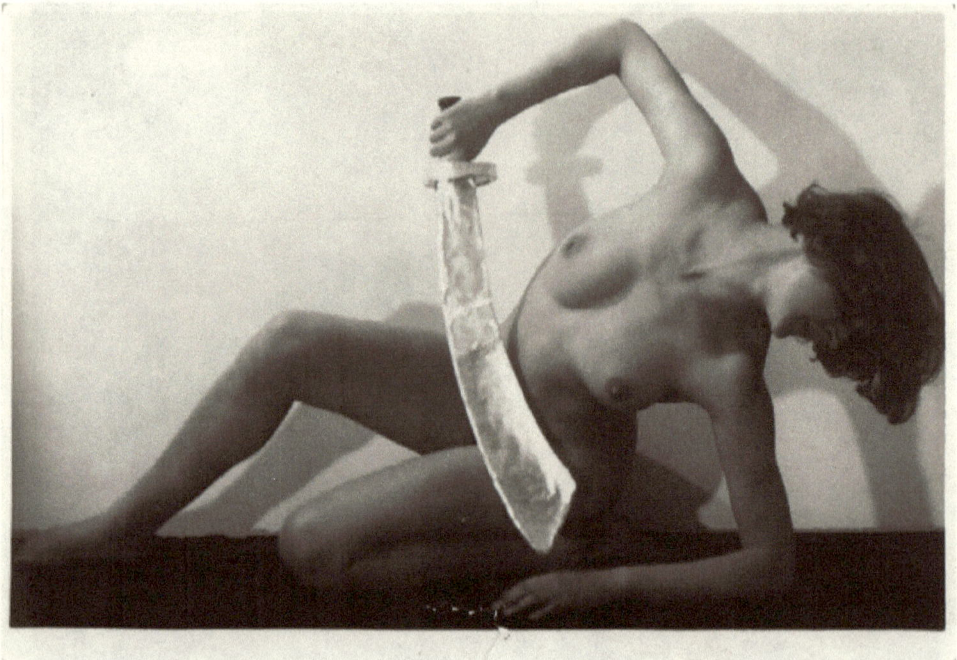

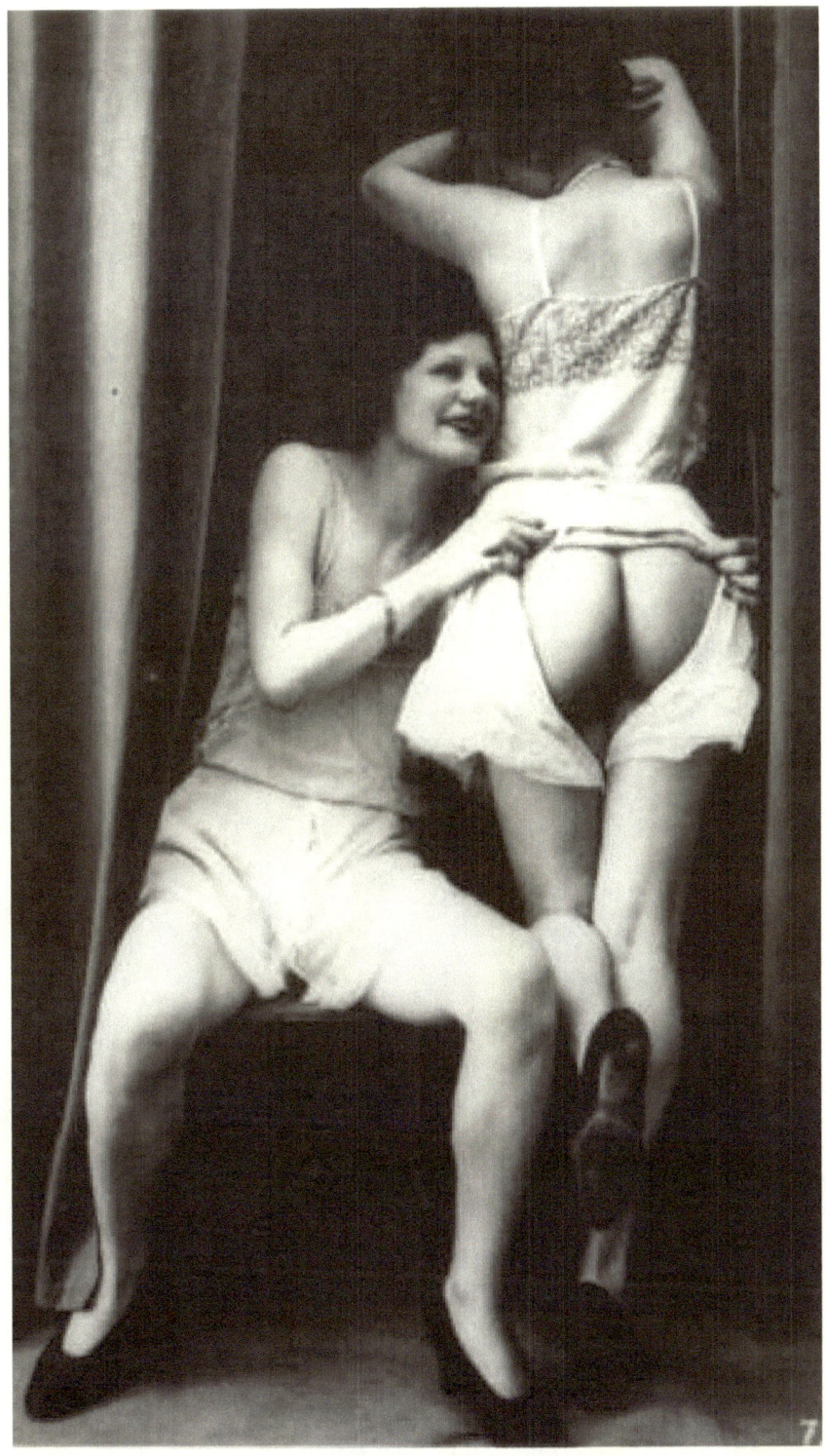

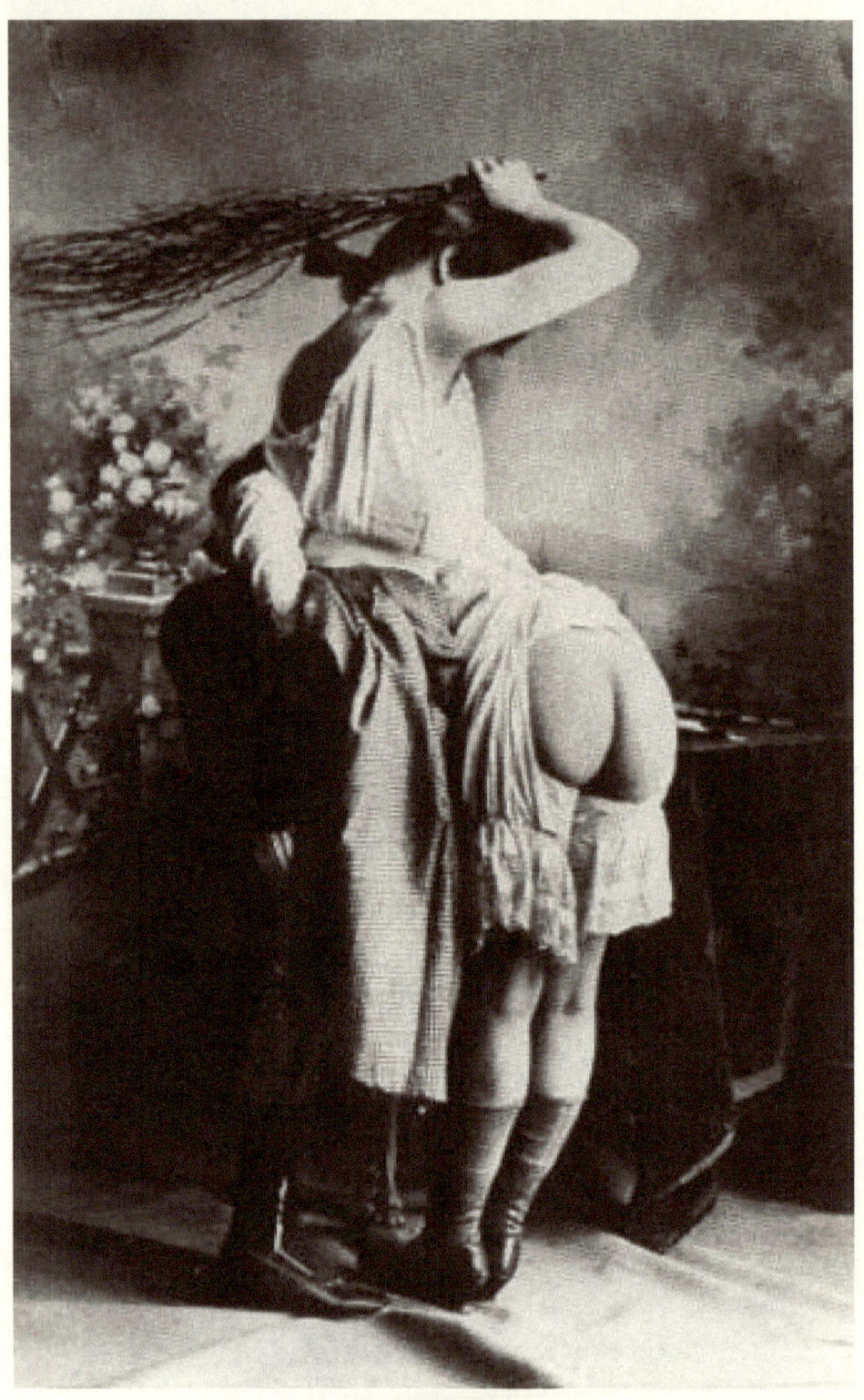

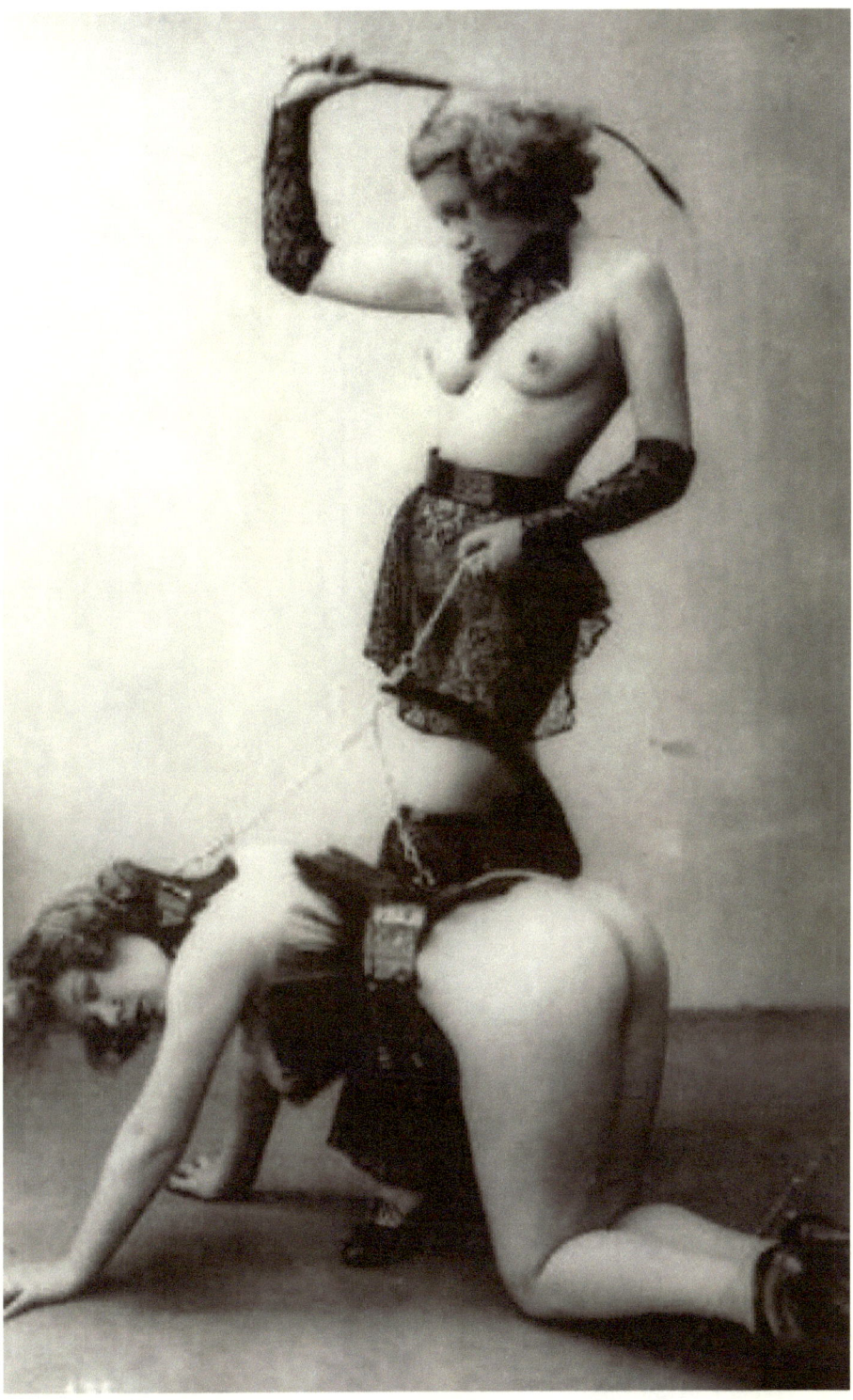

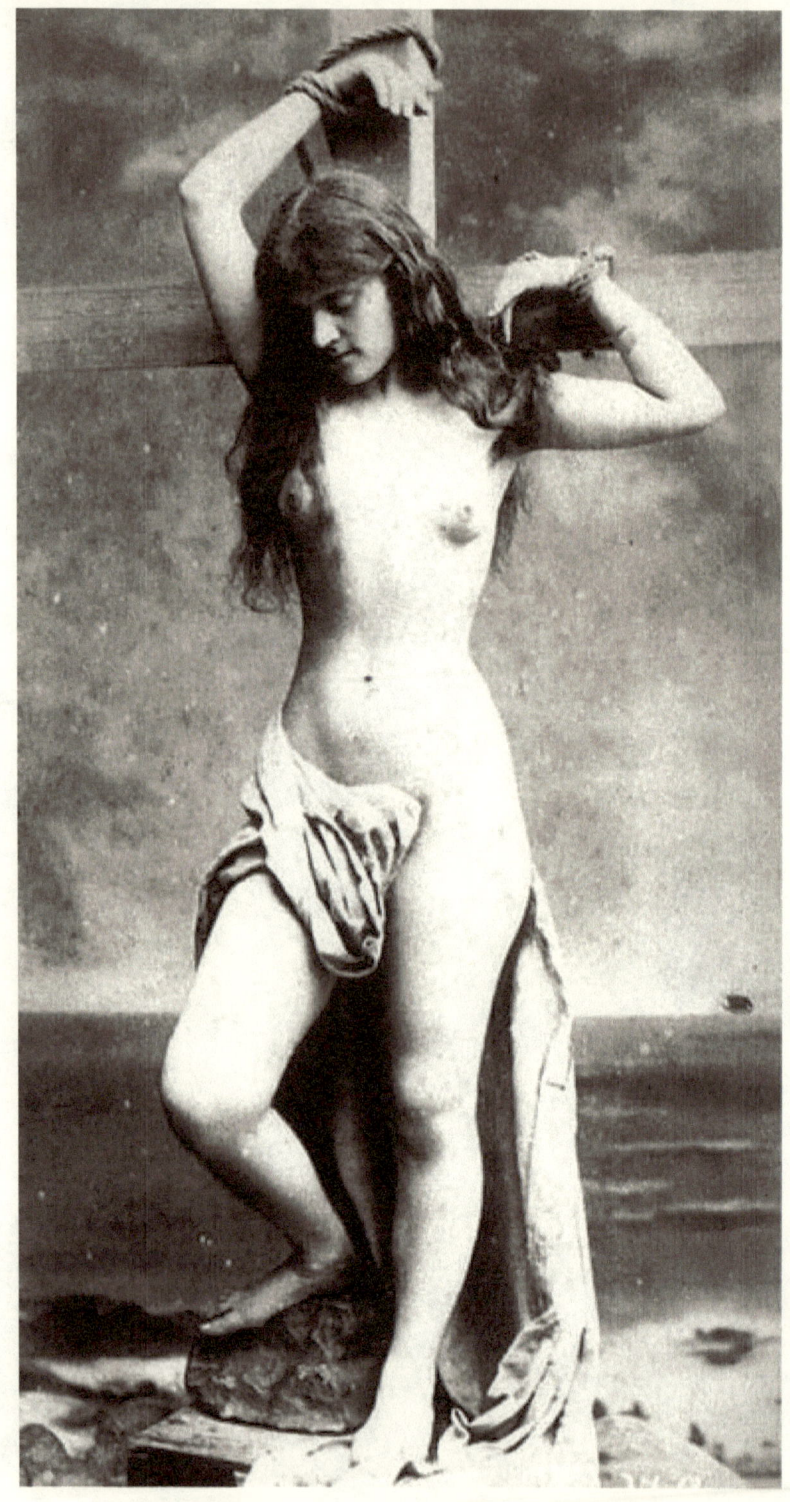

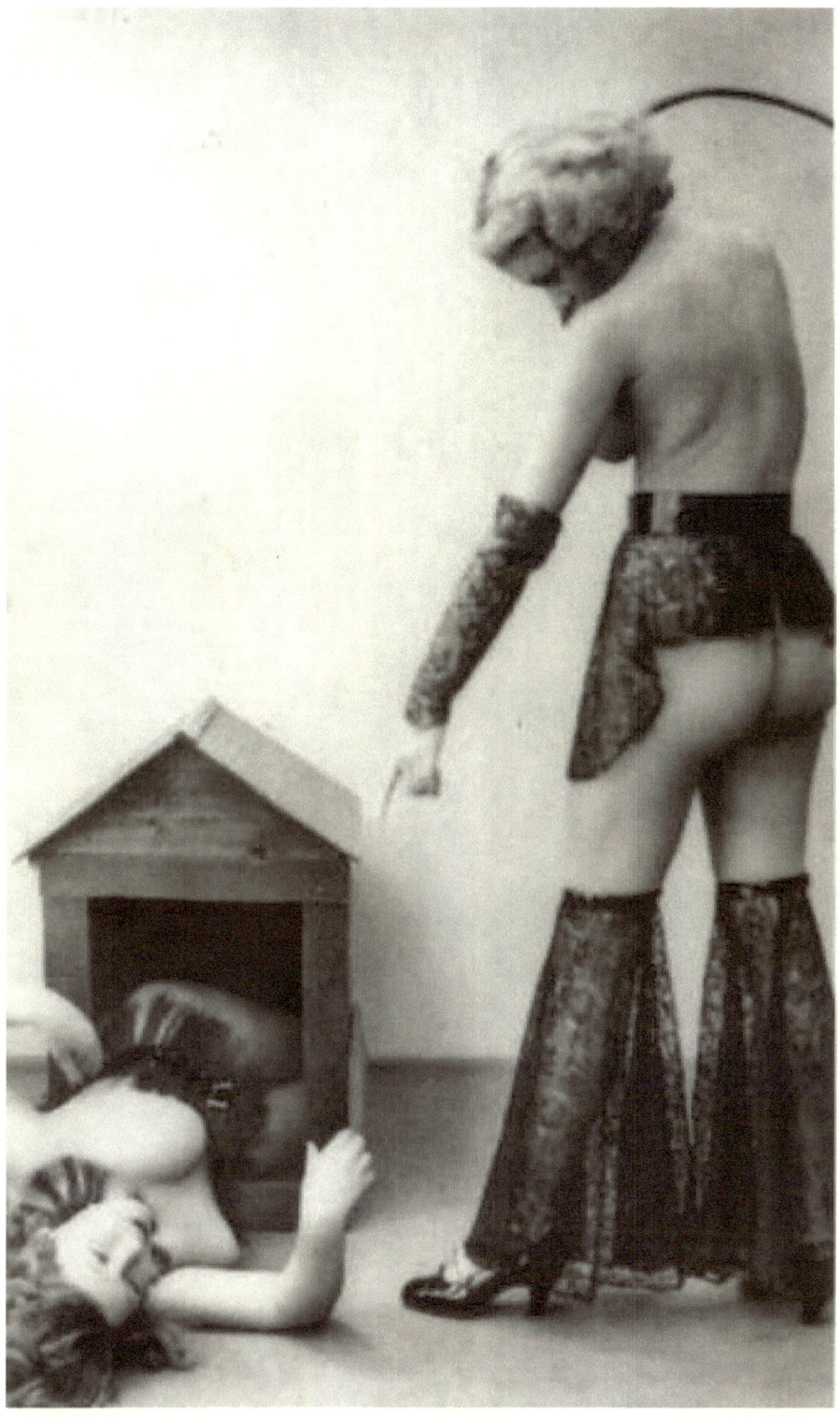

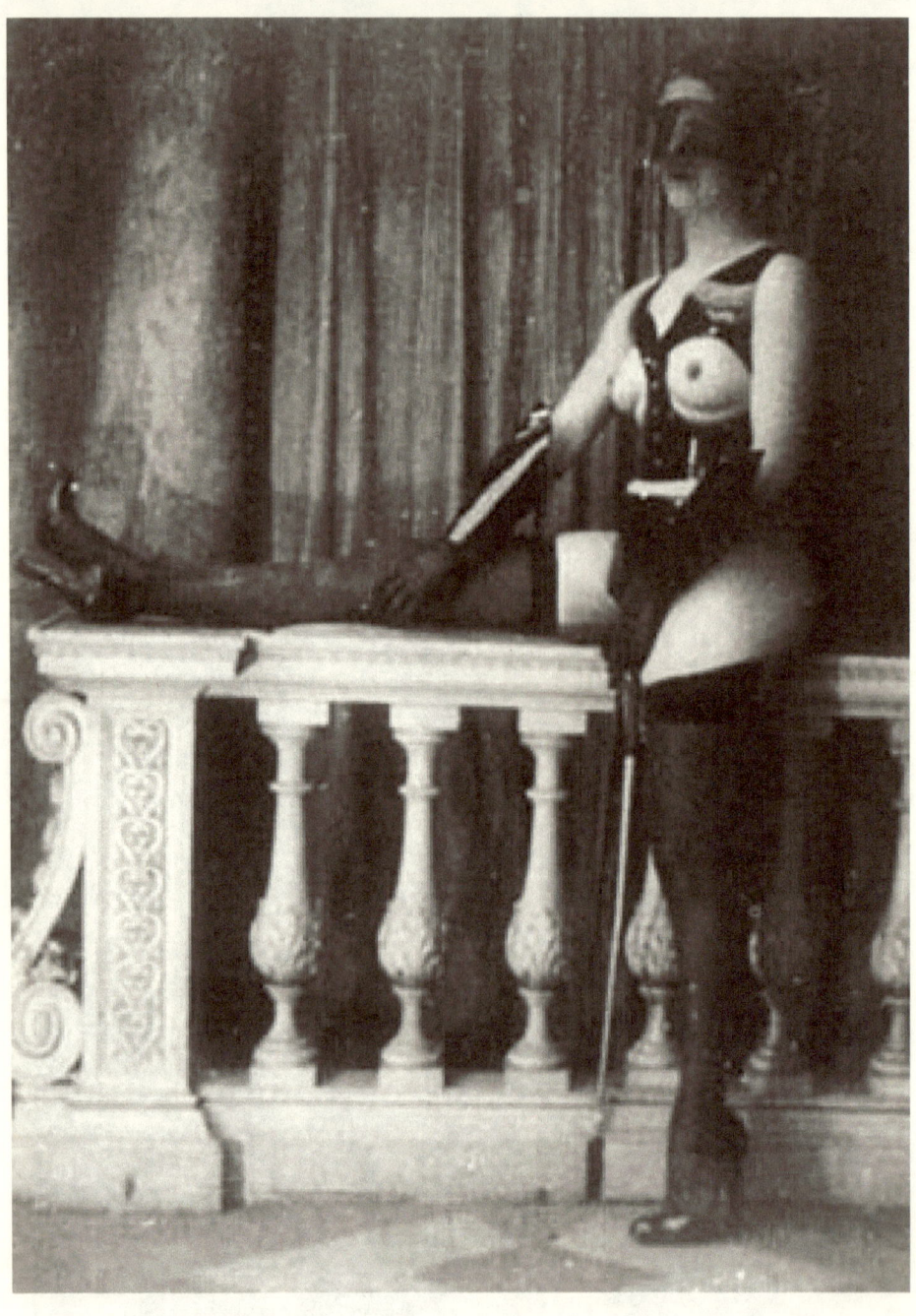

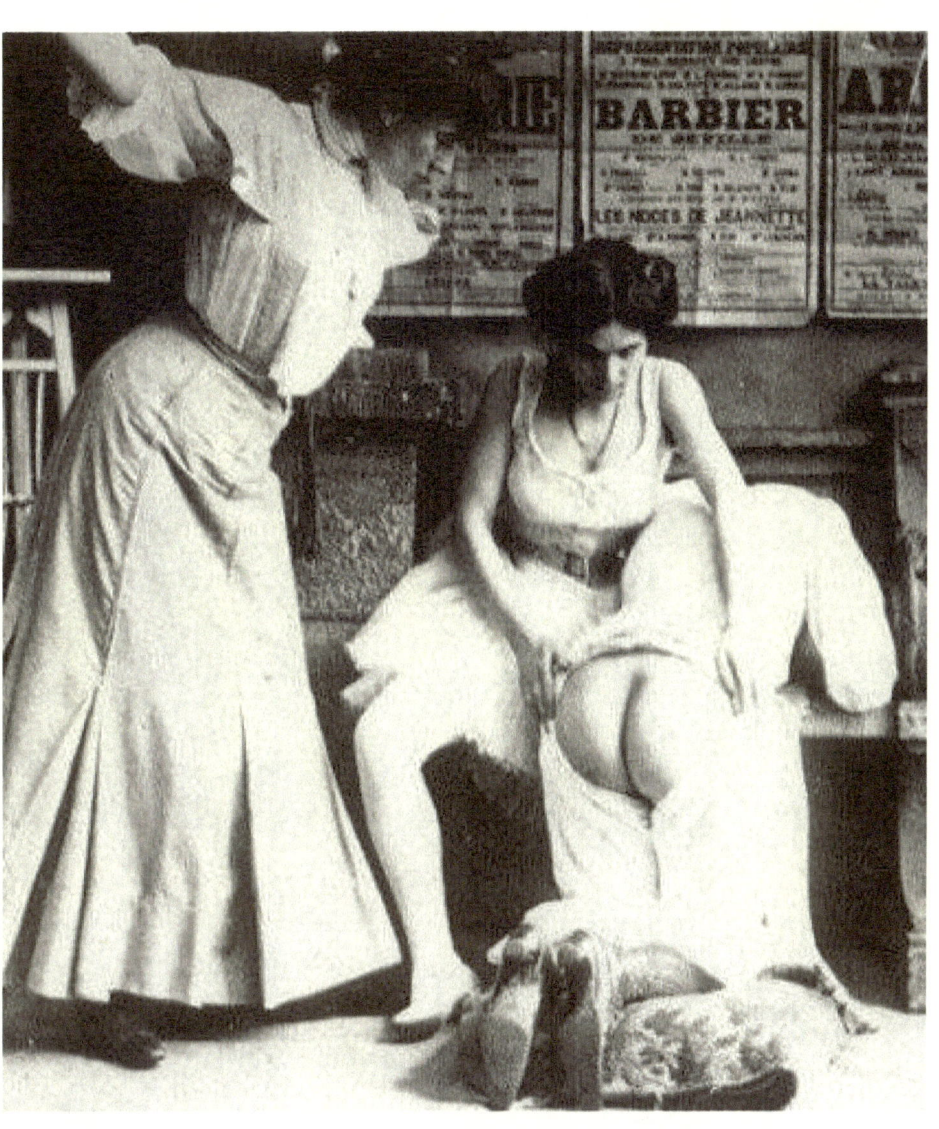

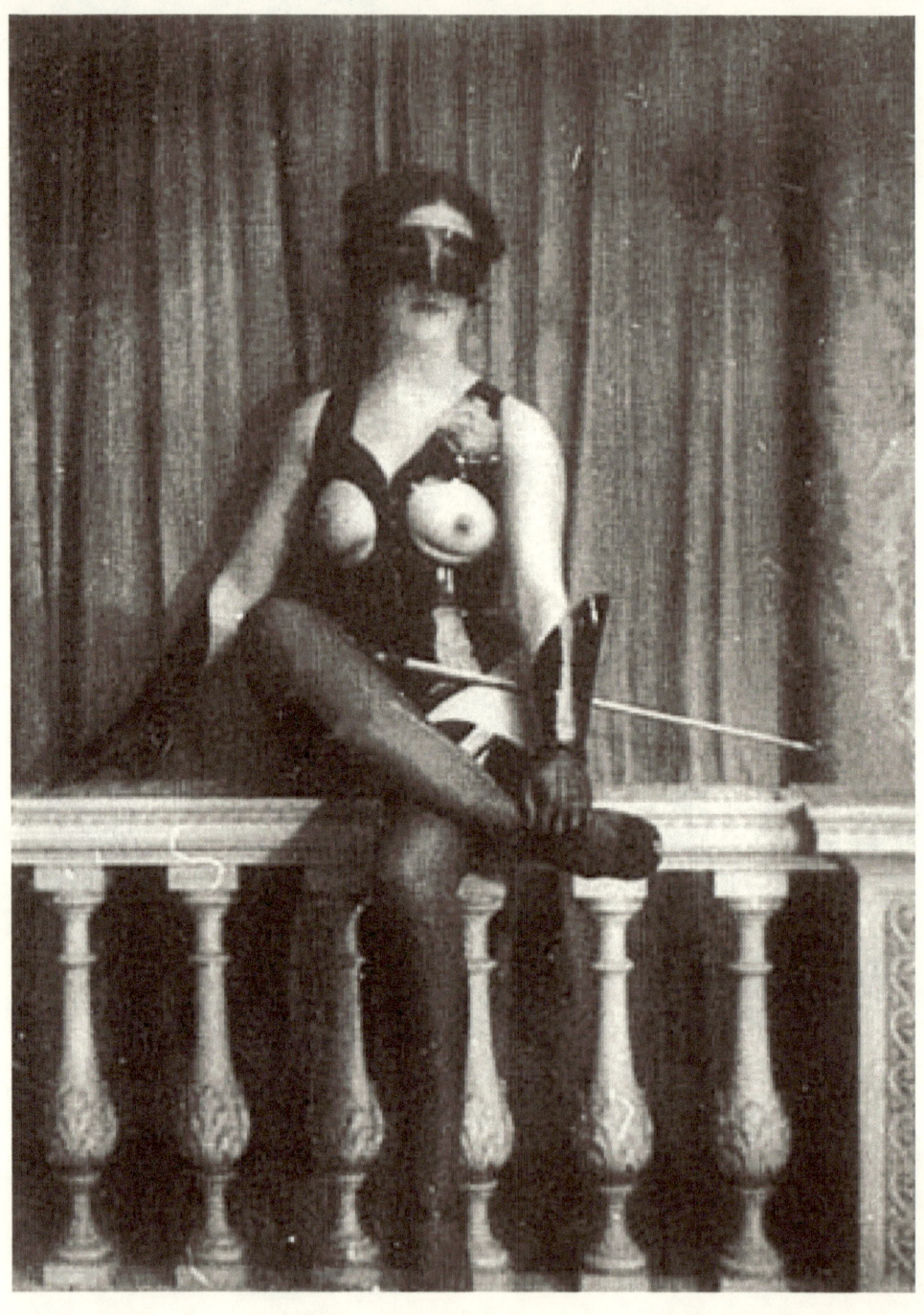

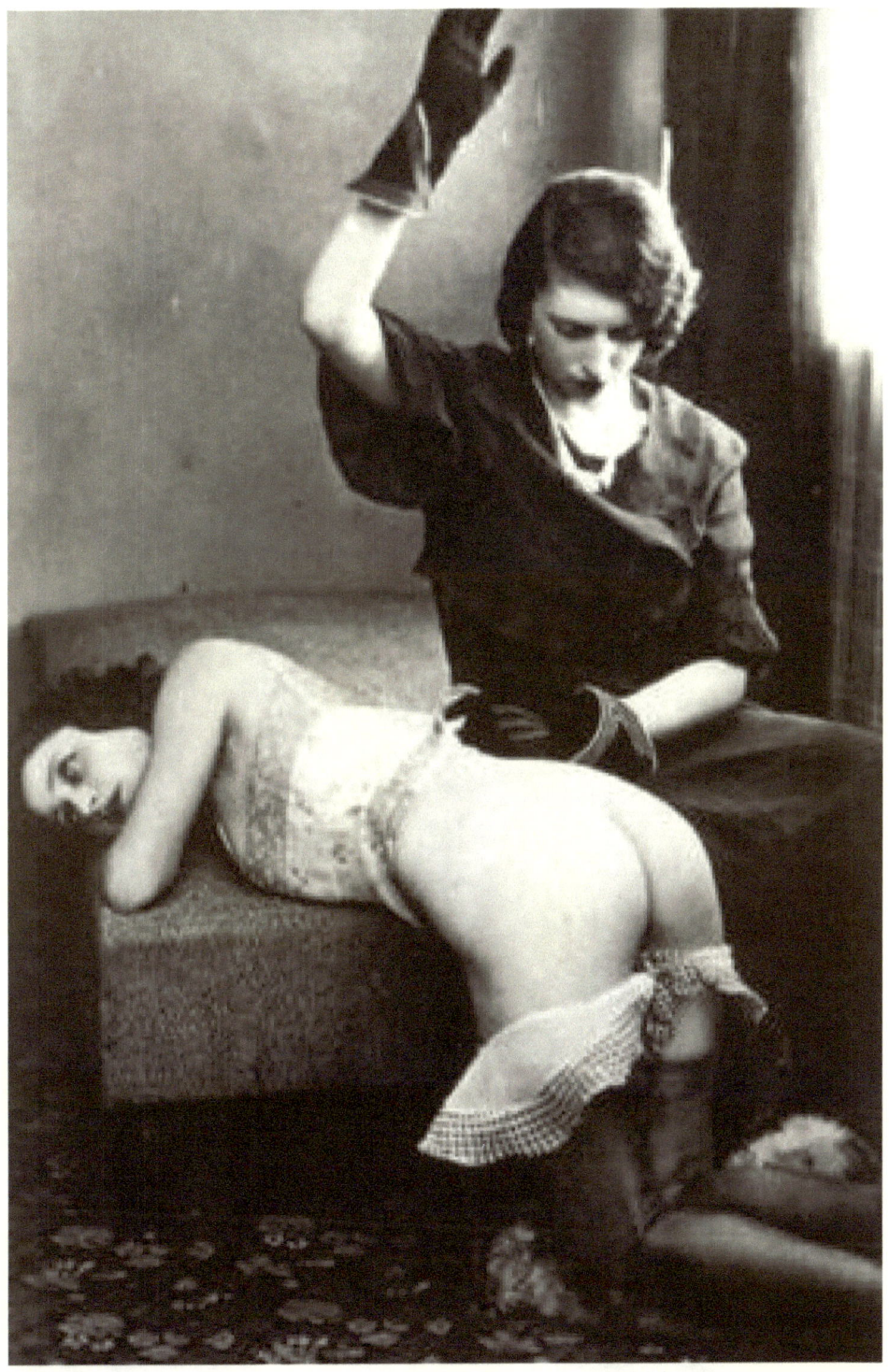

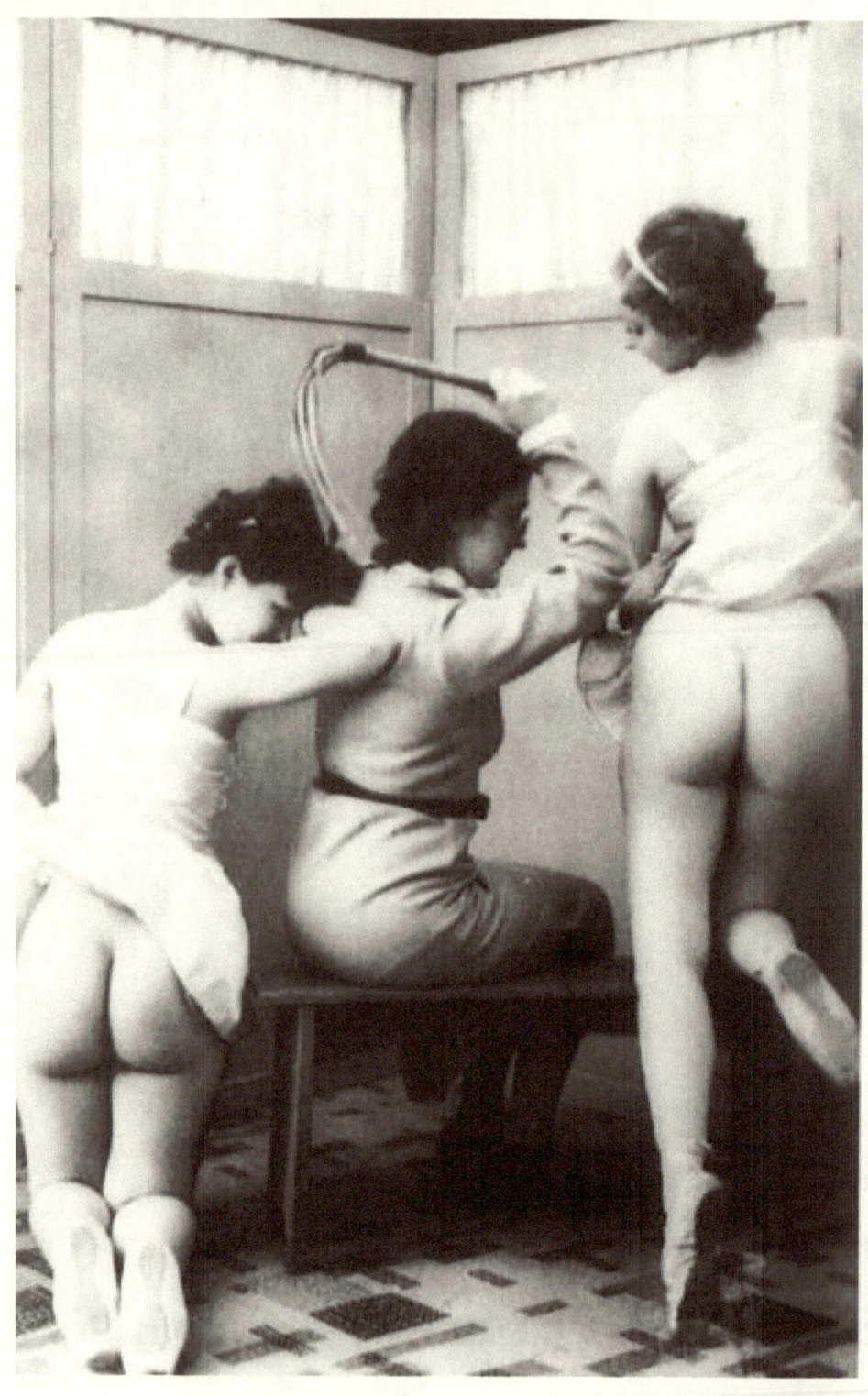

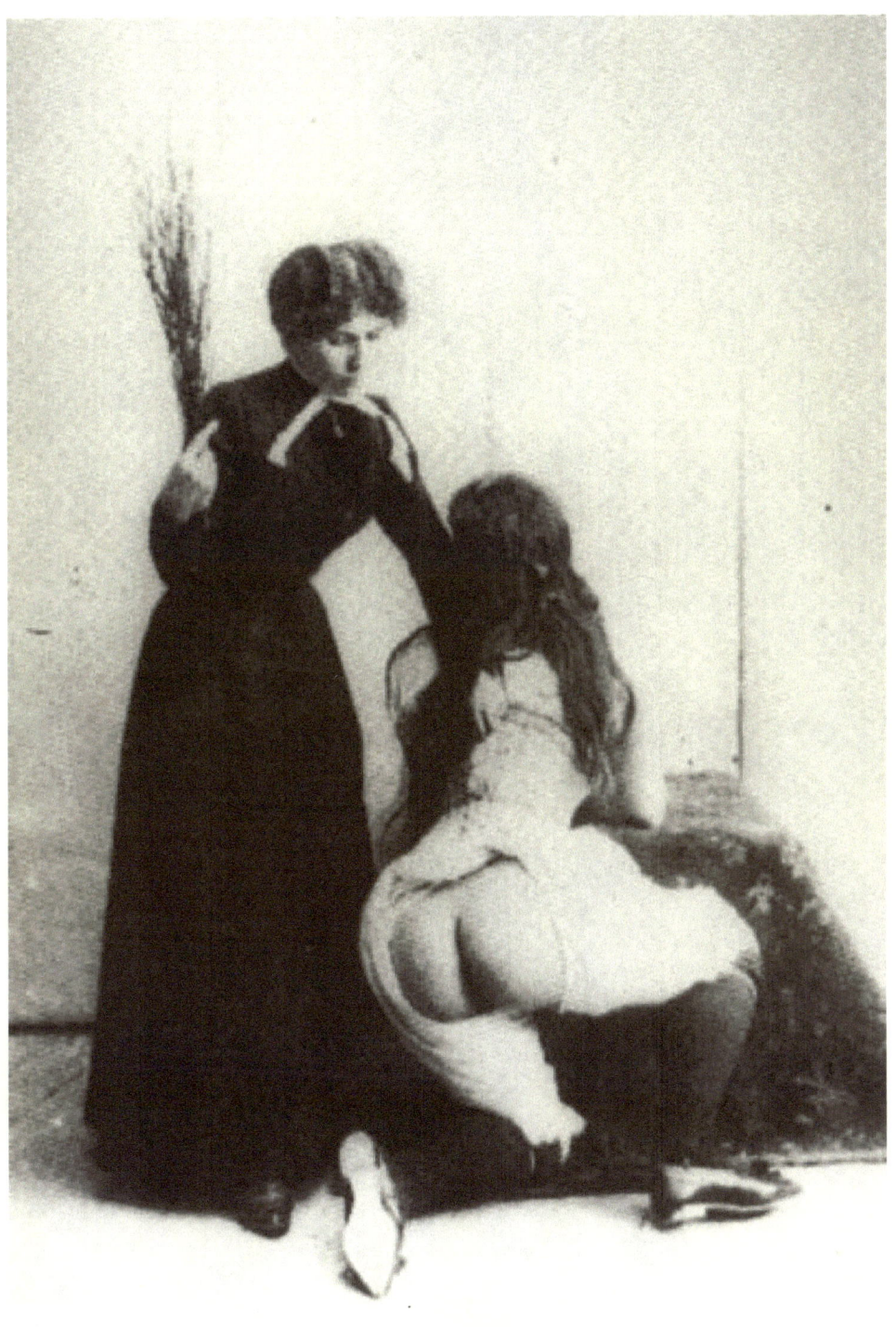

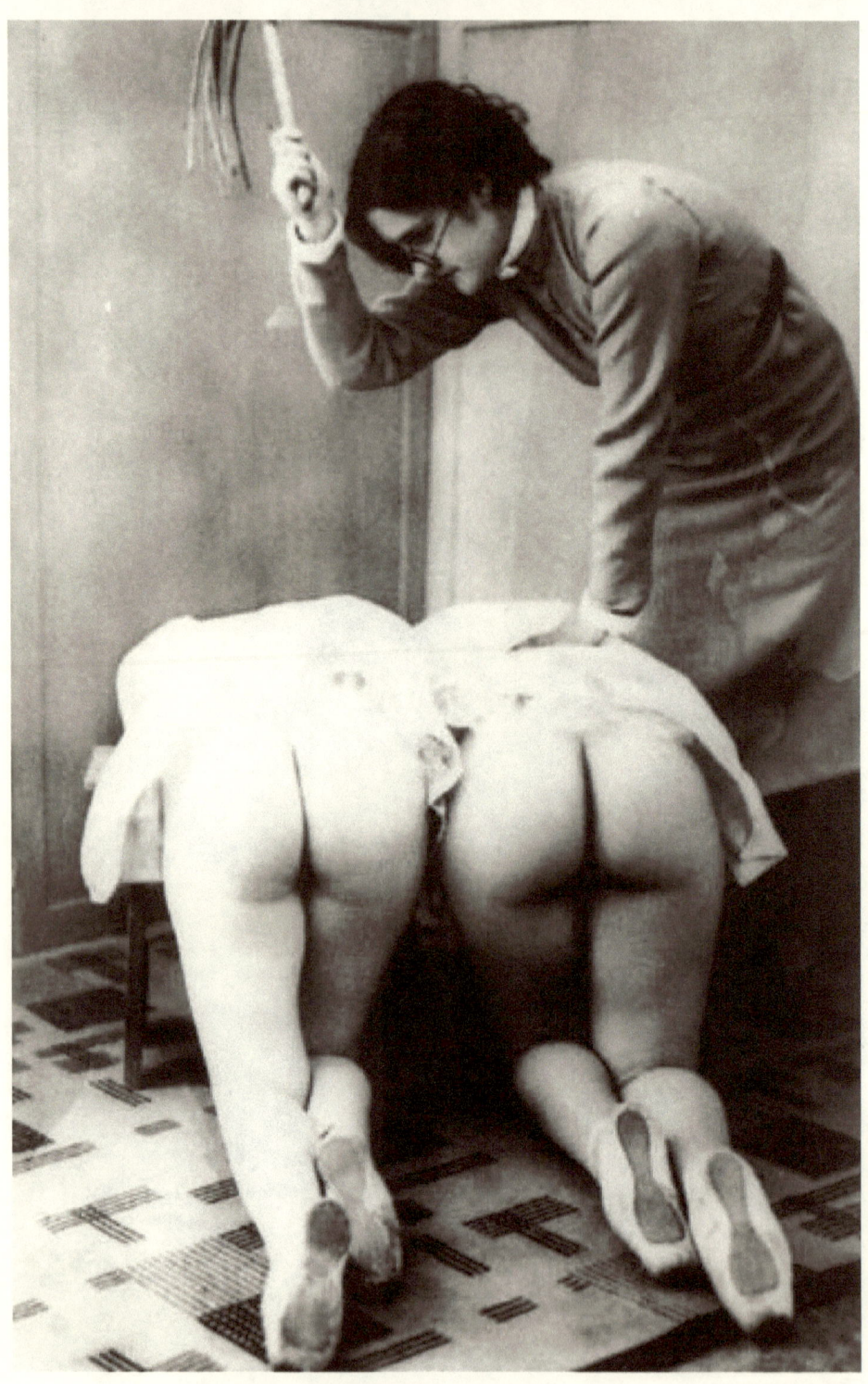

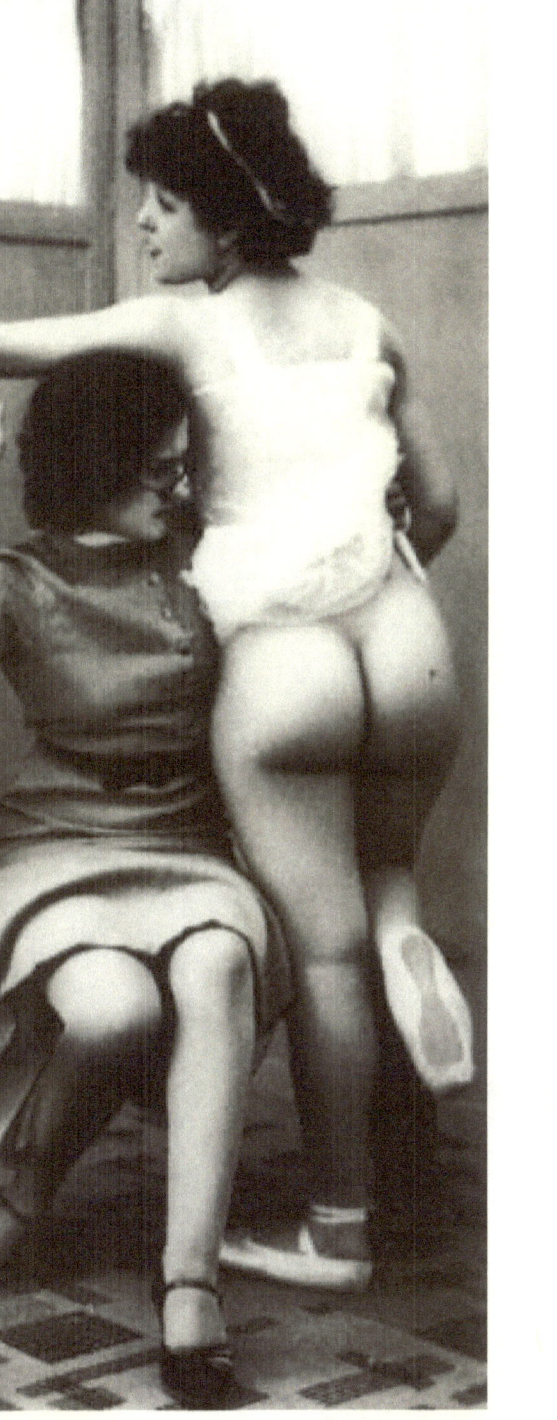

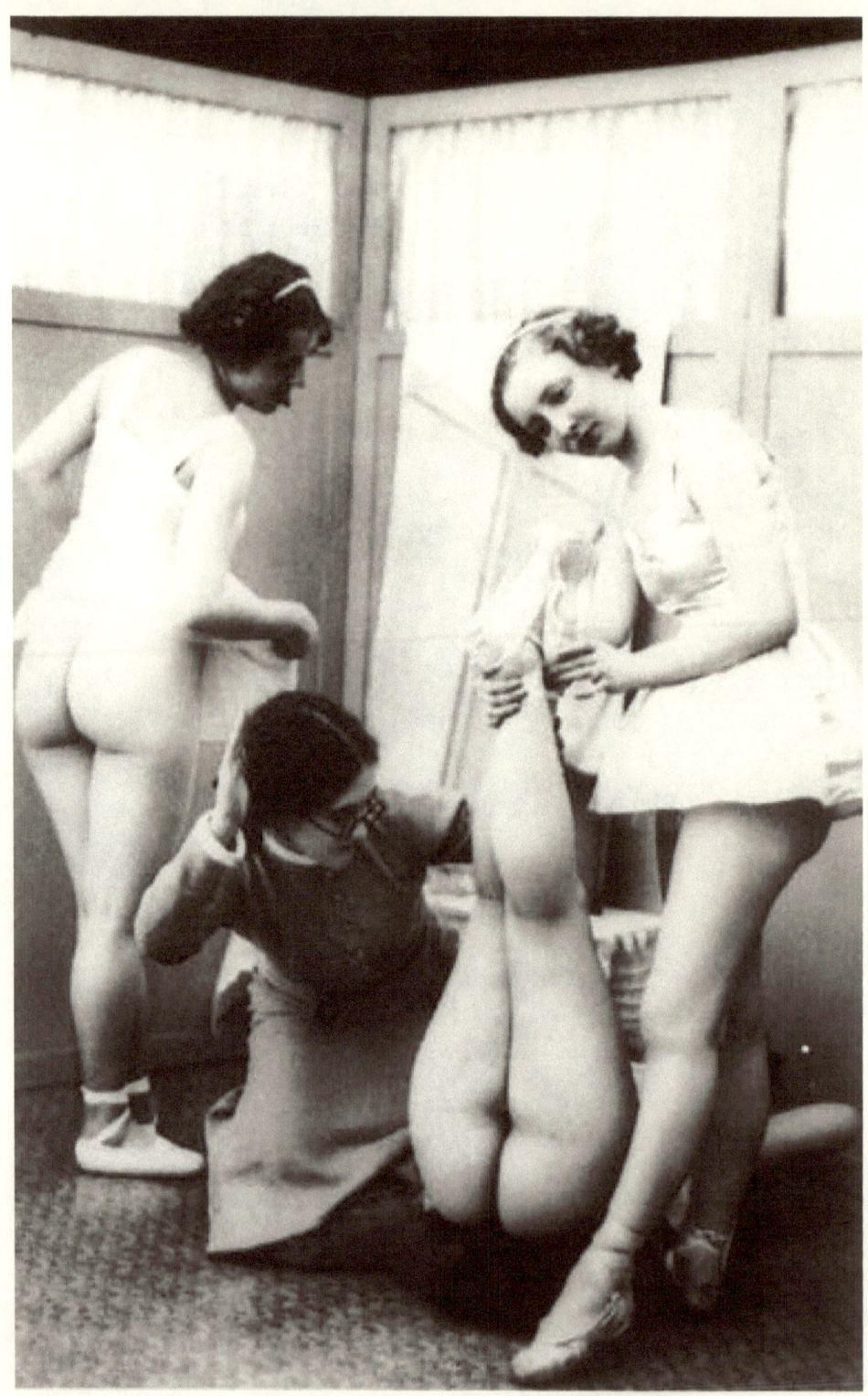

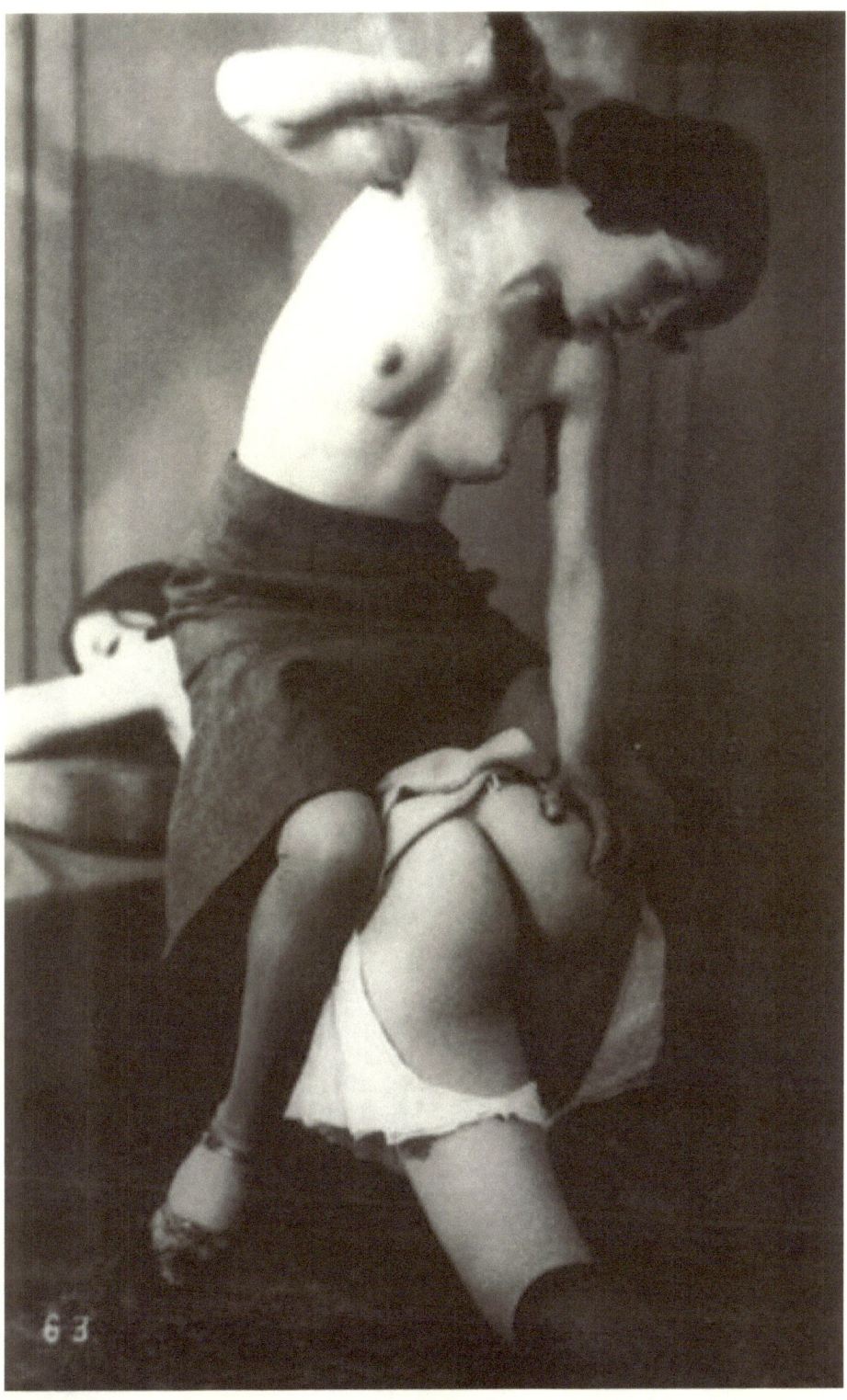

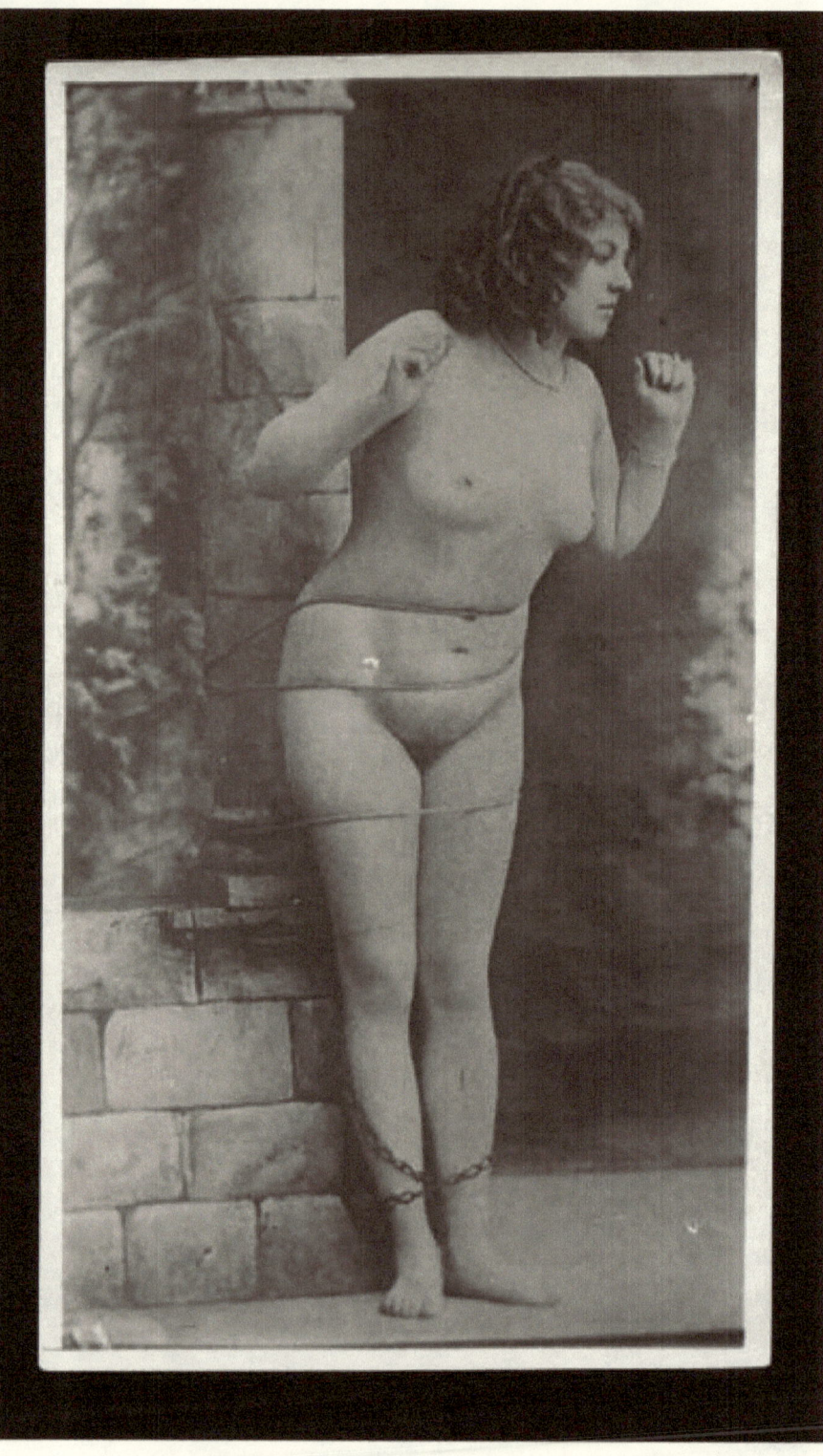

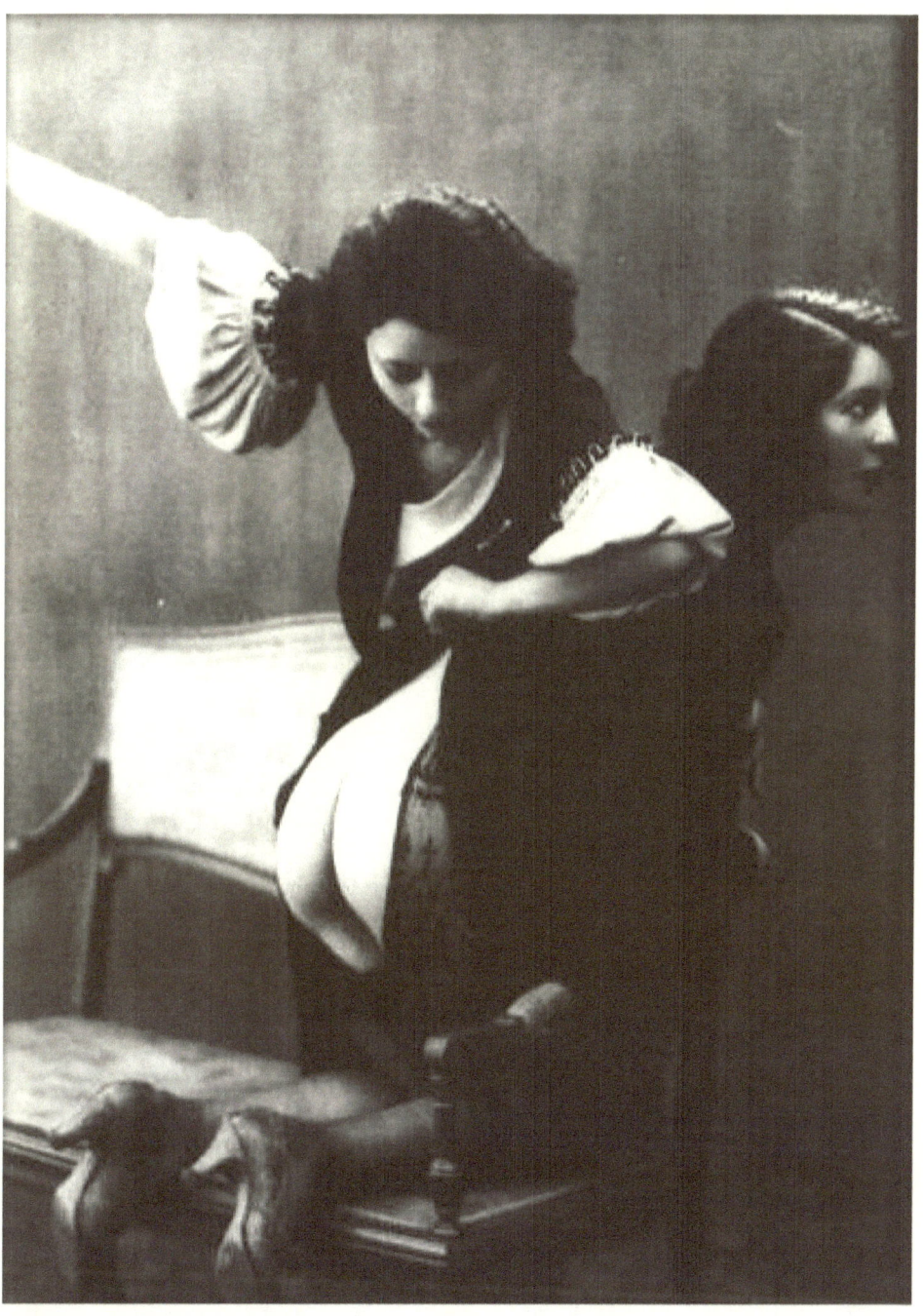

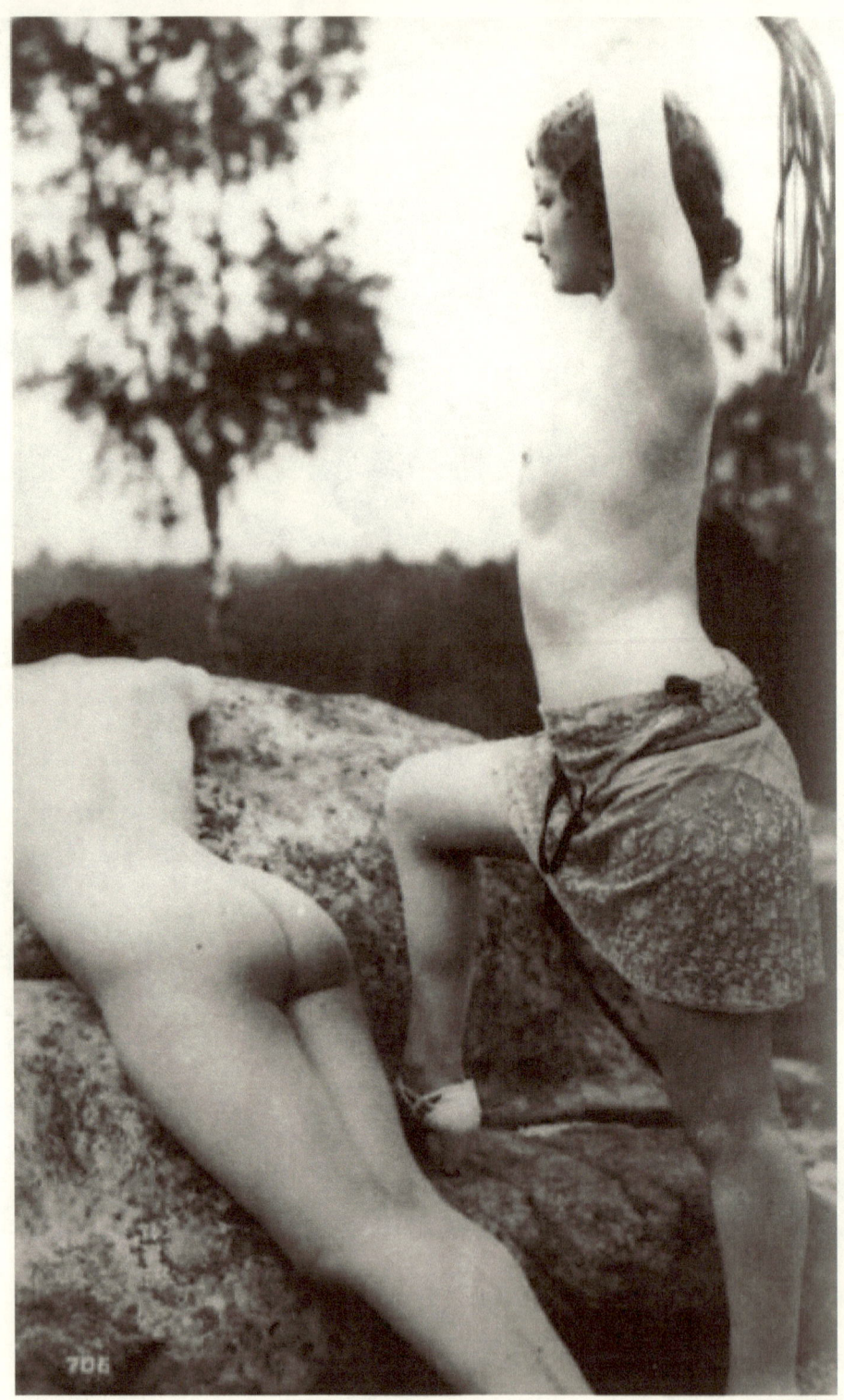

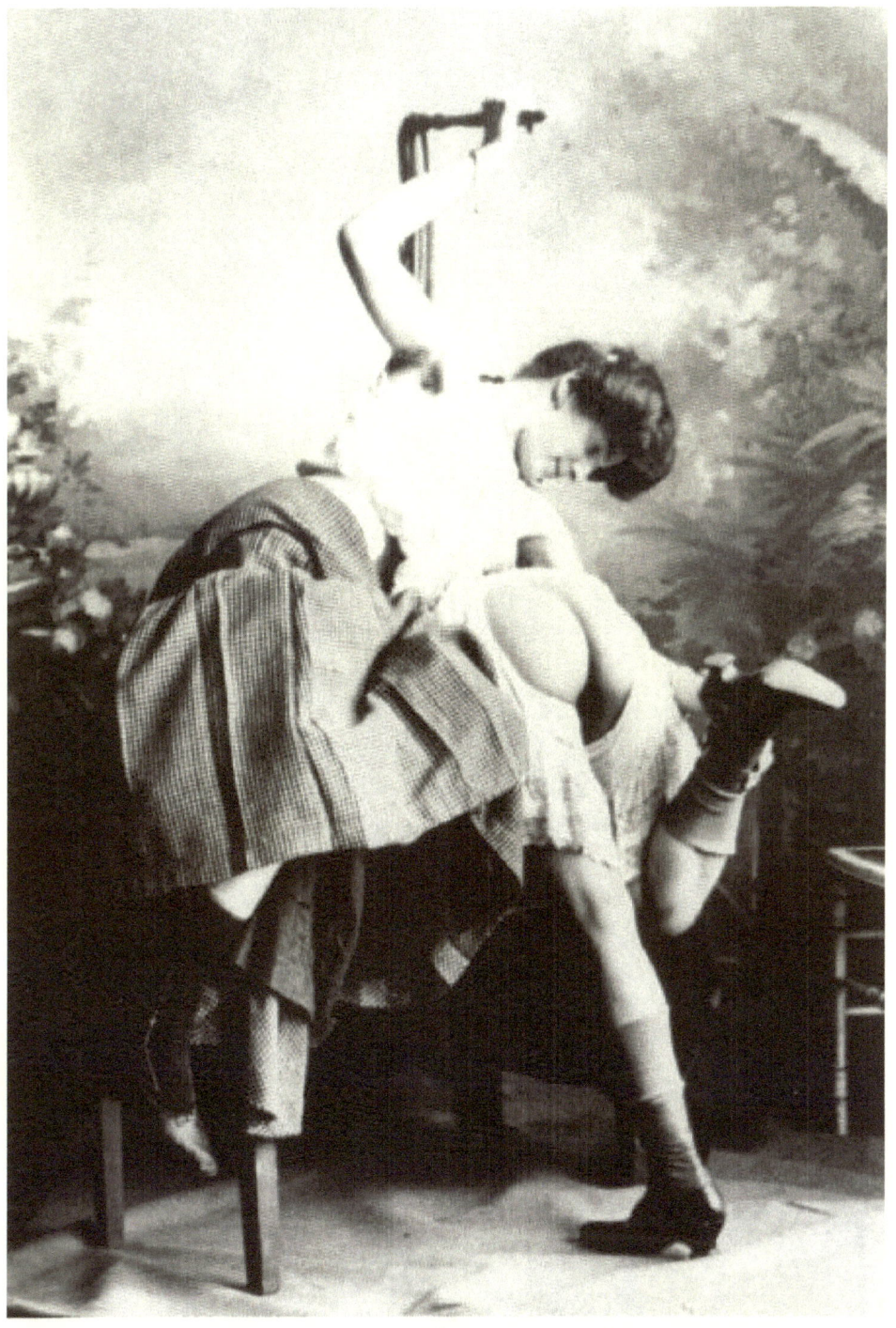

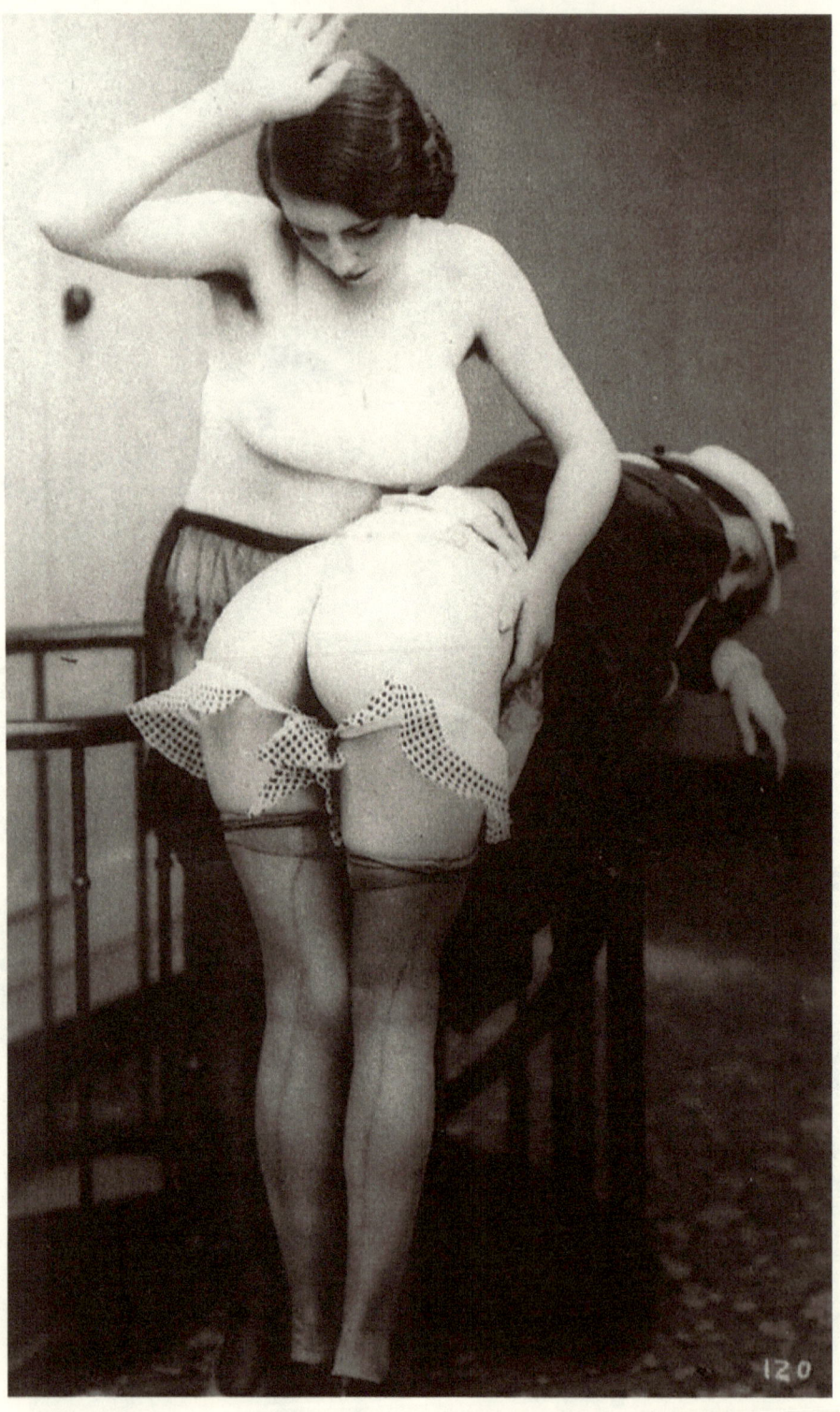

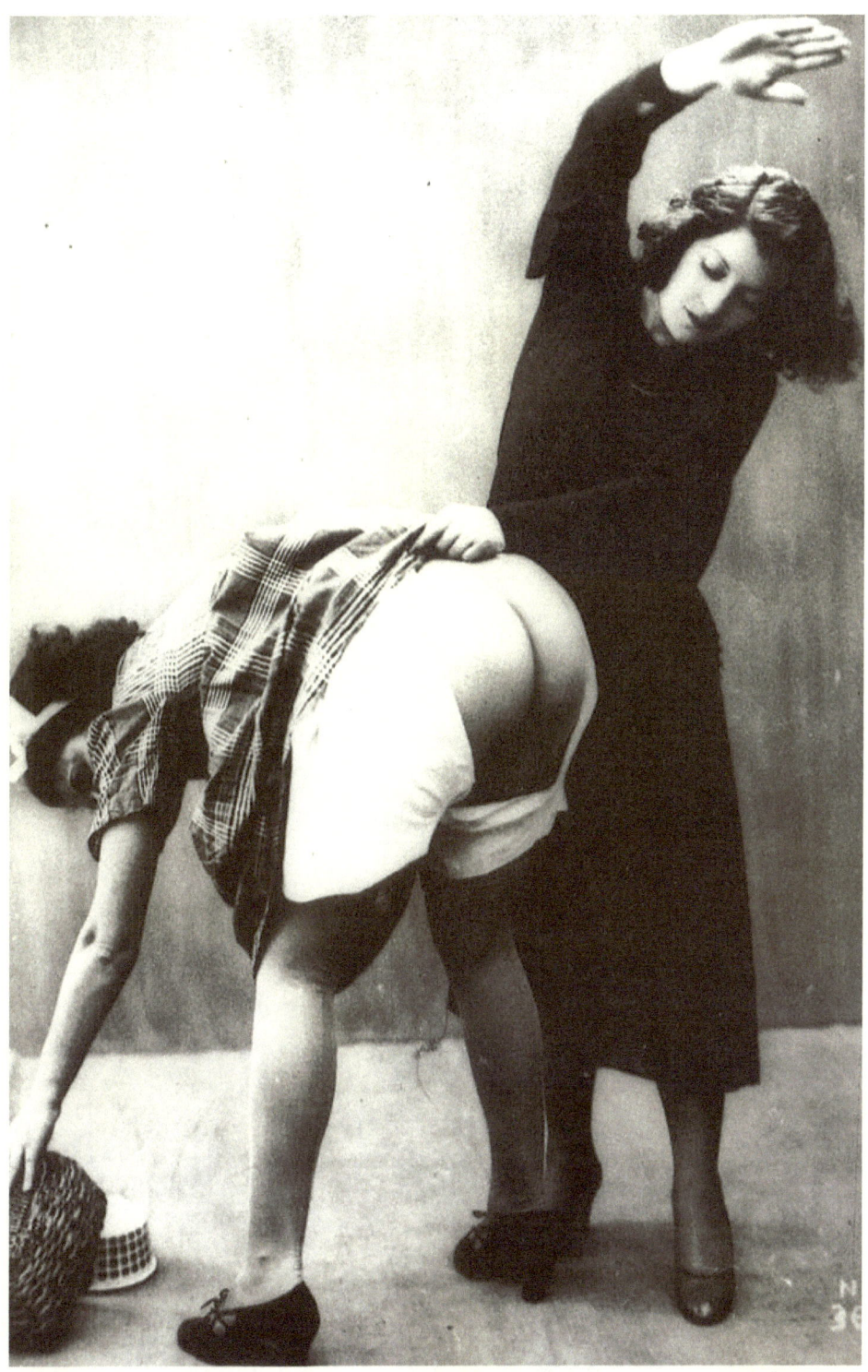

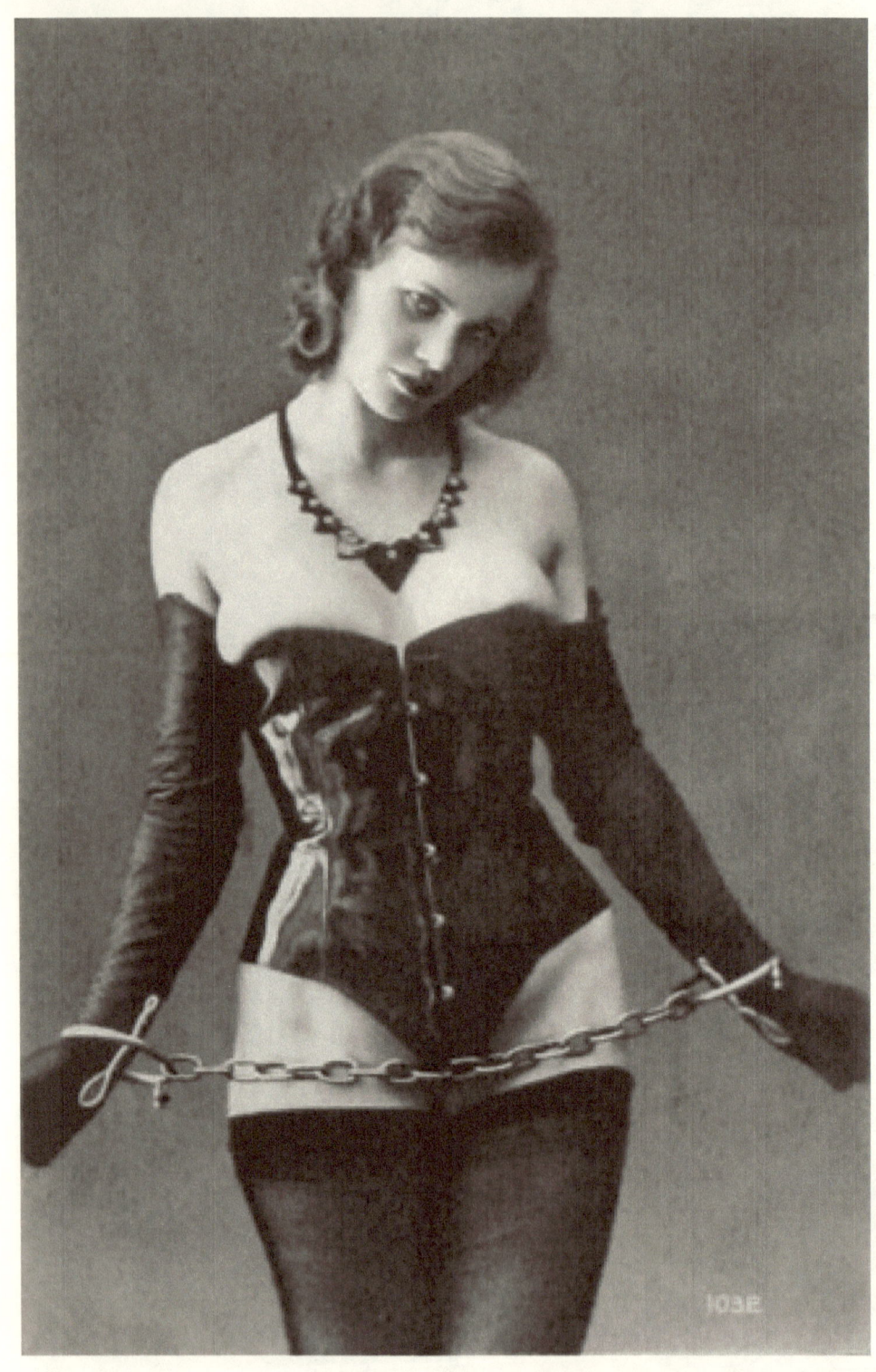

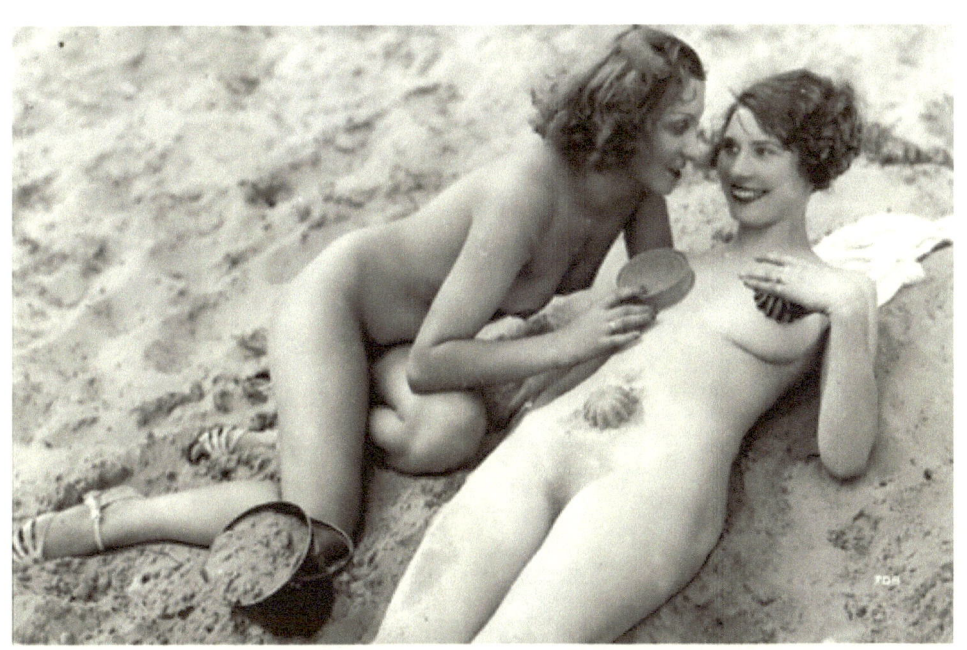

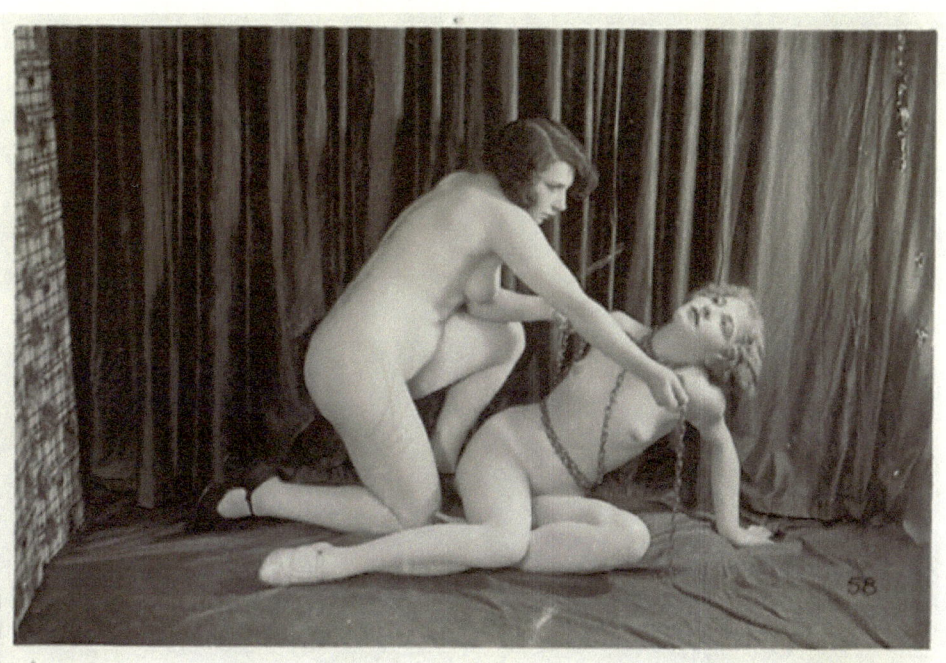

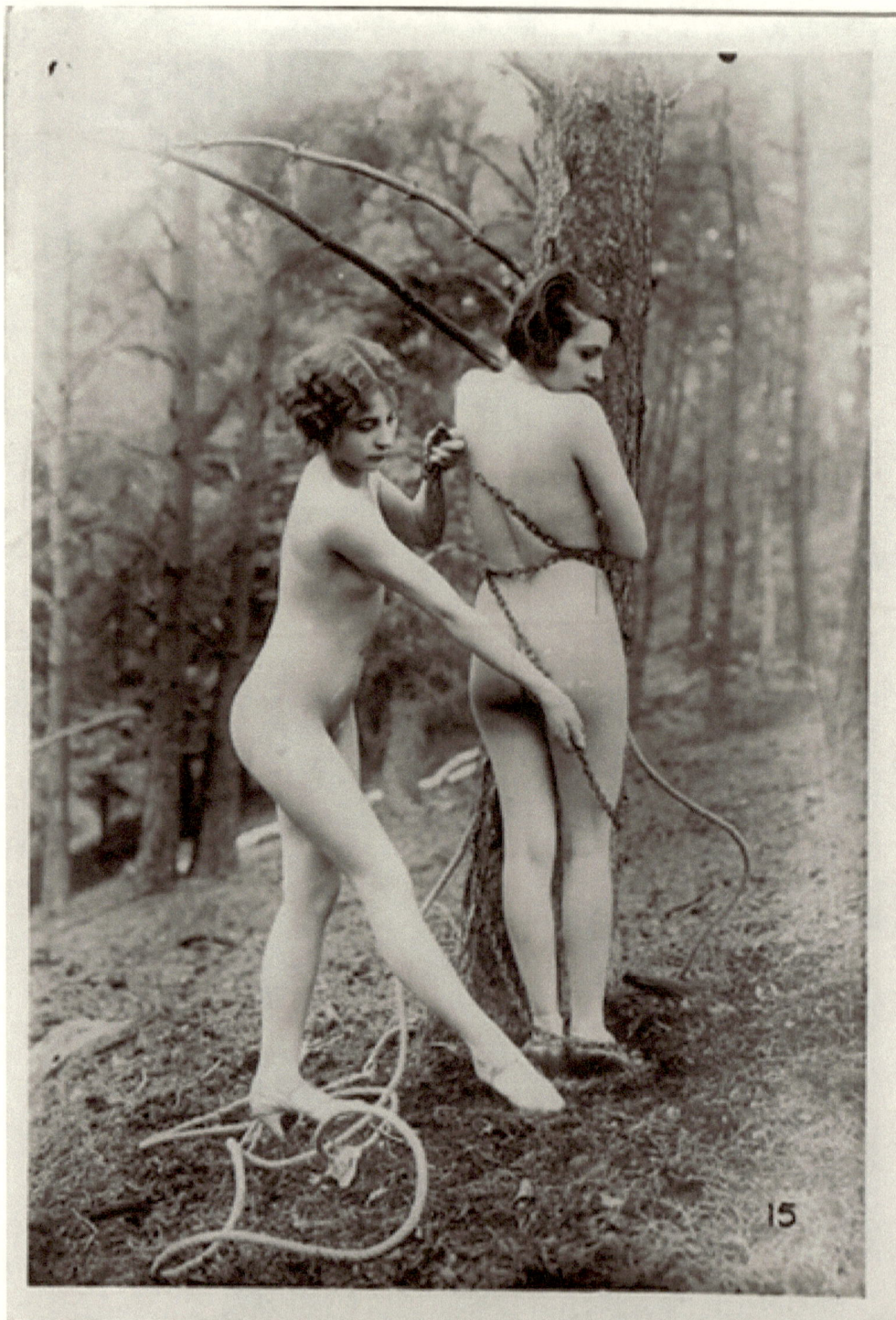

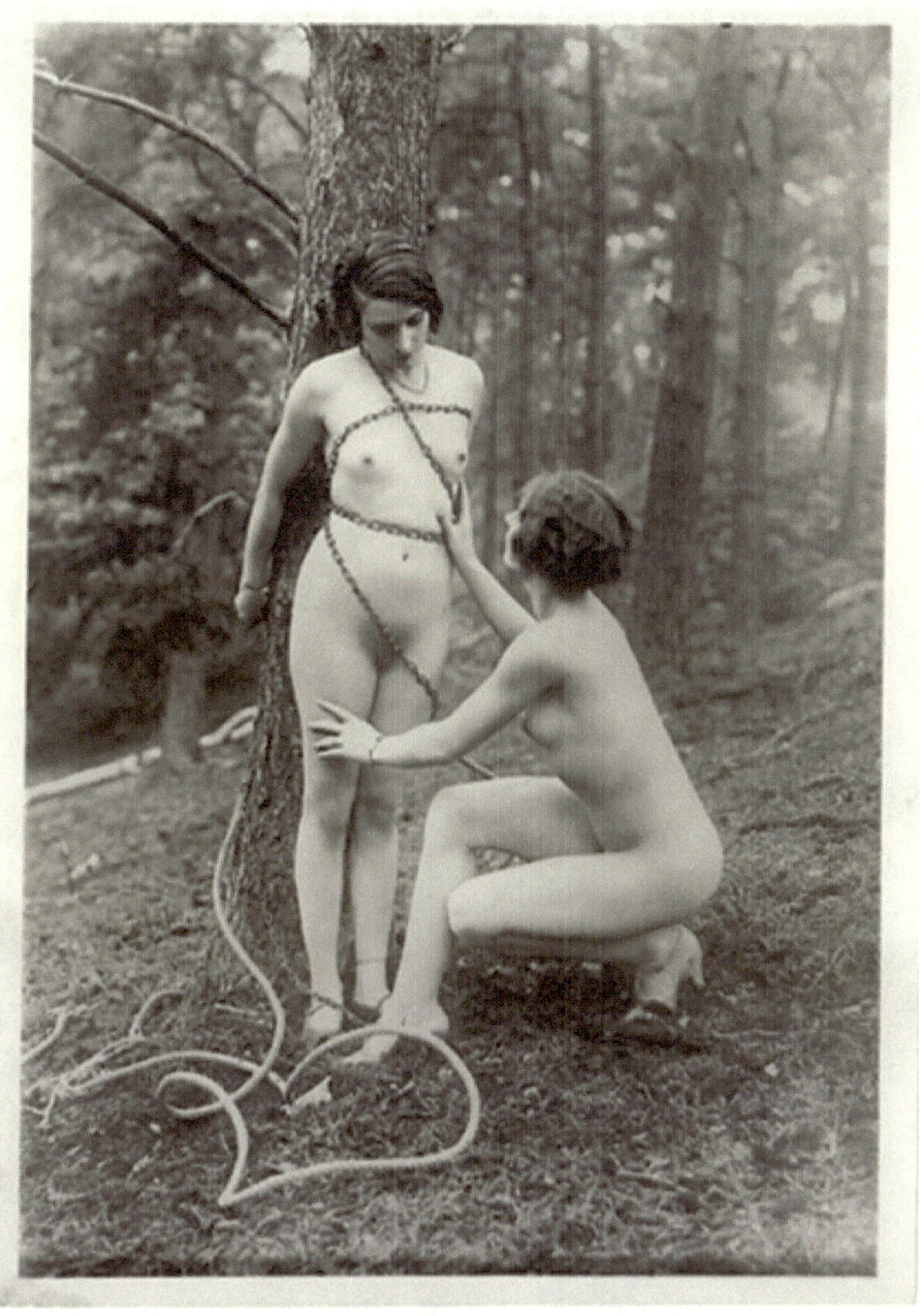

Yomikiri Romance

Presented by Seiu Ito

The following pictures were published by the Japanese magazine Yomikiri Romance.

Kinbaku is a Japanese style of bondage or BDSM which involves tying up the bottom using simple yet visually intricate patterns, usually with several pieces of thin rope (often jute, hemp or linen and generally around 6 mm in diameter, but sometimes as small as 4 mm, and between 7 – 8 m long). In Japanese, this natural-fibre rope is known as 'asanawa'; the Japanese vocabulary does not make a distinction between hemp and jute. The allusion is to the use of hemp rope for restraining prisoners, as a symbol of power, in the same way that stocks or manacles are used in a Western BDSM context. The word shibari came into common use in the West at some point in the 1990s to describe the bondage art Kinbaku. Shibari (縛り?) is a Japanese word that literally means "Decoritivley Tie"

The aesthetics of the bound persons position is important: in particular, Japanese bondage is distinguished by its use of specific katas (forms) and aesthetic rules. Sometimes, asymmetric and often intentionally uncomfortable positions are employed. In particular, Japanese bondage is very much about the way the rope is applied and the pleasure is more in the journey than the destination. In this way the rope becomes an extension of the nawashi's hands and is used to communicate.

Traditional Japanese bondage techniques use natural vegetable fiber rope (hemp, jute, or linen) exclusively, though contemporary Japanese Masters have been working with a range of rope materials. The natural fibers easily lock to each other which means the bondage can be held together by the friction of twists and turns or very simple knots. Traditionally, multiple 6-8 meter lengths are used.

Bondage as a sexual activity first came to notice in Japan in the late Edo period. Generally recognized as "father of Kinbaku" is Seiu Ito, who started studying and researching Hojōjutsu (this is the traditional Japanese martial art of restraining a person using cord or rope also used by military and police). He is credited with the inception of Kinbaku, though it is noted that he drew inspiration from other art forms of the time including Kabuki theatre and Ukiyoe woodblock prints. Kinbaku became widely popular in Japan in the 1950s through magazines such as Kitan Club and Yomikiri Romance, which published the first naked bondage photographs. In the 1960s, people such as Eikichi Osada began to appear performing live SM shows often including a large amount of rope bondage, today these performers are often referred to as Nawashi (rope master) or Bakushi (from kinbakushi, meaning bondage master).

In recent years, Kinbaku has become popular in the Western BDSM scene in its own right and has also profoundly influenced bondage, combining to produce many 'fusion' styles.

Kinbaku is based on fairly specific rope patterns, many of them derived from Hojojutsu ties. Of particular importance are the Ushiro Takatekote (a type of arm box tie), which forms the basis of many Kinbaku ties, and the Ebi, or "Shrimp", which was originally designed as a torture tie and codified as part of the Edo period torture techniques. Today the tie is used as part of SM play and can be considered a form of Semenawa, torture rope.

Generally speaking, Kinbaku is practiced with ropes of 6–8 meters (20–26 feet) in length. Due to the generally different physique of Western subjects, 8 meters (26 feet) ropes are commonly used in the West. The rope material is usually hemp (or jute) though many other materials are in use including cotton and various synthetics.

責められる女を写す
悦虐恍惚圖

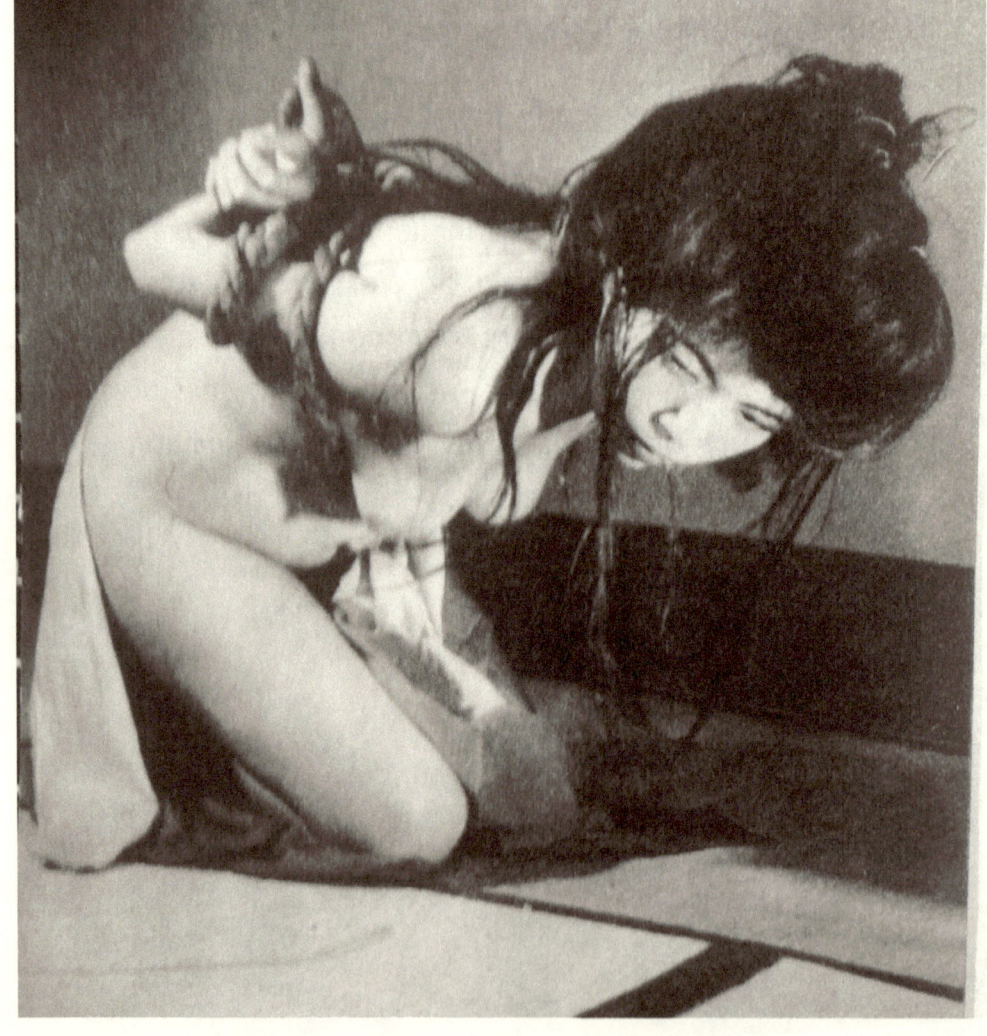

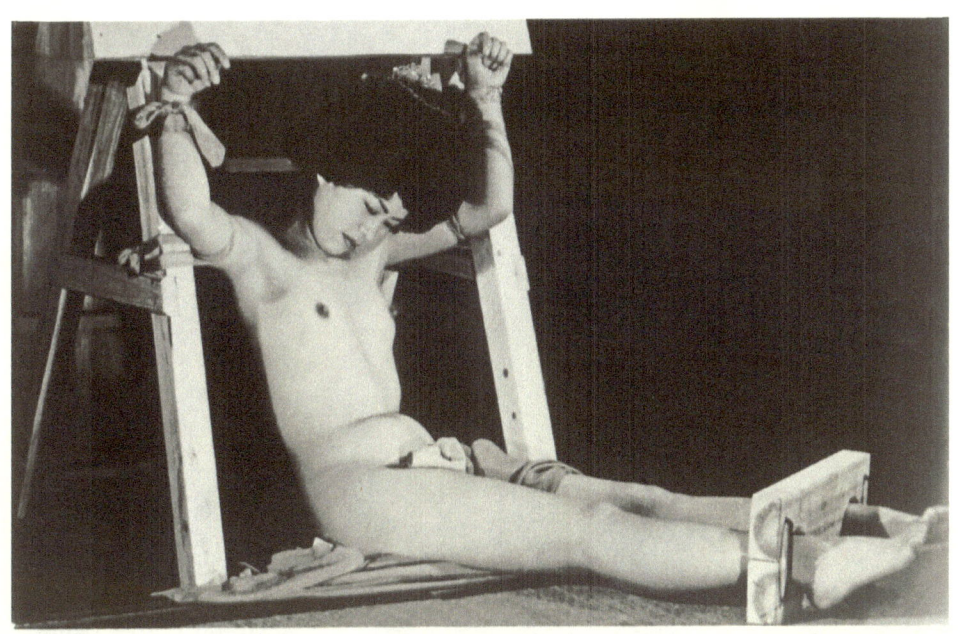

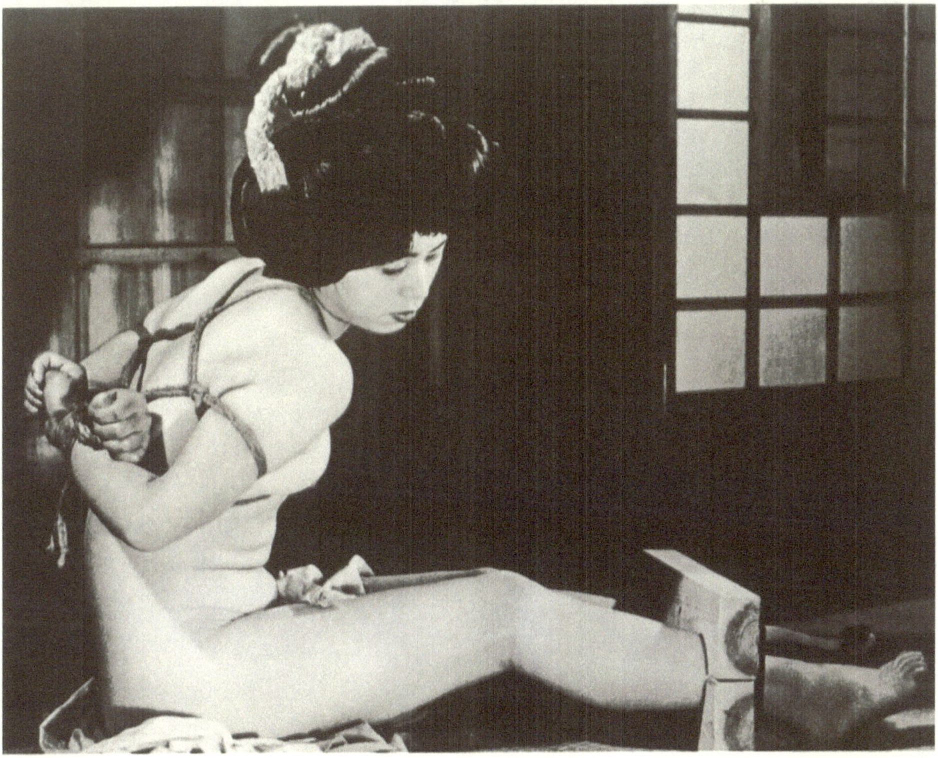

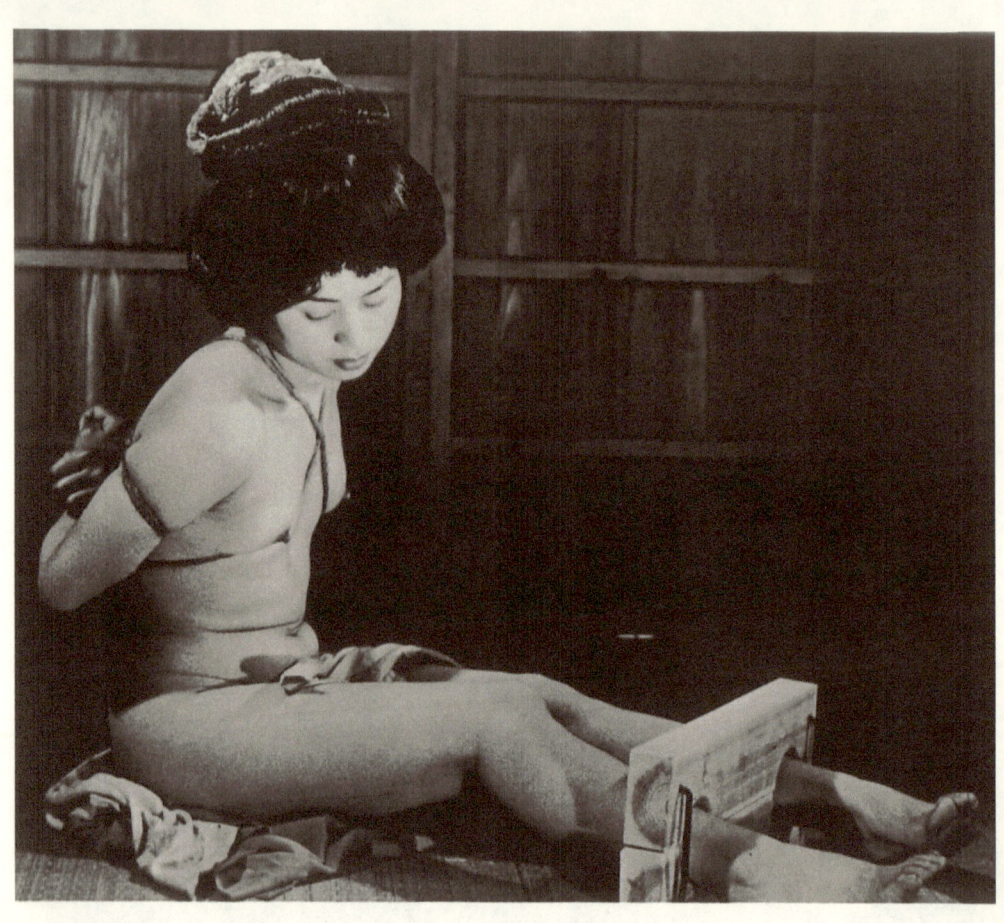

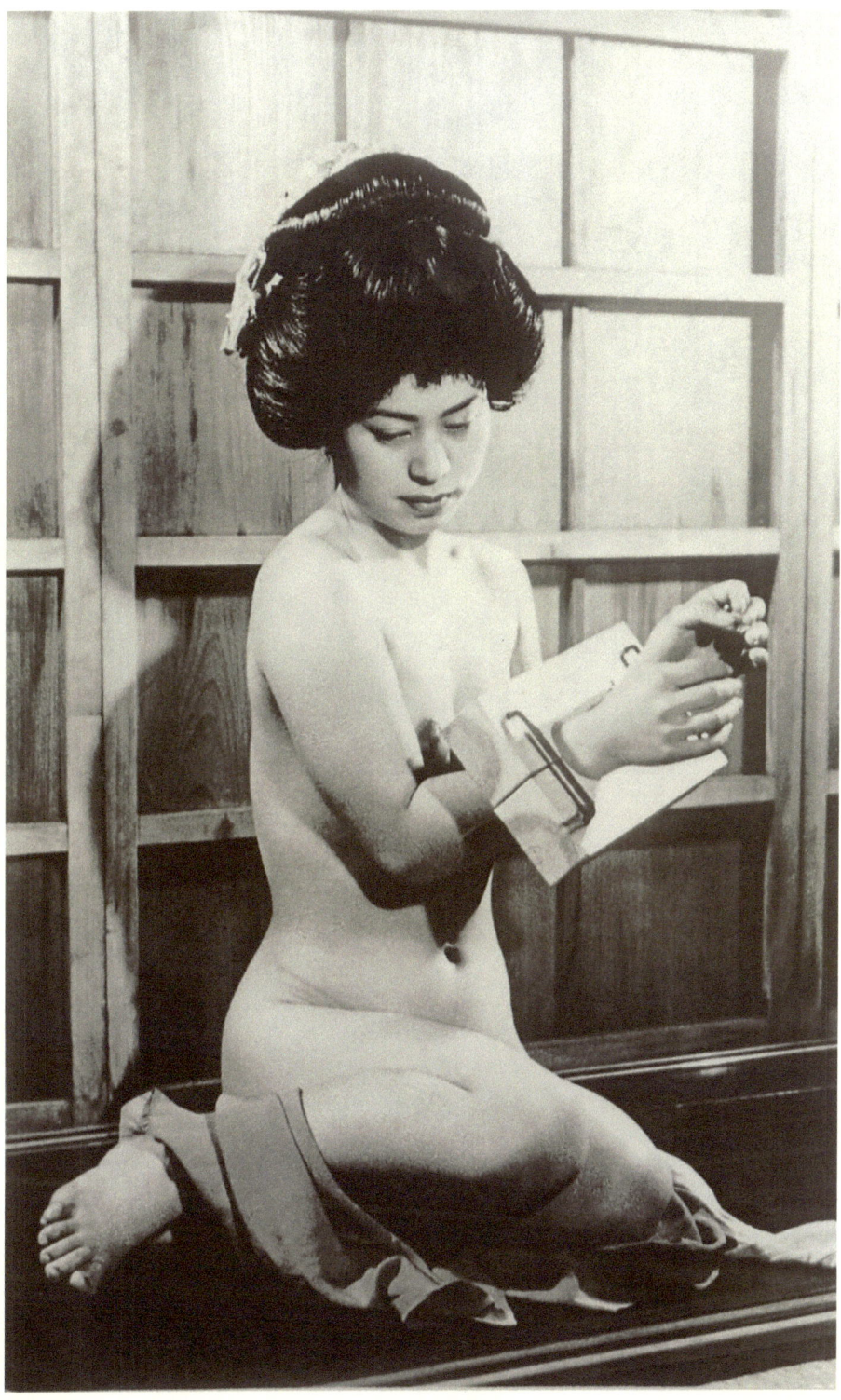

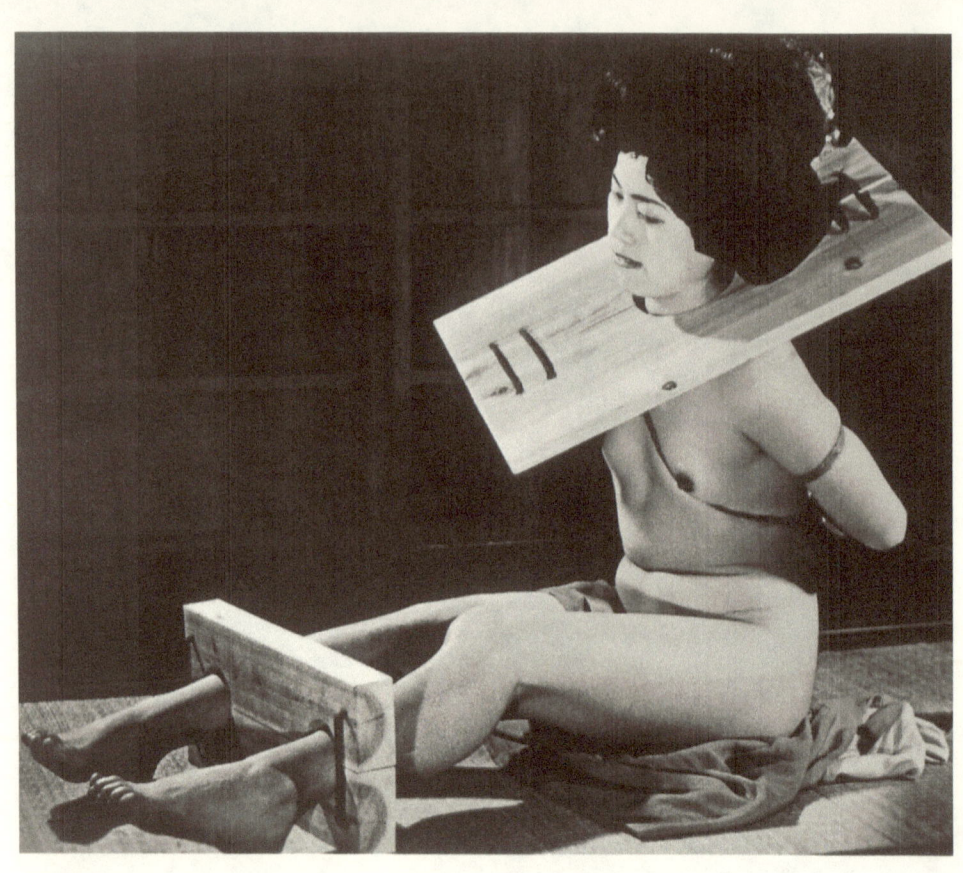

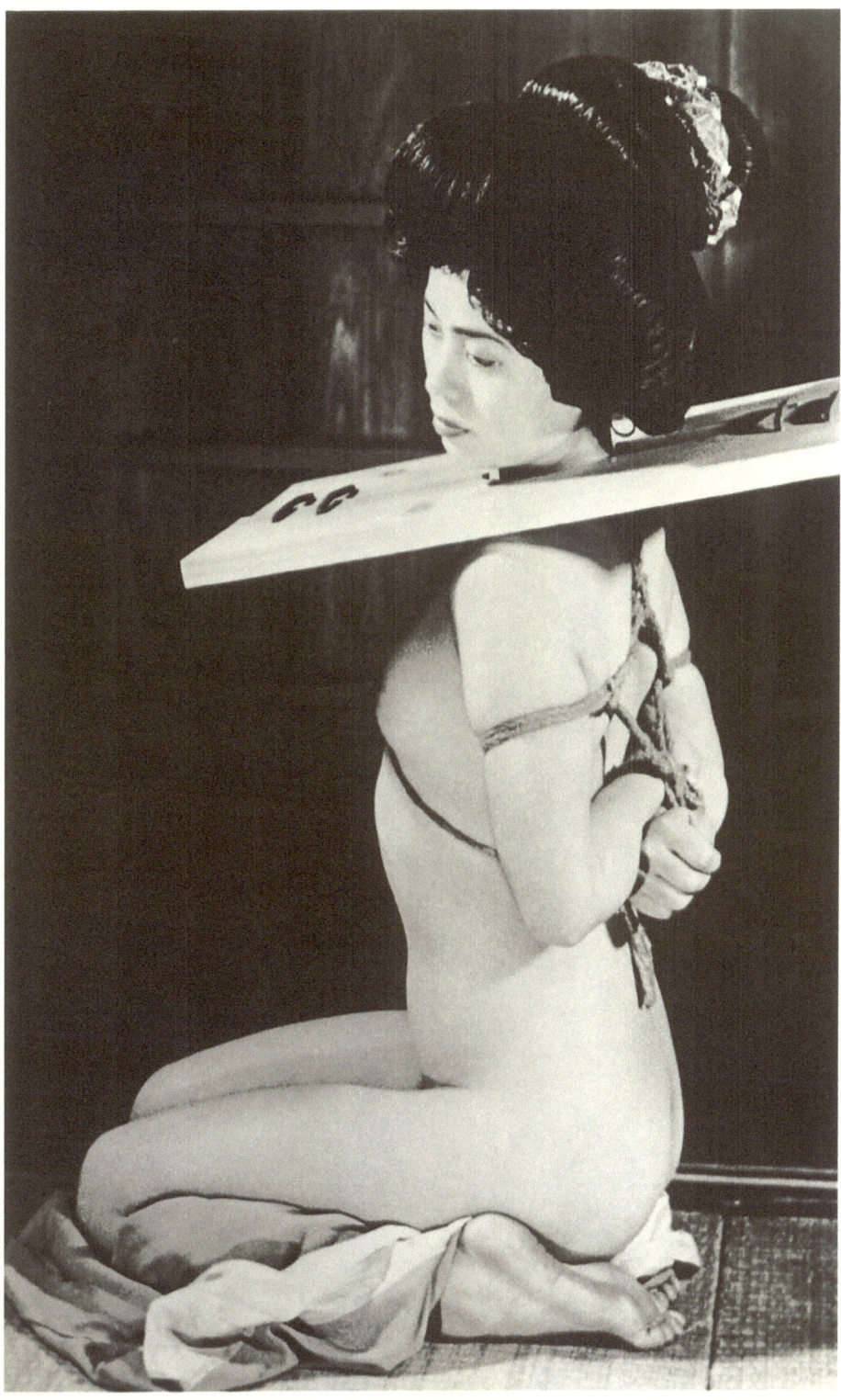

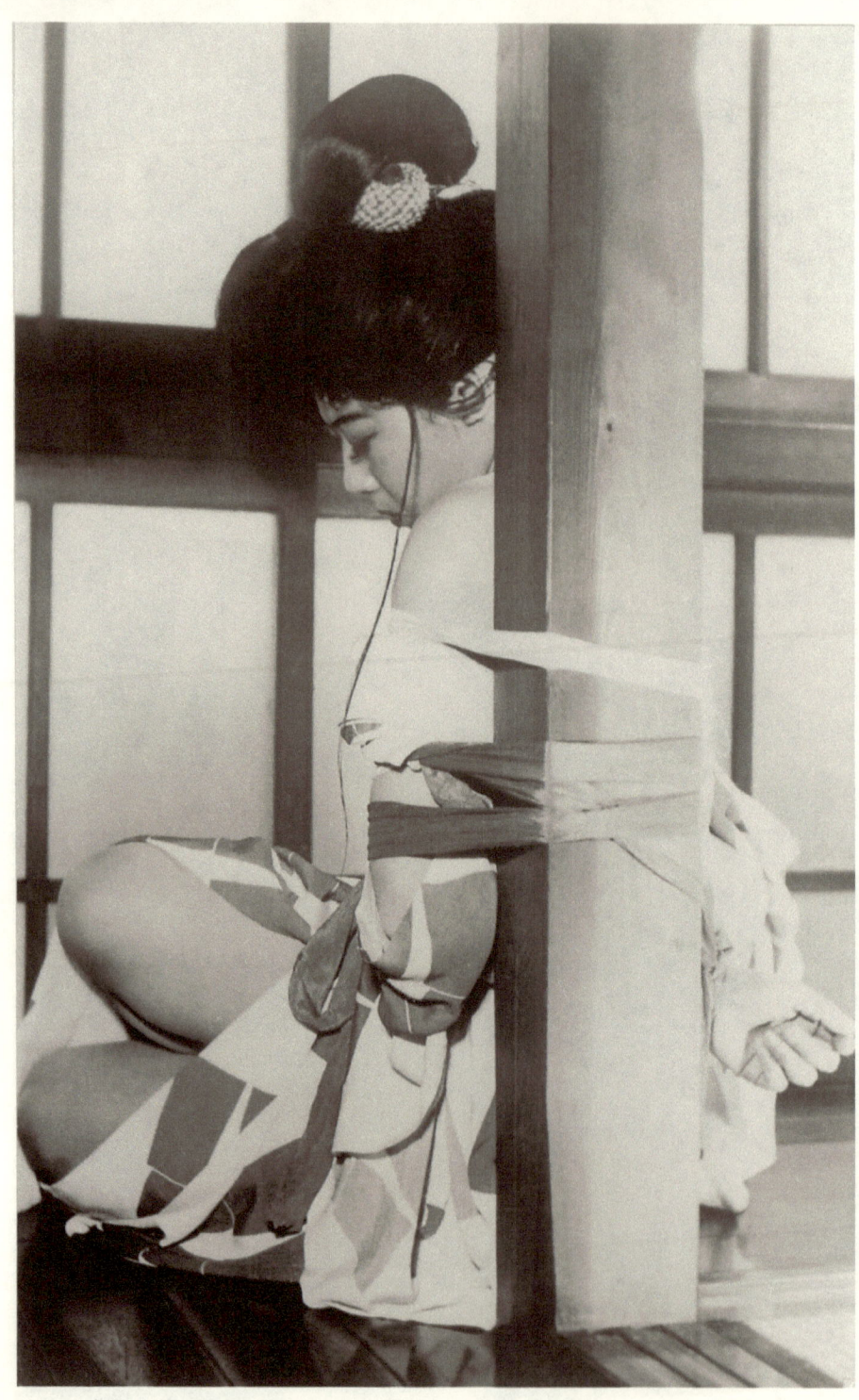

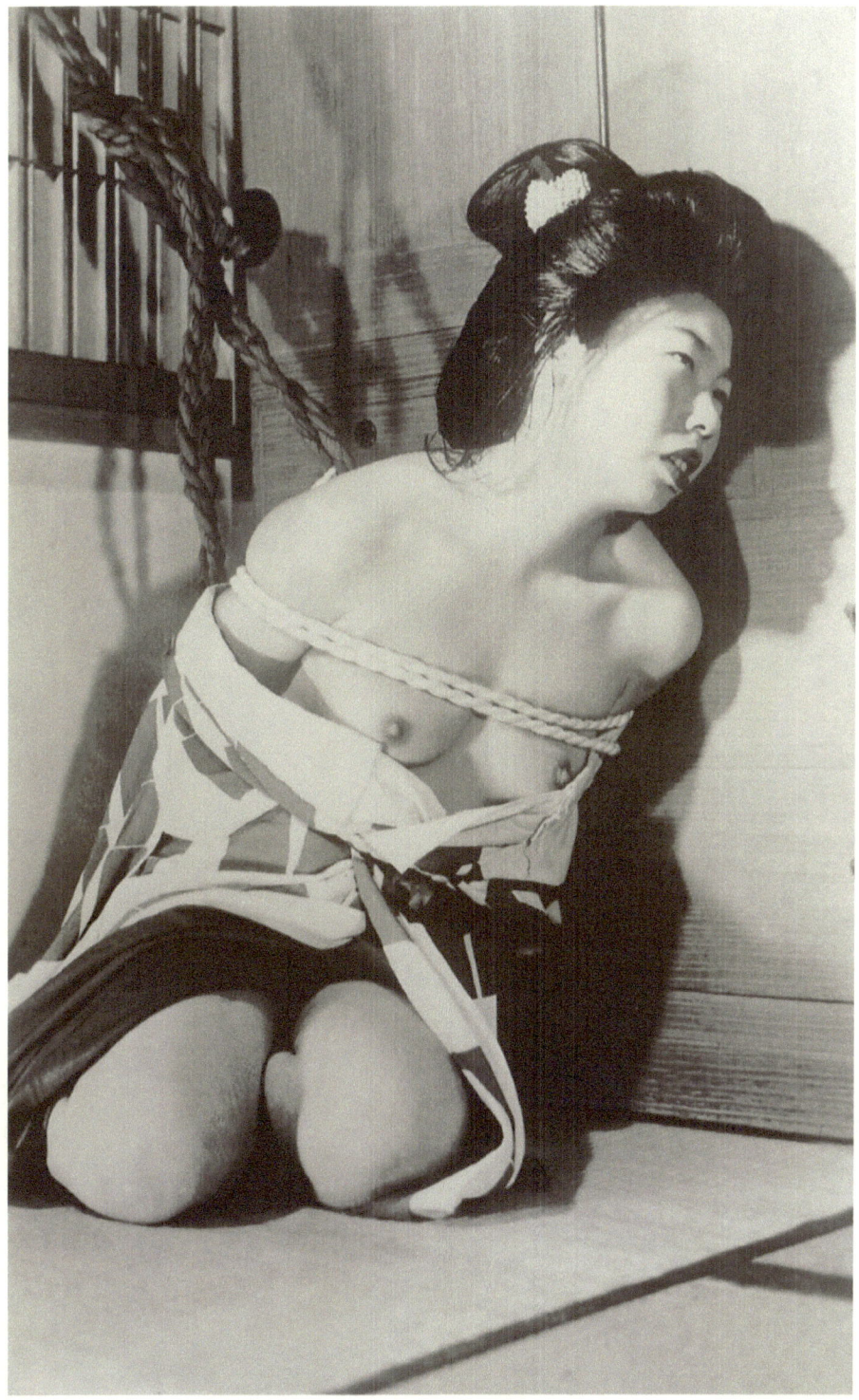

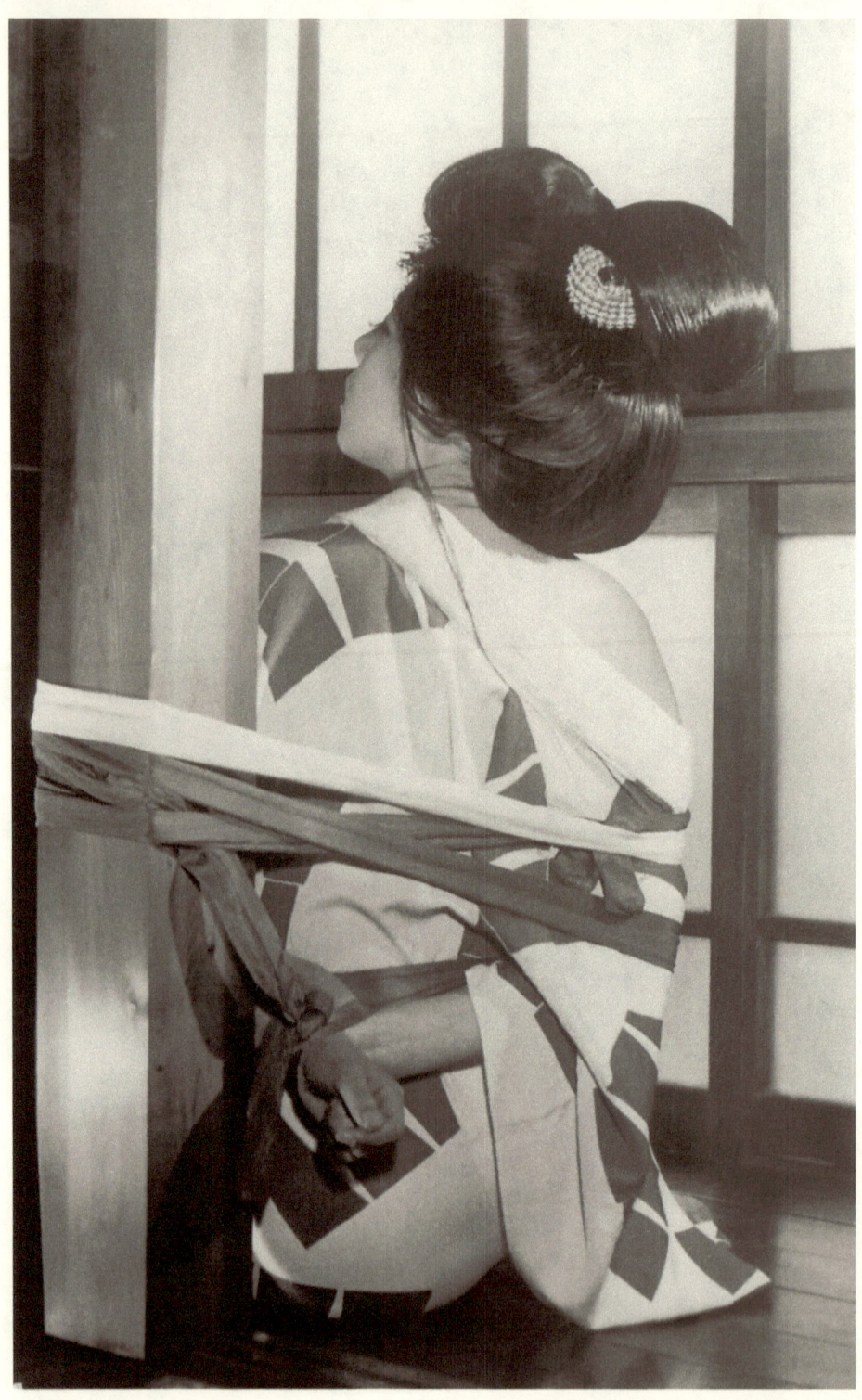

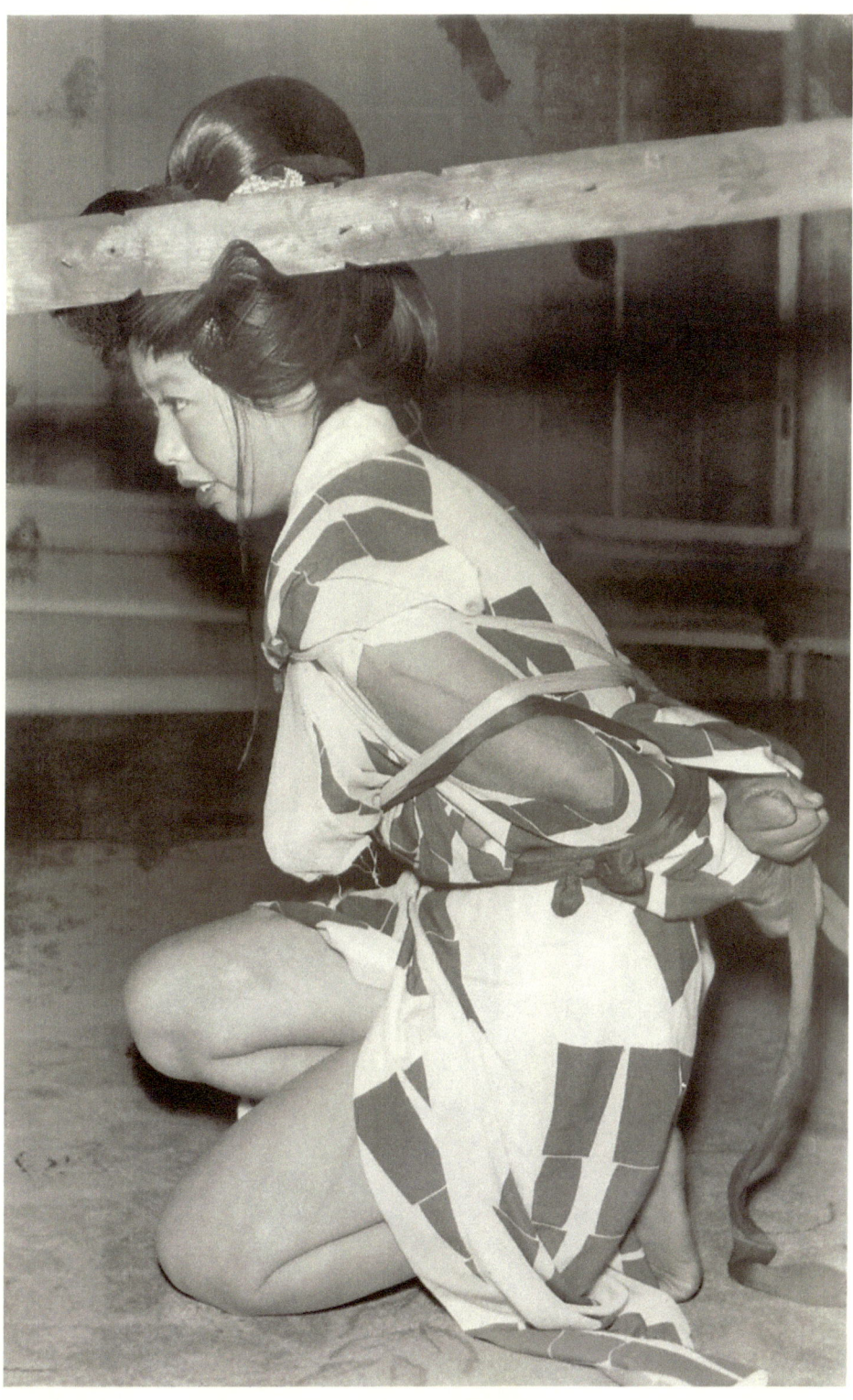

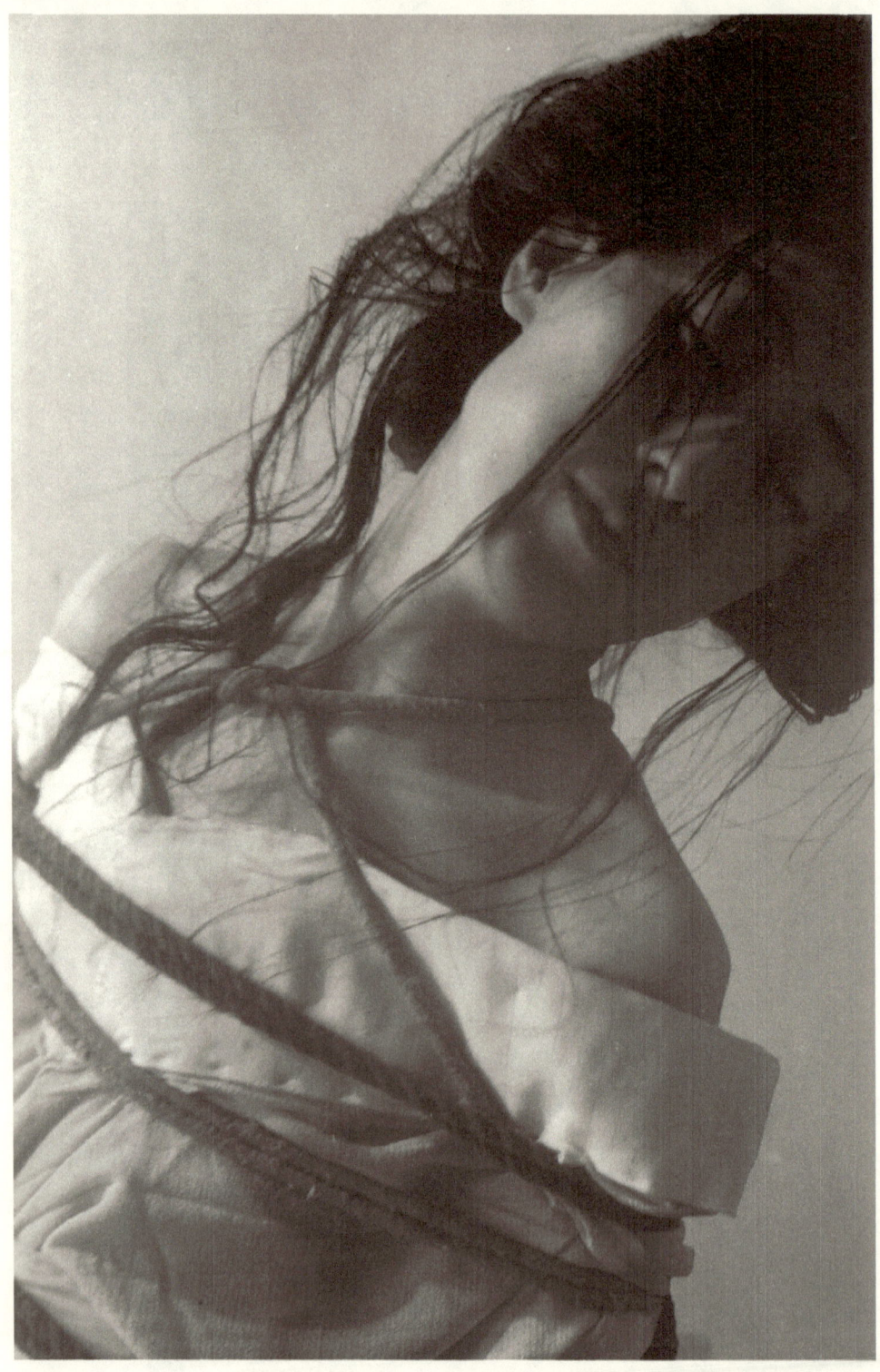

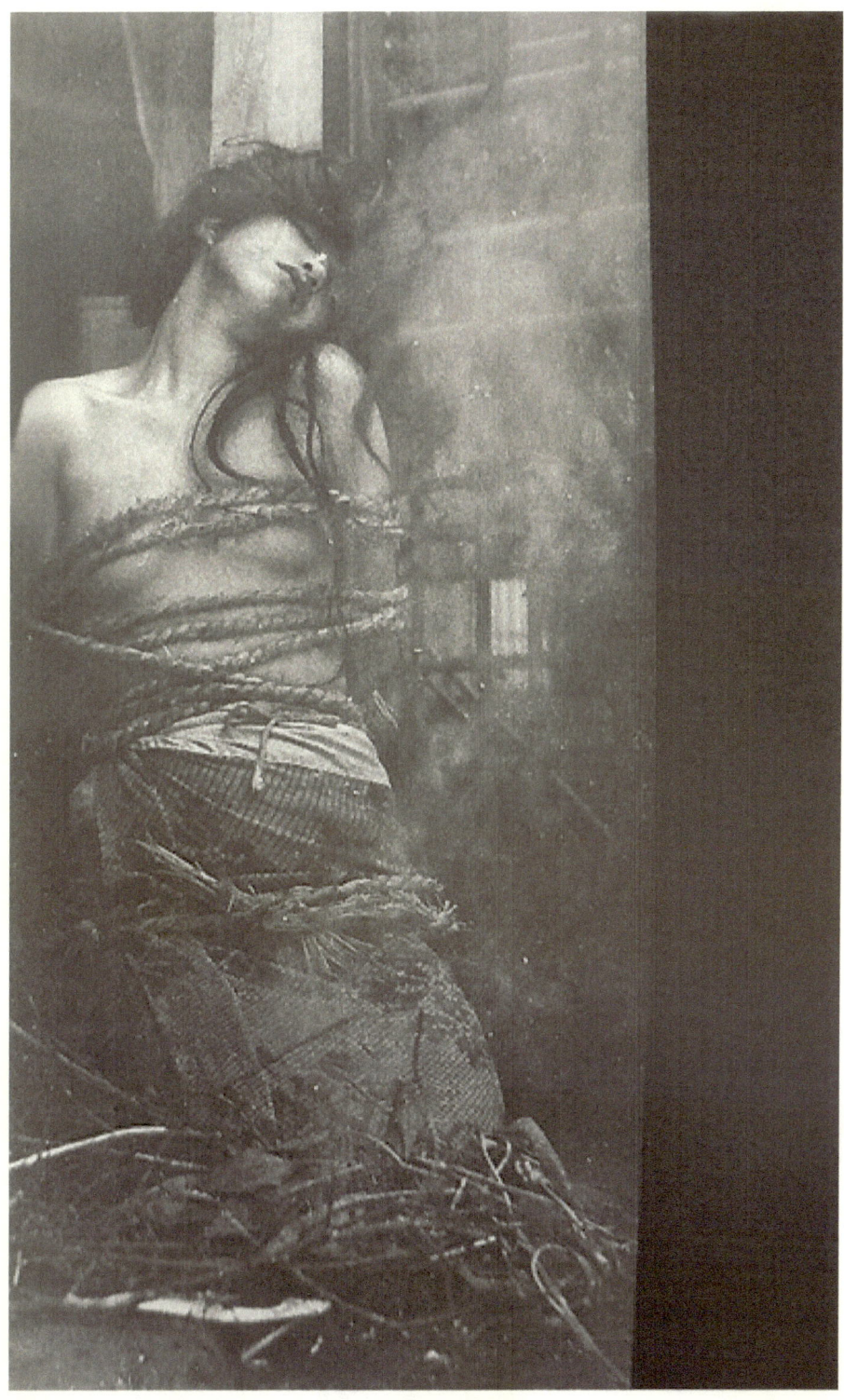

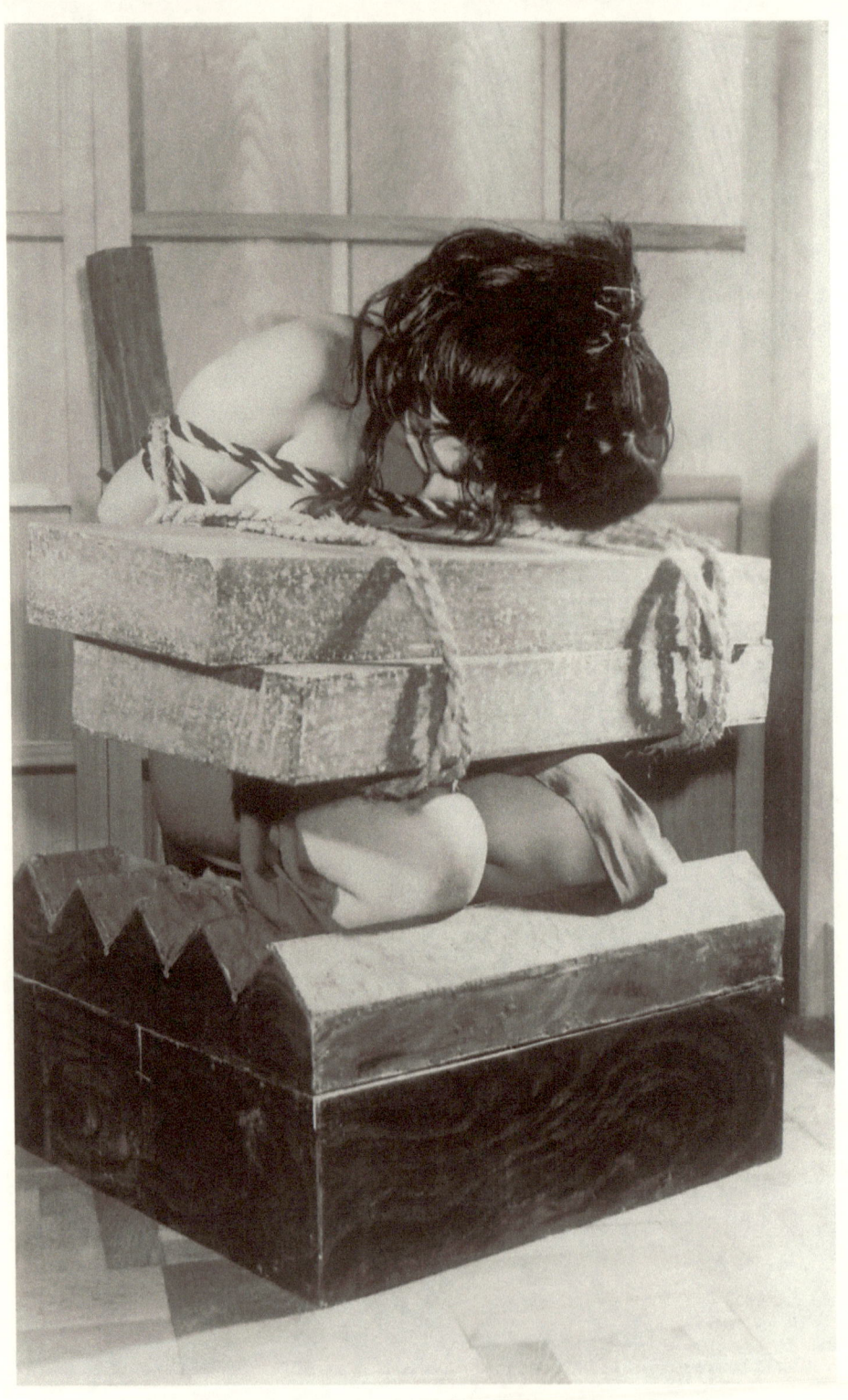

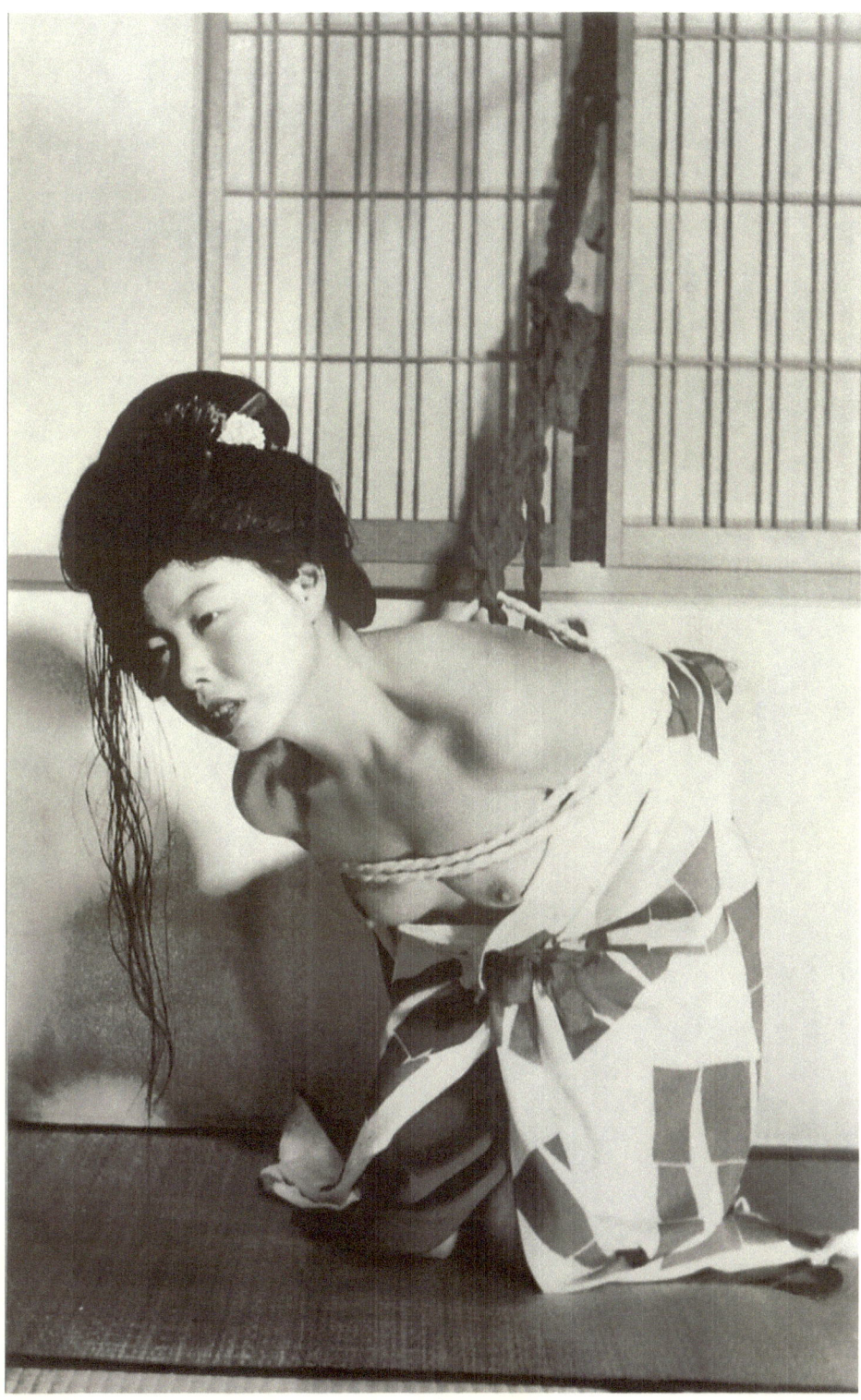

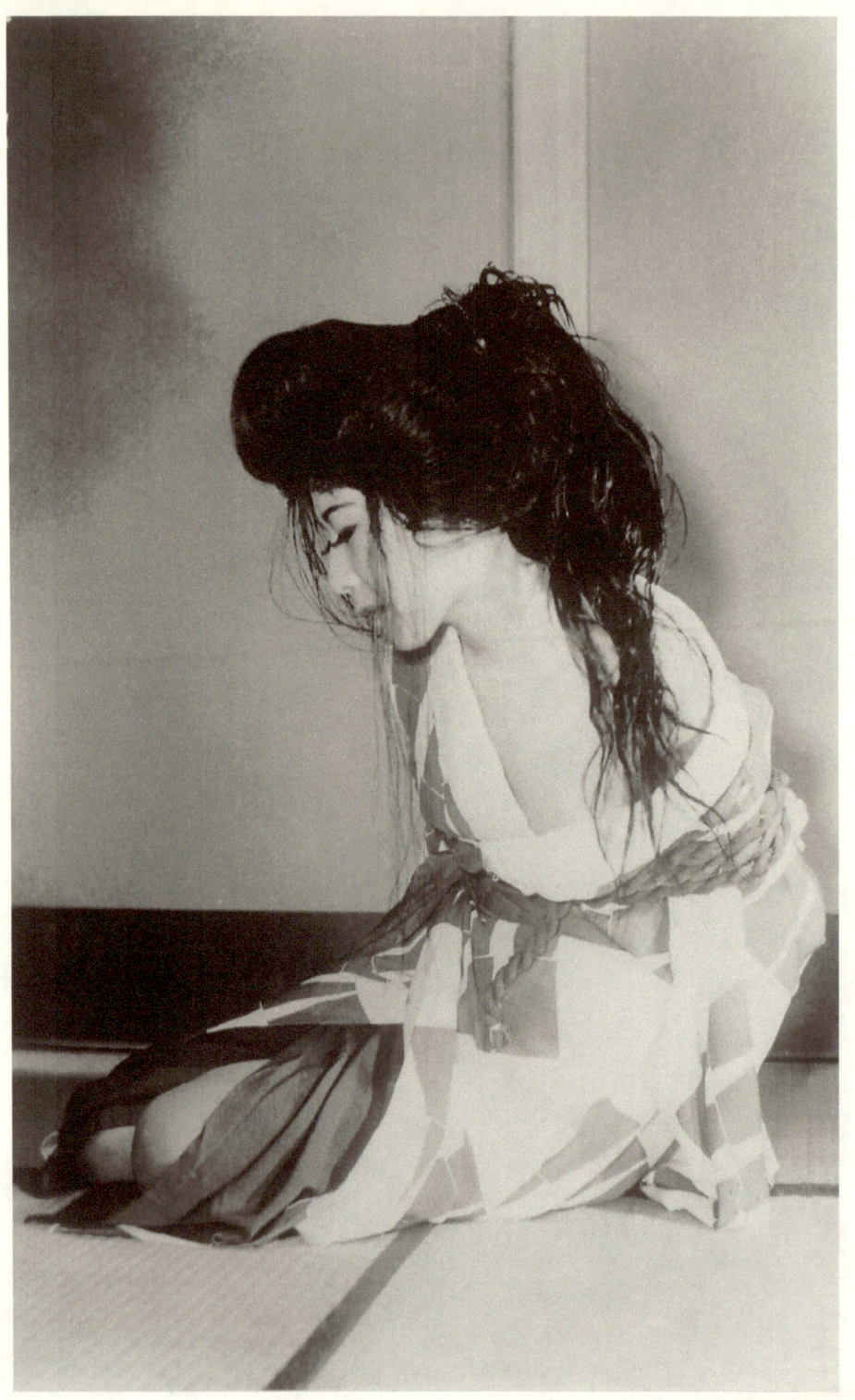

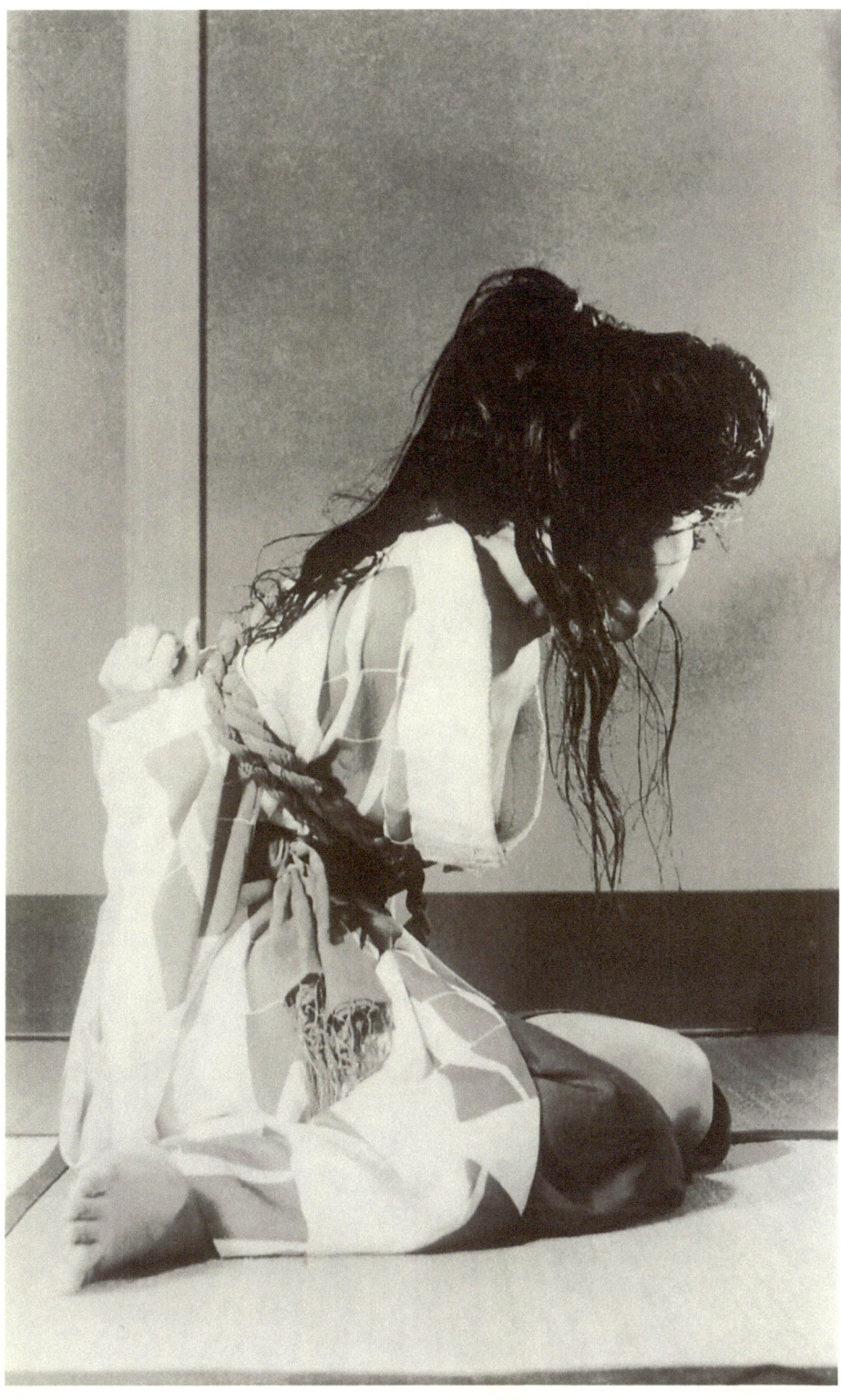

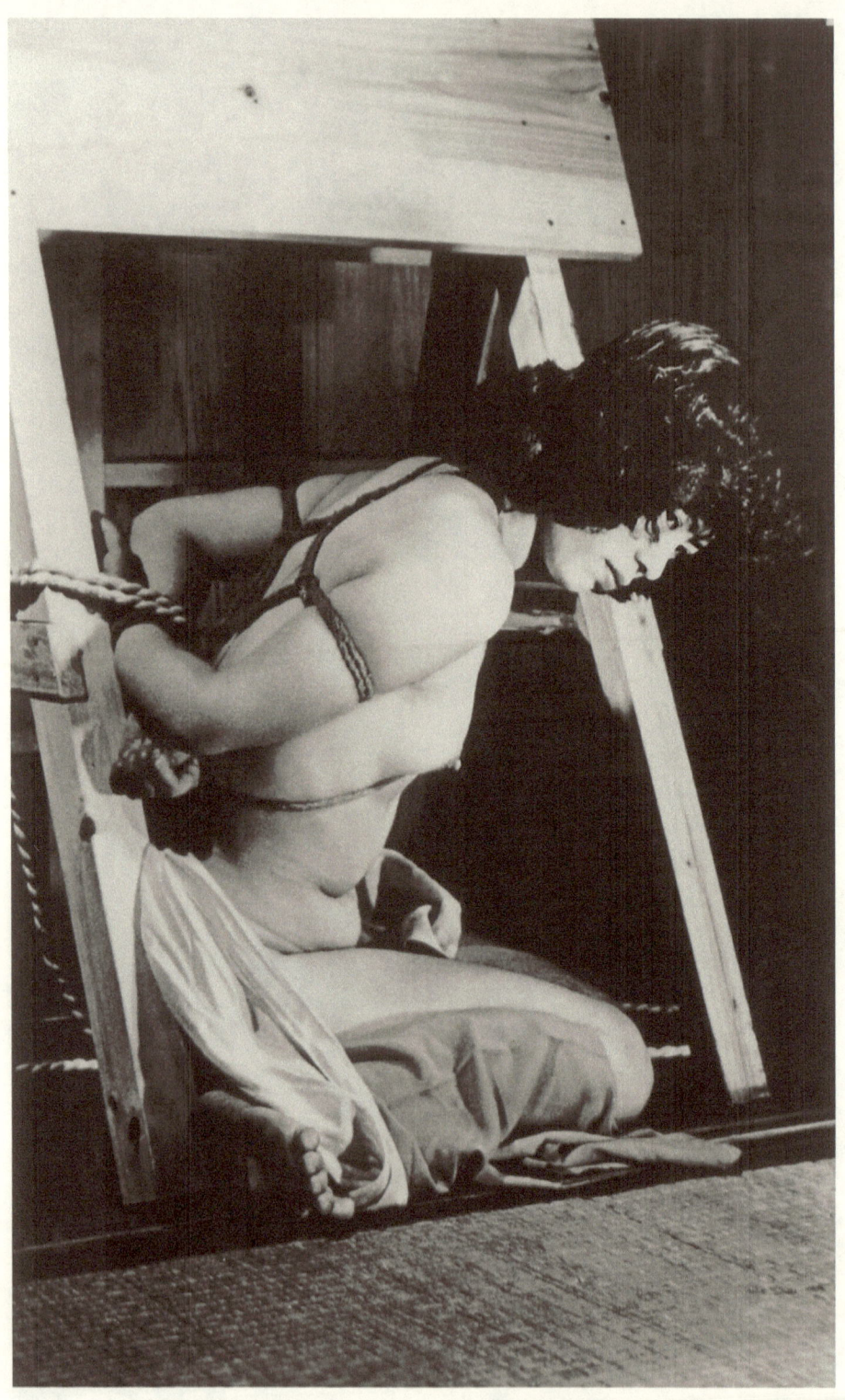

www.ingramcontent.com/pod-product-compliance
Lightning Source LLC
Chambersburg PA
CBHW030814180526
45163CB00003B/1278